what matters most

what

matters

BASIC
BOOKS

a member of the perseus books group

most

How a Small Group of Pioneers
Is Teaching Social Responsibility
to Big Business, and Why
Big Business Is Listening

jeffrey hollender

stephen fenichell

Published by Basic Books,
A Member of the Perseus Books Group

Library of Congress Cataloging-in-Publication Data
Hollender, Jeffrey.
What matters most : how a small group of pioneers is teaching
social responsibility to big business, and why big business is listening /
Jeffrey Hollender and Stephen Fenichell.
p. cm.
Includes bibliographical references and index.
ISBN 0-7382-0902-3
1. Social responsibility of business. 2. Social values.
3. Social responsibility of business—United States—Case studies.
4. Business enterprises—United States—Case studies.
I. Fenichell, Stephen. II. Title.
HD60.H65 2003
658.4'08—dc22
2003020345

Design by Jane Raese
SET IN 11-POINT JANSON

This book is printed on chlorine-free paper.

04 05 06 07 / 10 9 8 7 6 5 4 3 2 1

contents

CONTENTS

—————

The dog days of the Enron/Global Crossing/Imclone/Tyco/World Com/Martha Stewart Omnimedia summer of scandal found me in a rented house out on the South Fork of Long Island, surfing. During those stomach-churning weeks, the Dow dove to depths not seen for five years and the NASDAQ flopped helplessly around like a beached bluefish. I frequently felt a nearly irrepressible urge to press the panic button, to rush back to our Seventh Generation office in Burlington, Vermont, to mind the helm of the company I'd started fifteen years before, and guide it through these troubled times.

When I fell back into CEO default mode, I took a deep breath and reminded myself that we were now truly a *we*. Seventh Generation had an exceptionally strong management team comprising competent, experienced, and caring people who would have been capable of handling a crisis on their own, with minimal input or intervention from me. If there had been a crisis.

One reason that the adverse macro-economic climate was not affecting Seventh Generation was that in late 1999, following a disastrous experience with the public equity markets, we had taken the company private. Our relatively small pool of investors was likely to regard the stock market turmoil and plummeting corporate confidence as requiring a cool head, not a respirator. In fact, they may well have been thankful to have their money safely invested in a private rather than a public company.

Just about every morning during that August, while my wife and children slept, I'd get up before dawn to respond to a few e-mails over a cup of hot coffee. I couldn't resist scanning with appalled fascination the latest lurid headlines on the business pages. Each new revelation of acts that were invariably described as the aberrations of a few rotten apples but more likely represented the tip of a moral and ethical iceberg made me sigh and shake my head. Then I would start my car and slowly cruise down to the beach with my surfboard tucked behind the back seat. These were the same dark Atlantic waters I'd surfed as a kid, when my family owned a summer house in Westhampton.

I couldn't have been more than ten when our neighbor Frank Knoska taught me to surf. Frank was a full-fledged teenager, and on those mornings when we'd grab his long fiberglass board and strike out for the Atlantic, he seemed like the very essence of manhood. The local surf beaches were all named after a series of jetties that had been built in an attempt to protect the rapidly eroding beach. Frank possessed the detailed knowledge of a local kid. He was able to intuit where the waves would be big, but not so big as to intimidate an anxious novice. He taught me how to paddle out beyond where the waves were breaking—which can be surprisingly hard—and how to position myself in just the right spot to catch a wave without wiping out.

Surfing, I learned, requires not just balance and judgment, patience and skill, but a sharp sense of timing combined with the body knowledge that tells you when to wait for the next wave, or when to start paddling in, at a speed as fast or faster than the wave itself, to become one with the swell as it raced to the beach. You spend a lot more time sitting on your board, watching and waiting, focused obsessively on which wave is going to peak and when, than you ever spend actually riding the waves. You need quick responses to current conditions, but also slow, painstaking preparation. You need to know the hidden contours beneath the ocean as well as how to connect to a network of fellow surfers, who communicated—in my day, before the Internet—by a primitive form of bush telegraph known as the phone.

A good surfer needs to know what time the tide will change as well as the strength and direction of the wind. Wind affects the shape of a wave. An offshore wind creates a hollow wave by holding it back from breaking by a critical few seconds. A hollow wave is what every surfer wants so you can position yourself inside the hollow—called "the tube"—and ride for as long as possible in the "pocket." The ultimate surfer's high is riding so deep inside the tube that you actually disappear from sight and then emerge as the wave winds down and you approach the shore.

———————

During that summer of scandal I felt that we as a society were surfing a wave that had run aground on a sandbar. Never mind that certain things once skillfully hidden from sight were emerging into our surprised view; an entire way of thinking, a swell we'd been riding for a decade or more, had run out of steam. I found myself struck by Federal Reserve Director Alan Greenspan's belated discovery—in light of his previous pronouncements on the subject—that greed, on a corporate level, might be a bad thing after all: "It is not that humans have become any more greedy than in generations past," Greenspan piously assured Congress, "but that the avenues to express greed have grown so enormously." This from a man who not long before had espoused the thesis, "it is precisely the 'greed' of the businessman, or more appropriately, [his] profit seeking, which is the unexcelled protector of the consumer."

Greenspan acknowledged that "the incentives created"—he remained opaque about *who* created them—"overcame the good judgment of too many corporate managers." And he coined a new phrase—"infectious greed"—his post-millennial counterpoint to the boom decade's "irrational exuberance."

A good surfer is soon thinking about the next wave. At some point that summer, I began to adopt the minority view that the scandals presented American business with one of the greatest opportunities of the new century. The renewed emphasis on corporate responsibility and accountability that the scandals were beginning to spawn offers us all a chance to redefine the role of the corporation in society. In the wake of the scandals, a door was opened for a new way of looking at business and of thinking about the role that business might play in a better world. For fifteen years at Seventh Generation—one of the country's first self-declared "socially responsible" companies—we have been operating according to a different set of principles from those followed by the rogue's gallery of the late boom. All during the

Roaring Nineties, we had remained focused on offering people avenues not to express their greed and ambition but their idealism, passion, and commitment to a cause larger than themselves, and larger than the company. By "people," I mean our managers and employees as well as our customers, suppliers, partners, and every party along our value and supply chain. Not just our shareholders but our stakeholders.

In our business, we have gone to what some might regard as inordinate lengths to answer such imponderable questions as, "How can you measure how passionate people are or how safe they feel about walking into the CEO's office and saying what's really on their mind?" We've come to consider the company as a place in which to offer people an opportunity not just for material and economic growth, but spiritual and moral and personal growth as well. We've tried to create a corporate culture in which people are not drained by their work but energized by it, not alienated but fulfilled as members of an intentional community. We've tried to be, in the largest sense, a satisfying company to work for and do business with, and a major part of that effort is having a well-developed vision of what it means to be a responsible business and a good corporate citizen.

We are hardly alone in this. Global and local businesses—private enterprise—present the largest force truly capable of providing workable solutions, not just to business problems but to the daunting social and environmental challenges facing our planet. In the absence of large-scale government-sponsored reform, leading-edge businesses and not-for-profit organizations all over the world have responded not just to the current credibility crisis but to the greater long-term challenge of being part of the global solution by evolving a new corporate model that shifts the paradigm for the role that business can play in society.

This is the next wave. It is not a public relations ploy, a new financial model, or the next management and leadership trend, but a broad social movement, centered in the corporation much as the antiwar movement of the 1960s was centered on college campuses. It will, we believe, have deep and lasting effects on our values and beliefs as well as the world's future. From the celebrated Grameen Bank microlending program in rural Bangladesh, to a group of mid-sized companies that pioneered the concept of corporate responsibility in this and other countries, to a gratifyingly large—and growing—percentage of Fortune 500 companies, private enterprises of all sizes and shapes have embraced the concept of corporate responsibility as more of a challenge and an opportunity than a threat. As this new vision of the role of business in the world is fleshed out, it has also become a way of developing new markets, positioning products, gaining new customers, attracting the most talented workforce, building strong and lasting relationships with consumers, and building strong brands for a new century. Beyond even that, it has become a new way to be a fundamental part of the paradigm within which all business in the future is bound to evolve.

In *What Matters Most*, Stephen Fenichell and I explore the forces behind this new paradigm and the social implications it offers. There are still some who consider the phrase "socially responsible business" a contradiction in terms, and who feel that the notion of CSR (Corporate Social Responsibility) is a trendy hollow hoax, intrinsically suspect. Others believe that this emerging doctrine of deeper and broader accountability for business is fundamentally pernicious, because it distracts profit-making organizations from what they do best: making money for their shareholders.

One of the latter critics, Michael Prowse, recently argued in the pages of the *Financial Times*:

> The role of the corporation should be to provide individuals with the means to be socially responsible. Rather than trying to play the role of social worker, senior executives should concentrate on their statutory obligations. We should not expect benevolence of them, but we should demand probity: the socially responsible chief executive is the one who turns a profit without lying, cheating, robbing or defrauding anyone.

This formulation is not only inadequate but fundamentally misguided, and we will put forth the case for precisely the opposite of that argument: The adoption and infusion, throughout every phase and element of a business, of a vision and mission that embrace the values of social responsibility in all of its forms will increasingly become a necessity for organizations of every size. The corollary to this thesis is that managing the often daunting task of introducing this critical component into the day-to-day conduct of business activity, and of maintaining top management's attention and commitment to it, can be—*and has been*—as effective a means of re-engineering an organization and of creating opportunities for long-term stable growth and improved financial performance. Most, if not all, of the trendier change agents—downsizing, hierarchy-flattening, entrepreneuring, to name just a few of those employed over the past decades—have proved to be futile and often fleeting attempts to fundamentally improve the concept, content, and character of corporations. Responsible business is different from all other trends because at the most fundamental level it is responsive to significant changes in the macro-economic environment, otherwise known as the planet and all those who inhabit it. It is not driven by a desire to develop a new way to beat the competition, or to maximize profits, but by a compassionate and value-based response to the challenges facing our society and the new role that business is expected by that society to play in the world.

We will talk about the voguish term *synergy*. But the synergy to which we refer is not the sort so frequently invoked over the past decades to justify large-scale mega-mergers, which have for the most part failed to live up to their great expectations and have created short-term value largely limited to brokers and other intermediaries, a few senior managers, and other interested parties. The synergy we advocate integrates values and belief systems across a wide range of business units, partners, employees, and customers, and brings such disparate groups as investors and customers into a unique form of synchronization, a corporate community of stakeholders united by a common vision, which creates truly long-term value not just for shareholders but for all.

We will talk about transparency and disclosure, one of the foundational elements of this entire concept. Transparency not just in the sense of providing complete, accurate, and reliable financial information, but of a full disclose of every aspect of a corporation's impact on and relationships with all of its stakeholders, as opposed to its shareholders. This ranges from how it treats its employees and the workers at all the factories that manufacture the products it sells, to the environmental footprint of its operations, and the way it influences and interacts with NGOs (nongovernmental organizations) and local politicians in all the communities in which it operates.

We will also talk about *scale*, but from a different perspective than the one associated with the pet phrase *economies of scale*. Our sense of scale is more one of appropriate scale than of size at all cost. Scale is a two-way street: Size does matter, but not the way most people think. To refer to the once fashionable (perhaps soon to be revived) work of British economist E. F. Schumacher, small can be both beautiful and profitable.

We will be talking about ownership structure and the often overlooked and misunderstood differences between private and public equity. Venture capitalists and private equity investors play an important role in the constant jockeying of long-term versus short-term gains and expectations. Ownership structures *do* matter, and they must be understood in terms of their impact on management decisions.

We will be looking at the emerging ethic of social responsibility from the point of view of some of its early visionaries. We will take an intimate look at Ben & Jerry's, Patagonia, the Body Shop, Stonyfield Farm, Working Assets, Interface Carpet, and our very own Seventh Generation. We will ask these companies some difficult questions: How has Ben & Jerry's core mission survived as a subsidiary of Unilever? Are the mission and values of Stonyfield Farm, now a division of international food giant Danone, so deeply and indelibly "encoded into the brand," as its founder Gary Hirshberg maintains, that becoming part of a great global conglomerate really is an unmixed blessing? Is it the place of business to adopt controversial political and social positions, and if so, to what benefit to the business and at what cost?

From Intel and Hewlett-Packard to Chiquita and Nike, we will be looking at the transformations being executed by some of the world's largest corporations, and the difficulties they have faced as they rise to the challenge of embracing this new paradigm. In all of these explorations, our intention will be to uncover and carefully anatomize the pervasive compromises and complexities, as opposed to the simple and easy solutions, that being a good citizen on the corporate level inevitably requires in the twenty-first century.

- In what cases does an inflexible adherence to core values conflict—often painfully and publicly—with short-term and even long-term goals and commitments?
- How do companies resolve or fail to resolve such conflicts? Or, do they attempt to paper them over with rhetoric and bureaucratic BS?
- In what cases does it make sense to compromise, even to sell out?
- Why does the evolution and implementation of a value system take so long?
- Why is it so hard to sustain?
- Does being a responsible business really cost more money and adversely affect shareholder value?
- Where does disclosure and transparency conflict with competition, liability, and confidentiality?

All of these questions ultimately distill down to one: *What matters most?* Is it sustained, increased quarterly profits? Maximizing shareholder value and if so how quickly and steadily, at what cost to whom and how high is high enough? Is it growth—and defining positive, sustainable, responsible ways to maintain it? Or are the metrics that mattered yesterday evolving in new and different ways? To this end, we will look at the subject of *metrics*, guidelines, and yardsticks by which business is measured, and by which performance is judged in this new paradigm of responsibility and corporate citizenship. We will describe the evolving global consensus that new yardsticks are needed to reward and measure performance in this area, cutting across a far broader range of criteria than pure short-term financial gain.

A dizzying proliferation of standards and guidelines are now being drafted by national and local governments and NGOs around the world. These range from the Sullivan Principles to the United Nations' Global Compact to the Global Reporting Initiative (GRI) to a variety of protocols and compliance demands intended to increase corporate accountability and to broaden the range of corporate responsibility. All of these are elements of a massive shift from the shareholder to the stakeholder corporate model.

We will for the most part avoid talking about ethics—in the sense of individual behavior inside the corporation—because corporate social responsibility is not primarily an individual ethical issue. It is more of an issue of values and corporate culture against which individual behavior can be measured. Instituting a value system that places appropriate emphasis on accounting for social *externalities*—pollution, environmental degradation and resource consumption, health effects of the workplace environment on employees, the need to create a work environment that fulfills all the needs and aspirations of its employees, and finally sustainability in all its myriad forms—is no longer a luxury, a sideshow, or a shallow public relations exercise. It must become a critical part of every company's core competence and strategy, integral to their internal behavior and culture.

We will also describe the challenges posed by the proliferation of highly sophisticated nonprofit advocacy and activist groups (NGOs) and we will show why many companies have found that engaging in a productive dialogue with them is not only possible but desirable. We will describe Greenpeace's role in reforming the operations of the energy giant Royal Dutch Shell, the Rainforest Alliance's role in guiding the corporate makeover at Chiquita International, and Global Exchange's effect on the conduct of Nike.

We will talk about supply chains and value chains, and how attempts to align these with an organization's environmental and social goals can foster significant change. We will show how business practices are changing rapidly and dramatically to meet the needs of a new century.

Finally, we will talk about leadership and inspiration, soul and spirit, guts and heart, because even as a set of ideas grows more broadly accepted there is always the danger that in the very process of becoming the mainstream, the ideas themselves—once shocking and radical—will lose their capacity to inspire change.

The interlinked notions of responsibility, accountability, and transparency are driving forces not just among United States companies but of companies around the world. They presage a fundamental redefinition of private enterprise. What if we created a world in which the most powerful institutions in the world were truly trustworthy? Accountable, transparent, and progressive? They will never, of course, be perfect. Nevertheless, we hold in our hands the template, the model, and the guidelines for fundamental and positive change.

acknowledgments

No one could ask for a more talented, committed or able partner and coauthor than Stephen Fenichell, a friend from our days that began together in the fifth grade at Riverdale Country Day School, in the Bronx, New York.

This book couldn't have been written without the support and endless understanding of my wife Sheila, whose love and commitment create the space essential for the work I do, and my children Meika, Alex, and Chiara, to whom this book is dedicated. They inspire my passion to make the world a better place.

We would also like to thank our agent, Kristine Dahl of ICM. And at the Perseus Books Group, William Frucht, our editor, and Jack McKeown, our publisher, for their unflagging commitment to the project; and Christine Marra for her fine project management.

My amazing team at Seventh Generation, especially the Leadership Team, Jeff Phillips, Karen Fleming, and John Murphy, and my assistant Anita Lavoie, provide me with the time I need away from the office and the freedom to experiment with these ideas inside the company. I am also tremendously appreciative of the Seventh Generation Board of Directors, especially Arthur Gray and Peter Graham, who have supported this work, and provided me with both their confidence and wisdom. This book also would not have been possible without the openness and time that all the companies and nonprofits we interviewed have shared with us or the support I have received over the years from both the Social Venture Network and the Vermont Businesses for Social Responsibility communities.

I have had the luck to be surrounded by a wonderful group of teachers throughout my life, some of them being Alan Newman, my original partner at Seventh Generation, Yoram Samets, Gregor Barnum, David Levine, Wilson Alling, David Sundaram, Ray Ann Barry, and Stephen Viederman.

chapter one

The Making of a Movement

One summer day in 1990, I found myself in a Southern California retreat center sitting in a circle composed of Body Shop founder Anita Roddick; Ben & Jerry's Homemade founder Ben Cohen; Wayne Silby, chairman of the Calvert Group of mutual funds; and Joshua Mailman, a quirky, creative, quietly influential New York–based social investor and philanthropist who three years before had cofounded (with Silby) the organization responsible for the retreat: The Social Venture Network. SVN is a low-profile leadership group composed of socially progressive entrepreneurs, with a sprinkling of nonprofit participants, organized to promote the idea that business can and should be a vehicle for social change.

Three years earlier, Silby and Mailman had written a letter to about thirty-five potentially interested parties offering to host them for a "working weekend" at Gold Lake Mountain Resort, a rustic-style retreat about two hours outside of Denver, Colorado. As the letter explained:

> Our purpose will be to explore the idea of forming some sort of ethical investment banking network that can serve as a model for bringing emerging social values into a more collective sphere.

One reason the letter produced such an enthusiastic response—of the thirty-five invitees, seventy-two people actually showed up—may have been that 1987 was the year of Oliver Stone's *Wall Street*, which featured Gordon Gekko's memorable assertion, "greed is good." The source of this may be a well-known diatribe in Ayn Rand's *The Fountainhead*, disputing the notion that "money is the root of all evil." But whatever its source, this line—derived from an actual speech delivered by the financier Ivan Boesky—turned out to be a fitting slogan for the times. The heady free-market spirit of Reaganomics was very much in full swing, much to the distress of the majority of the conference's attendees. The conference organizers clearly hoped that by staging an event that ran culturally counter to the prevailing ethos, they might promote a valid alternative.

As a piece of social history, the agenda of that first SVN conference makes for some interesting reading. Following brief after-dinner opening remarks on Friday evening from Silby and Mailman, the participants were treated to a presentation by a social anthropologist, Dr. Frances Harwood, on the topic "The Entrepreneur as Shaman."

One of the many distinctive features of SVN conferences is the palpable presence of spiritual and religious leaders, including—on frequent occasions—Baba Ram Dass (born Richard Alpert and an assistant professor at Harvard and early disciple of Timothy Leary until he discovered his spiritual calling), Bernie Glassman, a Jewish Buddhist monk who runs a successful bakery in Yonkers, as well as the Venerable Chogyam Trungpa Rinpoche, a prominent Buddhist thinker and leader then based in Vermont, who attended the first SVN meeting.

This spiritual aspect reflects Wayne Silby's long-standing interest in infusing business practices with a spiritual, social, moral, and ethical dimension. He was clearly influenced by a 1979 Buddhist-sponsored conference in Vermont entitled "Right Livelihood."

Wayne was born in Iowa and traveled around India and much of Asia after graduating from law school. In his midtwenties, he founded the Calvert Investment Group, which he and his partners named after the street in Washington, D.C., where the fund had its first offices.

In the first of many incarnations, the Calvert Group dealt exclusively in "variable-rate securities," a Wall Street term for refinancing government-insured corporate debt. When interest rates spiked in the late 1970s, the Calvert fund gained a comparable boost, and before long Wayne and his young partners were managing over a billion dollars in assets.

Calvert's internal culture reflected Wayne's personal style. Employees wore jeans and bare feet to work, and "customers would come in," Wayne recently told us, "and put their life savings down on a cardboard table." Only after one of his staff members tried to steal $1.5 million in cash from the office did Wayne decide to tighten things up, at least sartorially. "I started wearing a tie the next day."

The Right Livelihood conference was a turning point not only for Wayne personally, but also strategically for the Calvert Fund Group. Before the 1979 conference, the funds were managed with no particular moral, ethical, or social criteria, which was the way nearly all mutual funds and financial instruments were governed at the time. But in Vermont it dawned upon him that "there was more to life than a few extra basis points"—basis points being the increments of 1/100th of 1 percent, which, then as now, ruled the world of mutual fund performance. "That conference turned my life around 180 degrees," Wayne recalled in the pleasantly chaotic living room of his Washington, D.C., townhouse, out of which he runs at least half a dozen for-profit and nonprofit organizations. "Nothing was the same after that."

Wayne's initial idea was to "somehow integrate the values of the Baby Boom generation into a financial product. We had money and resources which we felt needed to be deployed in keeping with our social values, which were themselves the product of the Civil Rights and anti-war movements of the late sixties, and the anti-apartheid movement of the seventies."

In 1981, Wayne had to overcome a certain degree of internal skepticism. "My partners told me in no uncertain terms that they thought I was on drugs. But I felt that this was really something I wanted to do, and I told my partner that I would throw a real tantrum if he—or they—tried to stop me. This was basically a chairman's pet project, because even though the vote at the meeting was five against one, as chairman I got five votes, so I won." Fortunately for Wayne and his investors (and for the future of the socially responsible investing movement), the renamed Calvert Social Investment Fund prospered.

Wayne Silby did not invent the idea of socially responsible investing (SRI). The first socially conscious investors on record belonged to the Society of Friends, better known as the Quakers, who began screening their investments according to moral and ethical criteria as early as the seventeenth century. The highly industrious Quakers tended to have a fair amount of money to invest, and they would steer away from companies that profited from activities of which they disapproved.

The Quakers were against slavery and against war—totally, utterly, uncompromisingly. In the seventeenth, eighteenth, and even nineteenth centuries, such a stance sharply limited your investment portfolio, because so many companies made their money through weapons production, other forms of military supply, or by growing the great agricultural commodities of the pre-industrial world: cotton, tobacco, sugar, coffee, and tea, nearly every one of which employed some form of enforced servitude.

By the 1920s, a number of religious institutions had taken up the idea of aligning their investing practices with their moral and spiritual principles. "Many Christians would never consider operating a casino, owning a liquor store, manufacturing weapons, using near-slave labor or operating a lending business charging usurious rates," wrote Gary Moore in *The Thoughtful Christian's Guide to Investing*, published in the midtwenties. Thoughtful Christians, Moore pointed out, would be well-advised to consider the potentially sinful purposes to which their stocks, bonds, and bank deposits might be put. Many religiously oriented people began to query their investment advisors as to how their money was making money.

In 1928, a financier named Philip L. Carret launched the Pioneer Fund in Boston to fill what he perceived as the growing need for a morally beneficial investment policy. Carret actively managed his fund for seventy years, until his death in 1998, with such consistency and quality of performance that "socially responsible investing" gained a degree of credibility based simply on Carret's track record. When *Mutual Fund* magazine rated the Pioneer Fund "the best mutual fund ever," the idea of socially responsible investing no longer seemed so off the wall.

Yet the universe of socially responsible mutual funds didn't really take off until nearly forty years after the founding of Carret's pioneering fund. The SRI idea lay dormant in the fifties and early sixties, but by the late sixties, a deeply divided and generationally polarized population was open to change in a variety of fields, including the rarefied and notoriously straitlaced world of money management.

Corporate complicity in environmental pollution, Ralph Nader's revelations of shoddy automobile manufacture, the successful consumer boycott of Dow Chemical for producing napalm during the Vietnam War—all began to change the moral and ethical lens through which corporate behavior was viewed in the United States. An increasing level of popular skepticism and hostility toward business—in particular big business—shifted the landscape to such a degree that gradually an emerging SRI movement began to take form. Steering your money into avenues where it might do some good, and away from avenues where it might do some bad, became more broadly perceived as a legitimate vehicle for social change.

In 1971, the Pax World fund became the first mutual fund to capitalize, as it were, on the burgeoning antiwar mood. Pax screened out defense stocks and only defense stocks, and successfully attracted investors who wanted to abide by this morally and ethically informed investment policy. That year marked a watershed in the evolving relationship between consumers, investors, and corporate managers, who up until then had treated both consumers and investors with a degree of disengagement that might charitably be described as paternalistic. The president of the Episcopal Church in the United States petitioned General Motors to cease all operations in South Africa, a shareholder resolution that to GM's shock and horror attracted widespread shareholder support. The walls were, as the song said, tumbling down.

Within months, a number of U.S. cities and municipalities (starting, not surprisingly, with Madison, Wisconsin) had begun passing local laws prohibiting governments under their jurisdiction from conducting business with companies active in South Africa. By the midseventies, these boycotts had begun to take their toll on management, on investor relations, on corporate reputations and goodwill, and eventually on share prices. When share prices suffered, managers were forced to sit up and take notice. This was no sentimental fringe fad.

By 1982, the year Wayne Silby launched his Calvert Social Investment Fund, a significant number of companies with operations in South Africa—including Mobil, Goodyear, RJR Nabisco, and Johnson & Johnson—had responded to the mounting consumer pressure by divesting themselves of their South African operations, often at substantial markdowns to their book values, and thus a loss to shareholder equity. The consumer boycott had irredeemably changed not only the operational profile of business, but its reputational profile as well. SRI, as it was soon to be known, had effectively rewritten the rules of a very old game.

For the first time in history, iconic American companies had been punished where it hurt most—in their balance sheets, and in their shareholders' brokerage firm statements—for failing to heed a moral imperative. Many managers and investors were furious at the unwelcome interference when into the fray stepped Leon Sullivan, an American clergyman, who forged an effective compromise to an increasingly polarized situation. His Sullivan Principles rewarded companies for good behavior with regard to South Africa, as opposed to simply punishing bad behavior. Though the term was not yet part of the popular parlance, the Sullivan Principles functioned effectively as a positive screen as well as a vehicle for social change.

When Wayne began soliciting funds for Calvert Social Investment Fund in 1982, he says now,

> We became the first fund to just say no to *all sorts of things*. We didn't say no to drugs, like Nancy Reagan, because for the most part, we were high on pharmaceuticals. But we did say no to defense stocks, no to stocks in companies in bed with South Africa, no to stocks that made money out of environmental degradation, no to stocks in companies that failed to respect human rights, no to stocks in companies that trampled on the rights of indigenous peoples around the world.

One of Calvert's contributions to what had by then become a burgeoning if still somewhat minor field was to create an advisory board of experts comprising a wide range of academics and activists. "Our

values were formed and informed by our advisory council," Wayne re-
calls. "We made sure to cast our net pretty wide. We had Amory and
Hunter Lovins and Bob Rodale from the environmental field, Hazel
Henderson from the field of environmental economics, and a number
of experts and anthropologists on the rights of indigenous people."
This last became one of Calvert Fund's special areas of concern.

At a pivotal moment in the evolution of the Calvert Fund, Wayne
met the young philanthropist Joshua Mailman through the Threshold Foundation. "Meeting Josh Mailman," Wayne recalled, "was like
a revelation, because it made me finally realize what it must have been
like for people to meet me." He and Joshua quickly discovered a spiritual and intellectual kinship. They soon concluded that where social
change was concerned, two were better than one, twenty were better
than ten, and four dozen might be better than two dozen. After hitting that number, they really weren't sure.

Wayne describes the Threshold Foundation, otherwise known as
"the dough nuts"—which remains active today—as "a group of people who want to get people to start thinking differently about money."
The organization to which I was briefly a member includes the children of some of America's wealthiest families from the original robber
barons to an eclectic collection of names that you might find today in
the *Forbes* list of the 500 wealthiest individuals in America. The foundation's Web site says much the same thing, in a bit more detail.

> Threshold provides a place where people with significant financial re-
> sources, a commitment to social change and an interest in their own
> emotional, psychological and spiritual development can come together
> to scheme, dream, learn, work, play and see what happens. We have
> observed that social change flows from personal growth so we work on
> our inner lives and social responsibility simultaneously.

One of the ideas being bandied about at the Threshold Foundation
was establishing an alternative investment bank, or possibly a venture
capital group, which would pool other investors' resources to support
socially responsible start-ups. That germ of an idea eventually
ripened into the Social Venture Network, which to Joshua's and
Wayne's surprise never did grow into a socially conscious investment

bank, but ultimately evolved into a support network for socially re-sponsible entrepreneurs.

Excited about their idea of an alternative investment bank, Wayne and Joshua sent off their letter to thirty-five people, which in turn prompted seventy-two interested individuals to converge on Gold Lake Mountain Resort in Ward, Colorado, over the weekend of August 7th, 8th, and 9th in 1987. Ben Cohen of Ben & Jerry's, recently told me his recollections of that landmark event.

"I got this letter out of the blue from these two guys I'd never met," Ben recalled over lunch at a French bistro in downtown Burlington, Vermont, "inviting me out to this ranch somewhere in the wilds of Colorado." He was particularly intrigued by a sentence that came about halfway through the third paragraph:

> An opportunity exists for us to build a new American story, a new American parable, a new American mythology, which can provide an alternative and renewing vision for some of the economic choices that face our culture.

"That was not the sort of language people used in those days to talk about business," Ben said with a wistful smile. "What really caught my eye about that letter was that here were these two financial guys putting their money where their mouths—and minds—were. Here were two guys who had never laid eyes on either Jerry or me, not only inviting us to this three-day-long conference, but offering to pick up the tab."

Given Ben's finances at the time, that last detail piqued his interest. Even after realizing, upon closer inspection, that Wayne and Joshua weren't paying for anyone's flight out to Colorado, he still really wanted to go. Ben talked the matter over with his business partner, Jerry Greenfield. Did it make good business sense for Ben to go? They hadn't the faintest idea. Could they afford it? Not really. "But Jerry and I decided to scrape the money together," Ben explained, "because even though we didn't have the money, it just felt like this was an opportunity to do something for society we simply couldn't af-ford to pass up."

Ben Cohen's last sentence is worth repeating. Listen closely to the voice of the socially responsible but financially strapped entrepreneur circa 1987:

> Though we didn't have the money, it just felt like this was an opportunity to do something for society we simply couldn't afford to pass up.

When representatives of businesses tell me—as they frequently do—that they would *love* to be more socially responsible, but their investors, partners, CFO, Wall Street analysts, board directors, mothers and fathers, what have you, wouldn't allow it, I'd like to respond with Ben's quote.

Ben was intrigued by the name Calvert Social Investment Fund on the invitation. A few months before, he had attended an SRI conference—a precursor to today's enormously popular "SRI in the Rockies"—because he wanted to attract more socially responsible investors, who might be more forgiving than conventional shareholders of his investments in socially responsible programs and practices.

Ben is a pretty easygoing guy, but he had a few intellectual disputes with the people he met at that conference. One of his problems "was that these folks seemed to be focused exclusively—you might say obsessively—on imposing negative screens on companies. I didn't think that it made sense to define social responsibility entirely from a negative perspective. They kept talking about steering money away from companies that profited from alcohol, from tobacco, from war, from environmentally nasty chemicals or petroleum. . . ."

This moralizing was an institutional leftover from SRI's origins in the religious convictions of many of its early participants. This Puritanical emphasis on sin and the devil and redemption and tobacco and alcohol all seemed a bit dour for a secularized Jewish guy from Long Island who likes ice cream and having fun. Ben basically thought that these folks should lighten up.

But he also had a strategic point to make: it wasn't enough to just say *no* to people doing bad things; it was profoundly important to be able to say *yes* to people doing good things. "*It isn't enough not to do the bad stuff,*" was how Ben kept putting it, and being a passionate and persuasive guy, he began to get through to them.

The two guys running the show and putting up the dough at Gold Lake Mountain Resort had bent over backward to avoid creating the impression that they wished to dominate the event. To avoid any mis-understanding on this front, Joshua and Wayne hired a professional meeting facilitator. This was the first professional facilitator Ben had ever laid eyes on. "We all sat in a circle and it was one of those deals where everyone said who they were and what they were about, and it just took *forever,*" he recalled.

Ben began to get impatient, and as he looked around that seated circle it dawned upon him that most of the people there belonged to a different tribe from his. Not necessarily ethnically—his tribe was the self-made entrepreneurs who had a passion and a mission and a set of values they cared about, but who also had realities like employees and a payroll and a production line to run.

People like Ben—people who ran "real businesses," as he put it— were scarce at that first meeting. Ben noticed a preponderance of "real-estate developers, philanthropists, private investors, private eq-uity guys"—the people who inhabited Joshua's world in New York and Wayne's world in Washington—and remarkably few small busi-ness progressives.

But then he ran into Bernie Glassman, a "Jewish-Buddhist nuclear physicist," as Ben described him, who had decided in his current rein-carnation to operate a business called Greystone Bakery out of an old monastery overlooking the Hudson River in Yonkers. Bernie was into baking brownies, and Ben and Jerry had been searching in vain to lo-cate a local supplier of brownie mix with which to make a brownie-flavored ice cream. "It was one of those marriages made in heaven," Ben said with a smile that became only mildly rueful when he recalled the temporary strain placed on this new relationship when the first batch of brownie mix arrived in Vermont stuck together in one giant block that turned out to be unusable as anything other than building material.

One of the great things about SVN, Ben quickly discovered, was that you could trust the people you met there. He and Bernie had done their deal on a handshake, ending up working out these minor kinks in a spirit of amiable partnership. It wasn't long before Greystone Bakery was one of Ben & Jerry's largest suppliers, and Ben & Jerry's had become Greystone's largest customer.

But Ben had other issues. The people he met at Gold Lake Mountain Resort tended to define a "socially responsible business" as one that made socially beneficial products. Period.

This definition really didn't work for Ben, in part because it left companies like his out in the cold. Now everyone knew that Ben & Jerry's was striving to be a socially responsible company, but virtually no one would have agreed that ice cream could be a socially beneficial product. Ben truly believed that what defined a socially responsible business was "a function of processes and practices as well as products."

Looking back over fifteen years, Wayne Silby recalled "the bifurcation that very quickly developed between the entrepreneurs and the financial people" at SVN conferences. "Josh and I had wanted to start a socially responsible investment bank, to do this thing together, while entrepreneurs are people who like to do their own thing. They wanted to be able to get together at regular intervals to share what they did on their own with other people like them."

By the time I attended my first Social Venture Network meeting in 1990, the socially responsible entrepreneurs had clearly gained the upper hand, but the financial folks like Josh and Wayne remained an important influence, in part because the SVN did end up functioning as an informal clearinghouse for entrepreneurs to raise capital from like-minded investors, and recently spawned a more formal offshoot called the Investors' Circle. But the latter function had clearly taken a second seat to the role of SVN as a safe haven and refuge for socially progressive entrepreneurs to come together and share their experiences of what it felt like to try to run a socially responsible business. It became a place to thrash out one's problems in an environment where having these problems at all—which often involved balancing profit and principles—was likely to illicit not merely sympathy, but empathy.

"What I think really happened at SVN," Wayne Silby explained, "is that we were inventing a language, a way of thinking and talking about these issues that has become so widely accepted today that it's easy to forget how original it was, how wild and strange and threatening to the status quo it once seemed."

When we first started Ben & Jerry's, we had no intention of going into "business"—we saw it as pretty much a lark. Then there came a time about five years ago when Jerry and I noticed that we were no longer scooping ice-cream cones behind a counter and working in the ice-cream shop, that we were bosses and administrators who were spending a lot of time on the phone and doing paperwork. When we were introduced to people and they asked, "What do you do?" there came a point when the answer was not "I'm a homemade ice-cream shop owner" but "I'm a businessman." And I had a hard time mouthing those words.

—Ben Cohen, cofounder of Ben & Jerry's Homemade Inc.,
in "Coming of Age," *Inc.*'s 10th anniversary issue, 1989

I think a lot of us would have slit our wrists if we ever thought we'd be part of corporate America or England. Big business was alien to me. What I wanted to do was create a livelihood, and I think women are quite good at that—probably better than blokes. We mush up an interest and a skill, and that's a livelihood.

—Anita Roddick, founder of the Body Shop,
in "Can Business Still Save the World?" *Inc.*, April 1, 2001

Over the years, the Social Venture Network has spawned a number of successful spin-offs beyond the Investors' Circle, including the World Business Academy, Net Impact, SVN Europe, BALLE (Business Alliance for Local Living Economies), and Students for Social Responsibility. But the new venture that has probably gained the most visibility and acceptance within the mainstream business community has been Businesses for Social Responsibility. BSR was launched in 1992 by a group of SVN members, one of whom was Ben Cohen. The original idea behind the venture, Ben recently recalled, was that "it was going to become an alternative Chamber of Commerce, an alternative voice in the nation's capital for socially responsible business, so that if the media wanted to take the pulse of business, they could go to someone else other than the National Association of Manufacturers."

Just as the SVN never evolved into a socially responsible investment bank, BSR never evolved into an alternative Chamber of Commerce. Instead, it has become the preeminent forum—not only in the United States but worldwide—for large businesses eager to learn the basic tenets and practices of corporate social responsibility (CSR) from a distinguished roster of experts.

Needless to say, this mission has raised a few eyebrows among those who consider the term "socially responsible business" a contradiction in terms, at least when the business is not only big but multinational. The fact that people like Ben Cohen and Anita Roddick and those of us who attended all those early SVN meetings have created a fashionable acronym (CSR), their own private language—the semantics of environmental footprints, sustainable development and eco-efficiency—and a visible seat on the *real* Chamber of Commerce gives some folks on the more radical side of the fence the jitters. What some welcome as signs of the movement's maturation others see as co-option, compromise, and corruption. The rise of CSR and the overwhelming evidence that some very large companies are starting to take this stuff seriously has also generated a cynical response among those already predisposed to believe that CSR is itself deeply cynical and deceptive. Curiously, CSR tends to get viciously attacked from both the political far left and from the right. From the left-wing perspective, CSR is often regarded as "greenwashing"—a term for promoting oneself as "green" and a good corporate citizen by adopting a few positive measures as window dressing, as a means of deflecting public attention from other, deeper, structural shortcomings. In this view, CSR is a lot of hype and PR—a fig leaf for the fundamentally destructive and rapacious character of unbridled free-market capitalism.

To its detractors on the right, CSR is a sop to sentimentality. Perhaps the most vociferous exponent of this point of view is the economist Milton Friedman, who in his 1963 book *Capitalism and Freedom* denounced the then-emerging doctrine of CSR as "fundamentally subversive." In a free society, Friedman argued, there is one and only one social responsibility of business—to use its resources and engage in activities designed to increase its profits so long as it stays within the rules of the game, which is to say, engages in open and free competition without deception or fraud.

Friedman somewhat hysterically criticized any attempt to make business responsible to society (as opposed to merely its shareholders) as "socialist" and "collectivist":

Once this [CSR] is adopted, the external forces that curb the market will not be the social consciences, however highly developed, of the pontificating executives; it will be the iron fist of Government bureaucrats. Here, as with price and wage controls, businessmen seem to me to reveal a suicidal impulse.

Leave it to business to make the money and make the products, the free-market fundamentalists say, and leave it to government to clean up the mess. Which would be all very well if government did or even could clean up the mess. But these same voices also argue strenuously for smaller government and oppose most efforts to address social and environmental problems.

Businesses for Social Responsibility, for its part, stays entirely aloof from the political debate. It sees its mission as "bringing big business to the table, and then moving the table." At least that's how Ben Cohen sympathetically summarizes its current position. According to Bob Dunn, the current director of BSR and a former executive at Levi Strauss, the best metaphor for BSR's influence is the Glide Memorial Church in the Tenderloin district of San Francisco, which is a church for sinners in which the topic of the sermon is always virtue, and every sinner is welcome to attend, without guilt.

BSR describes itself on its Web site as "a global organization that helps member companies achieve success in ways that respect ethical values, people, communities and the environment." The main way they go about doing that is by providing "information, tools and advisory services to make corporate social responsibility (CSR) an integral part of the business operations and strategies" of its members.

As for its members, most are household names. The BSR member roster reads like a global Chamber of Commerce, including (I provide here a fairly random selection), Levi Strauss (which provided substantial support to get the organization up and running), Polaroid, AT&T, Chiquita Brands, Agilent Technologies, Ford Motor Company, L.L. Bean, Eddie Bauer, the Gap, Federal Express, Hallmark, Hasbro, Starbucks, Nike, Reebok, Coca-Cola, Wal-Mart, Monsanto, McDonald's, and Philip Morris (Altria).

Some people believe that BSR is not sufficiently selective about admitting applicants to its table. They're right. BSR does not see its role as being selective or exclusionary—it sees its role as encouraging change in companies that have faced intense criticism for their practices. For BSR, the company is responsible for change, getting its act together, and possibly even taking it on the road. BSR doesn't criticize if one of its members produces cigarettes that cause cancer, soda that destroys teeth and fosters Type 2 diabetes, burgers high in cholesterol or French fries that—until they changed the formula—were fried in beef tallow, without disclosure, to the dismay of horrified vegetarians.

BSR's 700 corporate members pull in combined annual revenues of over $2 trillion and employ six million people worldwide (let's make that 5.5 million after the latest round of layoffs). What matters is that McDonald's takes the issue of CSR seriously by signing a deal with Newman's Own to supply dressings for its new salads, opening a non-ozone-depleting restaurant in Denmark, and issuing a CSR report. That its French fries clog arteries is, from BSR's point of view, a problem that McDonald's evidently has the desire to solve, but it's up to McDonald's to decide on how and when to solve it. After all, Ben & Jerry's ice cream also clogs arteries with its high butterfat content, although no one—as yet—has sued them for contributing to heart disease.

To get his take on what BSR does best, I had a lengthy conversation with Bob Dunn, which, if nothing else, left me impressed by the breadth and sincerity of the effort. To Dunn, the real driving force behind the emergence of CSR as a transformative factor in big business is that stakeholder groups in the more developed economies are insisting that attention be paid to these issues, while evidence is growing that "the reward and penalties associated with dealing with these issues effectively or not effectively" has become clearer to corporate managers. A third reason that CSR has become a contagious trend is that "large global companies have been putting pressure on their business partners to comply with new standards in both the environmental and social arenas," which adds up—in his view—to a virtuous circle, although he is the first to admit that the movement, worldwide, remains very much in its fledgling stages.

"As recently as five years ago," Dunn added, "when interacting with companies, the common starting point was having them ask us to *prove* to them that this was an effort worth making. Today, the starting point tends to be, 'Given our limited resources, what would be the most effective way to address these issues effectively?'"

That the big companies tend to see CSR as an incremental endeavor, and are highly conscious of the reputational (PR) dimension, makes some people cringe. But from Bob Dunn's perspective, "The broadness of the challenge still tends to be off-putting to some people. And when you're talking about large global companies, executing any change is daunting."

What BSR basically does best, according to Dunn, is to work closely with big companies to promote an emerging set of "best practices" in both the environmental and social areas. Nothing matters more to big companies, he insists, than the fact that other big companies are doing something, so every time he or one of the people he works with gets a big company to sign on to the program, he can feel pretty confident that other big companies will come snooping around, hoping to get in on the act. It's corporate nature, but it's also human nature, and a very effective tool for change. Is the change broad enough or fast enough to please everyone? Obviously not, but that is not the same thing as saying that encouraging the big companies to change—even at their own pace—is a bad thing.

Most left-leaning critics of CSR see it as a substitute for more effective government regulation of big business. Which is to some degree true. But some changes are best left to the theoretically free market, if it is a free market that forces companies to respond to such critical pressure points as class-action lawsuits and shareholder resolutions, a few of the tactics that outsiders use to get insiders to do things differently.

The problem ultimately boils down to whether you believe there is any alternative to big business—meaning big global business—and whether the "transnationals" can ever be truly beneficial to society. This has become something of an ideological, even religious dispute, dividing those who believe that it is possible and desirable to reform big business—because there is fundamentally no alternative—from those who unequivocally do not. Those who believe that big business should be eliminated all together are largely left out of the debate.

I believe that it's a question of *scale*—a term that first came into popular parlance in business as a derivative of the economists' term "economies of scale." The principle of economies of scale has been used—to great profit from certain interested parties—to justify mergers that enrich only the senior executives and the investment bankers who drove the deal. It has been used to justify the layoffs that invariably flow from those mergers, few of which yield the "synergistic" results promised by their proponents.

The computer industry has conceived of yet another use for the term "scale." Products and services designed for small-scale applications and local enterprises are said to be "scalable" if they could be expanded to a wider platform. When the members of the Social Venture Network—most of whom ran small, socially progressive companies—began to wonder if their ideas might apply in larger, less intimate settings, they were essentially asking: *Would corporate social responsibility scale?*

The Judy Economy

One of the most passionate proponents of the small-is-beautiful school of CSR is my friend Judy Wicks, the founder and proprietor of the White Dog Café in Philadelphia and a long-time SVN board member. The White Dog Café occupies a row of four beautifully restored nineteenth-century houses in the university district, near the campus of the University of Pennsylvania. Judy established what has

17

since become a great Philadelphia institution in 1983 as a tiny walk-in, take-out muffin shop. She only just barely scraped the money together to buy the building—in which she originally rented an upstairs apartment—when the university threatened to tear it down.

Today, her elegantly funky fancy-casual restaurant—the style entirely derived from Judy's taste—can accommodate more than a hundred diners at a single sitting, on multiple levels. Judy employs more than a hundred people and grosses $5 million annually. She is one of the most articulate proponents I know who believes that "reforming" the capitalist system, as currently constituted, won't be enough to solve the world's problems. She insists that CSR as practiced in the Big Business setting can only be a distraction unless there is fundamental and structural change in society.

I recently visited Philadelphia to sample some of Judy's all-natural cooking and to get her perspective on this issue of scale. When she started out, she told us, she had no interior kitchen and in winter she was forced to set up a plastic tent around a charcoal grill in the backyard, while her chef prepared food wearing a parka and boots. After a few years, the restaurant began to take off, and she doubled her sales annually and began to learn more about alternative sourcing—buying ingredients from local farmers as opposed to agribusiness. At some point in the late eighties she went to hear Ben Cohen deliver a speech at the nearby Wharton School of Business. Ben's topic, not surprisingly, was "the social responsibility of business," and Judy went to the talk with a cousin who happened to be an old college friend of Ben's.

After Ben's talk, the three discussed the question of "what sort of impact a small company can have on the larger society." How effective, in other words, could a small company be at influencing change on a larger scale? Ben insisted, to Judy's surprise and delight, "you didn't have to be a large company to make a major impact."

Nevertheless, Judy recalled, "compared to Ben Cohen and his company, Tom Chappell and his company [Tom's of Maine], Anita Roddick and her company, and even you, Jeffrey—and *your* company—me and my company felt small and insignificant." She suffered from what she called a "small company complex."

Not long after that conversation, Judy met David Korten, the Seattle-based author and thinker about business and the world economy.

18

In his best-known book *When Corporations Rule the World*, Korten argues that globalization, as currently constituted, is effectively a process that only benefits big wealthy companies and big wealthy countries, and that it shuts everyone else out of the prospect of a sustainable prosperity. During Judy's discussion with Korten, she said, "David told me that what I was doing was *great*. He even came up with a name for what I was doing. He called it 'the Judy Economy!'"

What David Korten and Ben Cohen said was intriguing, but Judy's own instincts and core convictions led her to the great and motivating insight of her life. The idea of small-scale local businesses developing organically within a particular community, built on personal relationships, could be a valid model for a type of business that, she believed, represented the only hope we have as a species for surviving on the planet and creating a just and sustainable society.

From her point of view, even the gospel of growth with social responsibility espoused by her good friends and fellow SVN members Ben Cohen and Gary Hirshberg of Stonyfield Farm is fatally flawed. Under the onslaught of big agribusiness, small farms are being inexorably driven out of business, as are small local businesses when the big discount chains roll into town. She can see no positive outcome of the success of Starbucks, and insists that the world economy would be far better off if it were torn apart by centrifugal forces and the globalization trend was replaced by a countervailing trend, namely, localization.

According to Judy, as long as companies are obliged by law to serve the short-term needs of their shareholders—which, as Friedman states, is the conventional view of many managers' fiduciary duty to their shareholders—companies will continue to maximize profits regardless of other costs. This inevitably means raping the land, mistreating communities, and generally acting as very bad apples. Without some fundamental shift in the managers' role of the company in society, all the CSR in the world, according to this argument, will remain just so much window dressing.

As Judy told us, fretfully, over lunch:

My fear is that if current trends continue, we're all going to end up as serfs on global plantations. I believe in economic democracy, and I regard large companies as fundamentally undemocratic. Big corporations want access to cheap labor and cheap raw materials, cheap resources. My argument is that even in cases where individuals within these monoliths are passionate about change, that without some fundamental change to the structure, we won't see any real change, only cosmetic change.

When I asked her if there was anything being done by large global companies that she felt good about, she smiled and said: "Yes, that they are imploding. Look at Enron and WorldCom and all the others—don't you think they're just the tip of the iceberg?"

I left the White Dog Café feeling, on the one hand, optimistic that Judy had created a successful model that was truly worth replicating, and pessimistic about her model's chances of ever prevailing against the onslaught of globalization. It was hard to argue, philosophically, with her point that the "gospel of growth" espoused by even the most socially progressive businessmen, myself included, was riddled with contradictions. One of the points she so eloquently made, in fact, kept nagging at me after we left her restaurant:

> What needs to be examined more closely is this obsession with *scale*, which has everything to do with knocking out your competitors. My point is that even a Stonyfield Farm or a Tom's of Maine or a Seventh Generation is operating under the same pressure; that the businesses that are going to get knocked out of the market are not the Procter & Gambles of the world but the small localized businesses that can't achieve the economies of scale of even these mid-sized progressive companies. While a local or a regional brand can cooperate with other local or regional brands, in the long run they won't be able to compete with the larger companies.

I knew, of course, that Judy was right, and that at Seventh Generation, we were guilty of seeing the problem of growth mainly through the lens of our own self-interest. Without thinking too self-critically about it, we have tended to regard every unit of our products sold as a victory against the monolithic corporations that made the petroleum-derived, hyper-synthetic, chemically ridden products that our products were created to displace.

So far, as we took a larger chunk of the market—in a narrow niche called "natural household products" in which we have as yet few competitors—and as we moved from the natural food stores into supermarket chains, we have in fact been hurting the small local competitors within that niche more than we are hurting Procter & Gamble. While our efforts are enlarging the market for natural household products, I can't see how some of our smaller competitors can survive in an increasingly professional, competitive, and ultimately much larger market niche. There will always be successful niche brands, but only the very smartest and innovative among the smaller competitors are likely to survive.

Gary's World

Just a few months after our stimulating gourmet encounter with Judy Wicks in Philadelphia, I traveled to California to exhibit our products at Expo West, the largest natural product show in the country. There, I ran into another old friend and fellow SVN board member Gary Hirshberg, the founder of organic yogurt maker Stonyfield Farm. Gary was brimming with pride at having just sold a big chunk of his company to the French food conglomerate Group Danone. Although he and his family had walked away with many millions in the sale, money wasn't entirely the issue. He regarded this deal as a heaven-sent opportunity to "infect" Group Danone—as he cheerfully put it—with the organic bug.

We will be dealing with the social implications of the phenomenon of small, socially responsible companies "selling out" to big, possibly less socially responsible companies in a later chapter. For now, I'll relate a fruitful exchange Gary and I had—over a shared plate of organic snacks—on the ever-contentious subject of scale.

Gary began his career as an environmental activist, as the executive director of a small Cape Cod–based nonprofit organization called the New Alchemy Institute. "We started out as a nonprofit organic farming school," he recalled over lunch, "devoted to closing the gap between farmers and consumers." New Alchemy's goal, he said, was to "try to teach consumers to be more aware of the importance of farmers, and also to teach them to be more aware of their own power to keep farming local. We also spent a lot of time trying to teach farmers to be more aware of consumers, and to make them aware of the quasi-religious adherence to quality standards that growing hormone- and pesticide-free organic foods demands."

Does this sound familiar? It did to me, particularly since we'd had lunch not long before with Judy Wicks. In other words, Judy and Gary—who are old and good friends—started out from pretty much the same place. Organic farming and agriculture is quintessentially local, and its roots lay in a rejection of factory farming and agribusiness, which proponents of organic contend is fundamentally unhealthy, not just to people, but to the planet.

At some point in those early days of running his nonprofit, Gary made contact with Samuel Kayman, who ran a school for organic farming based in Wilton, New Hampshire. Sam's organic yogurt was famous, but the fledging business he was trying to get started was far from flourishing. Taking a gamble on Gary, Sam Kayman asked him to help run the business that today is Stonyfield Farm, an $85 million-a-year organic yogurt business for which Group Danone paid $125 million for 40 percent, with an option to buy another 40 percent at the conclusion of a prescribed period.

Judy Wicks does not approve of Gary's "selling out," a point that she made to a reporter for *Mother Jones*, because she believes that Gary is fooling himself that he can, in effect, have his cake and eat it too. At the natural foods show, Gary struck me as a man who very much believed that he exemplified the "doing well by doing good" ethos of the small, socially responsible business community. He has grown rich by living off the fat of the land—land he believes he can simultaneously improve by treating it with healthier methods.

The moral and ethical bottom line for Gary, as he explained, is tangible: How many farms can you get to go organic? How many pesticides and herbicides and fungicides and hormones can you keep out of the sanitary systems and groundwater of our much-abused planet by promoting organic methods and practices?

The U.S. government has recently instituted a very strict regimen for farmers in order for them to qualify for organic status. Farmers must certify, among other conditions, that they have not used any pesticides on their fields for three years. Gary also sees the move toward organic as the ultimate salvation of the small, family farmer. The organic produce market is at present growing at a rate fully five times that of conventional—that is, pesticide-ridden—produce. This is a hard fact that has not gone unnoticed by "big food" companies like Group Danone, Kraft, General Foods, Coke, and Unilever, which have recently exhibited a strong interest in snapping up small organic food companies. Why? Because they are tapping into the fastest-growing segment of the food business and attracting a very loyal and committed customer base. Are the big companies getting into organic for their financial health or the health of the planet? According to most impartial observers, the answer to that question can only be: yes and no. Yes, they are getting "into" organic, but while individuals within those companies may ascribe to the environmental and moral dimension of the change, the primary motivation is to participate in any high-growth, profitable market.

According to Gary Hirshberg, this is a classic win–win situation; we should all be happy that organic produce has gone mainstream enough for the big food companies to want to get into it. As he proudly put it to me:

> What's happening in the mainstream world with McDonald's and Unilever and Kraft and Nestlé is happening to Danone. They recognize that our approach, what you are doing and what I am doing, and the depth of that relationship and bond with the consumer, is a model they're going to have to adopt if they're going to be successful.

The commercial success of a Stonyfield Farm or a Ben & Jerry's—which in April of 2000 was acquired by Unilever, much to Ben Cohen's chagrin—has "legitimized, rationalized, and validated our hypothesis" that businesses can be both successful and socially responsible, Hirshberg insisted.

"These big companies," he said—and I did not detect a defensive note in his voice—"can make more of a difference with *one purchase order* than I can make in a lifetime!" To Gary, the issue of scale has positive as well as a negative aspects. If organic farming takes off on a grand scale, he can't see the problem. "I hear these debates in places like *Mother Jones* with Judy Wicks saying that you have to do everything locally. And I say, 'That's great.' But quite frankly, I don't have a long enough life to wait for change to happen that way."

Within the last several years, Gary's wife was diagnosed with cancer and he lost two of his brothers. "My experience of the last two years," he said, "has taught me just how short and temporal life is. Waiting for capitalism to fail and waiting for big companies to disaggregate into millions of little companies is certainly not going to happen within my lifetime, if it's going to happen at all. The ecological let alone human cost of these companies trying to survive through some ecological catastrophe—I'd rather see a gentler transformation, kind of like the fall of the Berlin wall."

The path to more responsible business is fraught with conflicts and compromises. Most people are deeply sympathetic to the plight of the local business forced to close down when a Wal-Mart opens offering lower prices; or the struggle of the underpaid worker, whether he or she be a small Mexican landholder battered by the onslaught of U.S. imports under NAFTA—particularly while the United States cynically continues to promote the idea of "free trade" as it continues subsidizing its farmers to the tune of some $20,000 per capita per year; or the predicament of the owner of a local stationery store, whose business shrinks with the arrival of a Staples or Office Max in the neighborhood.

I have been known to patronize a Starbucks without guilt, and I have also spent more than a few years patiently growing our own business. Our motivating force is to improve human health and the health of the planet by eliminating harmful synthetic chemicals, many of them petroleum-based, from our environment. I also admit to feeling happy and proud when a chain like Kroger stocks Seventh Generation products, because—as it says right there on the label—for every bottle of vegetable-based dish detergent or laundry detergent we sell, or nonbleached paper products, we are keeping harmful chemicals away from children and out of the waste stream.

If Seventh Generation one day were to become the size of Procter & Gamble, would that be a good thing or a bad thing? To me, the answer is obvious: The more the demand grows for healthier products, the better off we all will be, especially our children's children. The greater the public support for businesses committed to social responsibility, the more likely it is that responsible business becomes the standard to which all business is held. The underlying premise of corporate social responsibility is that *all* business has got to do something urgently to keep humankind from destroying itself by using toxic chemicals, through excessive reliance on fossil fuels, from a failure to more equitably share the resources available to us all. If business fails at this task, there might not be any more business to maintain. I've got to agree with Bob Dunn that bringing business to the table—and then moving the table—is what matters most.

In our world where dishonesty and scandal make it into the daily headlines, where oil spills and excessive executive compensation dominate the news, it's hard to feel optimistic about the positive changes that remain mostly out of view.

Where individuals are most likely to disagree is at what speed the table needs to be moved, how to treat those companies who are still committed to doing business underneath that table, and what regulatory changes need to be made to address those issues that business is unable or unwilling to address itself.

We, the small, socially responsible entrepreneurs, should be proud to have helped initiate a fundamental shift in the way private enterprise is conducted. Big global companies have begun speaking our language and even emulating some of what we've done in other arenas. We are all on a journey, and the more our goals converge at the end of the day, the greater our chance of ultimate success.

chapter **two**

The Value of Values

As I look back on my life's work, I'm probably most proud of having helped to create a company that by virtue of its values, practices and success has had a tremendous impact on the way companies are managed around the world. I'm particularly proud that I'm leaving behind an ongoing organization that can live on as a role model long after I'm gone.

—William R. Hewlett, cofounder of Hewlett-Packard

This uplifting quote, lifted from the pages of James C. Collins and Jerry I. Porras's best-selling book *Built to Last,* is one item culled from nearly a decade of research conducted by the authors at Stanford Business School. Collins and Porras advanced the thesis that the major difference between "visionary" companies (not necessarily socially responsible ones) and their less visionary counterparts is that visionary companies operate according to a set of clearly defined "core values." Fundamental to these companies' operation is the creation of a "cult-like culture" that defines the genetic makeup of the company, internally and externally. Most importantly to Collins and Porras, "visionary" companies generate outstanding financial performances. These empirical findings did much to bolster former Johnson & Johnson CEO James Burke's more intuitive contention, made nearly two decades before, that "ethical" companies—what today we *would* call "socially responsible" companies—consistently outperform their less responsible counterparts and competitors, as measured by long-term TRS (Total Return to Shareholders).

Collins and Porras persuasively demonstrated a strong causal link between culture and values and financial performance. They created three imaginary portfolios, one composed of investments in a "general-market stock fund," a second composed of investments in a "comparison company stock fund," and a third composed of investments in a "visionary stock fund." The focus here is on long-term financial performance based on an imagined $1 investment in all three funds made on January 1, 1926. If you reinvested all dividends, the value of the three portfolios on December 31, 1990, would have been:

1. General-market stock fund: $415
2. Comparison companies: $995
3. Visionary companies: $6,356

Lacking comparatively hard research but possessed of a wealth of business experience, Johnson & Johnson founder Robert W. Johnson Sr. arrived at the same conclusion some decades before. He saw no conflict between upholding his fiduciary duty to his shareholders and deliberately ranking shareholder concerns *last* on his official list of corporate priorities. The result was that long-term shareholder performance and satisfaction inexplicably *rose* over time. The issue of time is fundamental in such cases, because the performance of socially responsible businesses can often only be amortized over a longer time horizon.

Contrary to business school doctrine, "maximizing shareholder wealth" or "profit maximization" has not been the dominant driving force or primary objective through the history of visionary companies. Visionary companies pursue a cluster of objectives, of which making money is only one—and not necessarily the primary one. Yes, they seek profits, but they're guided by a core ideology, values and a sense of purpose beyond

just making money. Yet, paradoxically, the visionary companies make
more money than the more purely profit-driving comparison companies.

—Built to Last

The underlying premise of *Built to Last* and its best-selling sequel *Good to Great* is adherence to well-defined and well-articulated "core values" is the key to enduring corporate success. This has become virtually axiomatic in management circles today and is exemplified by a dizzying proliferation of mission statements, ethics, credos, commandments, and principles, and by intense management interest in the discovery, articulation, and implementation of core values. This is all well and good, provided that there is no glaring disconnect between the core values, missions, and ideals being articulated internally and the firm's operations and behavior in the marketplace. Where I depart from Collins' and Porras' agenda is that they are largely agnostic as to what social or environmental ingredients might be contained in a company's core values.

Not all visions and values are created equal. For example, Collins and Porras have held up Procter & Gamble and Philip Morris (now known as Altria) as "visionary" companies that have achieved long-term success in the marketplace based on the single-minded pursuit of a values-based culture. I would not take issue with that conclusion. However, Philip Morris (Altria) might have the best-defined values in the world, and be one of the most philanthropic organizations on the planet—which historically they have been—yet if those values don't include the health and/or environmental effects of their products (ranging from chocolate to tobacco), surely those values need reexamining.

Procter & Gamble wins rafts of rewards for the excellence of its management, the consistency of its financial performance, and its generous philanthropic endeavors. But Procter & Gamble opens itself up to criticism from environmental advocates when it insists, contrary to a wealth of scientific evidence, that paper bleached with chlorine, soaps, and detergents made primarily from petroleum-based chemicals, and products that contain certain suspect chemicals or additives, pose no risks to human, animal, or environmental health.

This is why I was less than amused by Procter & Gamble's plan to spend millions of dollars promoting the fact that Dawn dishwashing liquid (the #1 dish detergent in the country with a nearly 35 percent market share) is used by wildlife groups to clean ducks and other seabirds covered by oil spills. "They're facing the classic problem of a mature product in a mature market," opined one professor of business, who praised P & G's resorting to "cause related marketing" as a classic solution to that problem. The executive in charge of the campaign at the ad agency described a touching scene filmed at the International Bird Rescue Research Center near San Francisco "attempting to show that Dawn . . . is a brand that cares about community and the environment." At no point did the company see fit to mention that Dawn is a petroleum-based detergent, and that simply by virtue of its formulation it is, along with all petroleum-based products, a direct contributor to the very oil spills it is helping to "clean up."

Are Procter & Gamble and Altria (Philip Morris) socially responsible companies? By some definitions yes, by others, clearly no. Defining a socially responsible company involves invoking any number of normative judgments—yes, those "values" again—that are inherently subjective. A useful definition of corporate social responsibility appears in *Business: The Ultimate Resource* (2002), which helps us in rendering some of these judgments. Although "there is no single definition of CSR," the author of the entry points out:

> The term generally refers to an ongoing commitment by business to behave ethically and to contribute to economic development when demonstrating respect for people, communities, society at large, and the environment. In short, CSR marries the concepts of global citizenship with environmental stewardship and sustainable development.

What truly constitutes corporate social responsibility remains largely defined in the mind of the beholder, since no firm social consensus has yet formed as to what constitutes an appropriate level of responsibility of business to society. Apostles of Milton Friedman insist that the only responsibility of business is to generate maximum profits for its shareholders. Any other social goal, they maintain—particularly one that might deprive from the immediate concern for profit—betrays management's fiduciary responsibility to its shareholders. But Bill Hewlett and Dave Packard, the founders of Hewlett-Packard, have just as firmly argued that the primary purpose of business should be to serve and improve society, and that money-making should come in no higher than second. Robert Wood Johnson and his successors at Johnson & Johnson—most notably James Burke—have added an intriguing wrinkle to this argument by insisting that a business that consciously puts the needs of society *above* the needs of its shareholders may well end up making more money for its shareholders, over the long term, than a business that seeks only to make money.

Lynn Sharp Payne, a Harvard Business School professor, looks at the question from another perspective using the framework of morals and ethics:

> In the end, whether we ascribe moral personality to the corporation is not a question of metaphysics but of pragmatics. As a purely pragmatic matter, a society cannot survive, let alone thrive, if it exempts its most influential and pervasive institutions from all notions of morality. This, more than anything, explains why society has, in effect, endowed the corporation with the moral personality that many theorists have long insisted it could not have.

Can CSR actually comprise part of a core business strategy? In short, can being a socially responsible company contribute to the bottom line? I think the fairest answer to that question, based on the latest empirical evidence, is a qualified yes. Again, Lynn Sharp Payne presents the most comprehensive analysis:

> Perhaps the best perspective on the ethics–economic performance issue comes from a recent review of some 95 academic studies of the relationship between corporate financial and social performance.
>
> Although there is much to question about these studies, it is worth noting that only 4 of the 95 studies found a negative relationship between social and financial performance. Fifty-five studies found a positive correlation between better financial performance and better social performance. Twenty-two found no relationship between the two; and 18 found a mixed relationship.

The good news is that as more and more companies have consciously set socially responsible goals—and the evidence has begun to build—adopting an ethic of corporate social responsibility that cuts across all segments of a business can form the basis of a winning long-term strategy.

You are not here merely to make a living. You are here to enrich the world—and you impoverish yourself if you forget the errand.

—Woodrow Wilson

The fact that you can purchase a brass plaque bearing the Enron Mission Statement* on eBay—for a dollar—has certainly not escaped the critics of CSR. Enron was, in its time, highly touted as a socially responsible company, and proudly held in any number of socially and environmentally screened portfolios. Of course, its success in pulling the wool over the eyes of the sort of people who give out social responsibility awards should not be considered surprising. These are hardly green-eyeshade types, and Enron was an extremely professional put-up job that fooled hard-nosed analysts well outside the CSR crowd.

Enron conspicuously embraced a new business model held up in its era as the essence of socially responsible business practice. It was widely praised by analysts and the financial press for transforming itself from a collection of "hard assets"—traditional energy company properties such as pipelines, oil and gas wells, and the like—into a twenty-first-century post-industrial trading operation more like a Wall Street brokerage house (in retrospect, more like a bucket shop). It doesn't take a rocket scientist, or a former McKinsey consultant like ex-Enron president Jeffrey Skilling, to realize that an authentic energy production operation generates a lot more pollution than a trading floor.

---

*"We treat others as we would like to be treated ourselves. . . . We do not tolerate abusive or disrespectful treatment. Ruthlessness, callousness and arrogance don't belong here. . . ."

This fact addresses one of the more complex issues facing socially responsible investors: What constitutes a socially responsible company? A company, for example, that shifts all of its production to low-cost overseas subcontractors can claim to generate little to no pollution. But of course, this argument is truly specious, the company has shifted its traditional sphere of responsibility off its balance sheet. But this is truly a case of passing the buck, along with the muck.

One of the more unfortunate aspects of the corporate scandals of 2002 was that the irresponsible behavior regarded as so outrageous ended up being narrowly defined in terms of strictly *financial* misconduct, which meant that the victims were mainly shareholders and employees. That executive compensation had reached obscene levels by the turn of the century, that shareholder rights had been eroded, that pension funds were being destroyed and companies looted, all of this was understood to be tragic and terrible, but for the most part, legal and even defensible. By reporting and framing the issue as essentially a financial and legal matter, the media—misled by the U.S. government—was spun into missing the boat. Because if these were simply "accounting scandals" equivalent to the savings and loan scandal of the 1980s, the solution was obviously a tightening of accounting regulations and, in some cases, the introduction of new legislation. Then back to business-as-usual.

But what was truly going on in the corporate boardrooms wasn't limited to financial finagling. It wasn't just a matter of scale, although scale was clearly involved. A large part of the disease underlying all of these symptoms was management becoming captive to a stingy time horizon. A nation of day-traders, taking a myopic, short-term snapshot of the prospects of a company, had forced managers to do all sorts of silly and sleazy things they would otherwise never have felt compelled to do.

Traditionally and historically—although not consistently, as the quote from Woodrow Wilson cited earlier indicates—companies have been held responsible and accountable by investors, by government, by nonprofit groups, and by consumers solely for producing goods that functioned effectively and did not cause bodily harm, for making a reasonable profit, and for turning that profit—after management takes its share off the top—over to shareholders for distribution, in the form of dividends, a higher stock price, or both.

Traditionally and historically, companies paid workers the wage that was less than the cost of recruiting and training replacements. Companies bought raw materials as commodities at the lowest possible open-market price, and produced goods and rendered services as cost-effectively as possible. If they generated toxic waste or pollution or any other form of disposable effluent, they disposed of it appropriately—which meant by the cheapest means possible. And in those not uncommon cases when companies were exposed, a fairly limited menu of recourse and punishment was available, with redress through the courts or limited government action. The old trio of enforcement: legislation, regulation, and, if all else fails, litigation.

Traditionally and historically, some companies practiced corporate philanthropy, mainly as an extension of public relations. Few people noticed. Today, many companies have been called upon, and have in fact called upon themselves, to cast the net of responsibility wider, to set the bar higher, to do good for others, not just themselves. Traditionally and historically, companies possessed human resources departments, investor relations departments, marketing departments, and even environmental compliance or health and safety departments. Today, many have corporate social responsibility departments.

CSR represents the attempt to integrate all of these functions into a holistic, cross-disciplinary pursuit premised on a common set of agreed-upon social values—transparency, diversity, equity, and sustainability to name a few—driven by a broad vision of corporations as positive social citizens that takes twenty-first-century global realities into account. Today, the definition of responsibility has become immeasurably broader than ever before. Today, if you buy a pair of running shoes made by Nike, as Sarah Severn, Nike VP for CSR, recently advised us, "you aren't just buying a pair of running shoes; you are buying a product based on your knowledge of the people who made it, how much they were paid, how clean was the factory, how many toxic chemicals, if any, they were exposed to, what processes were used to make it, and what they will do to the air if they're incinerated, or to the soil or groundwater if they're buried in a landfill."

33

Today the amount of information available about every company and organization in the world is so immense—much if not all of it available from the organizations' own Web sites—that consumers and investors feel capable of rendering sophisticated and informed judgments and decisions about the companies from whom they purchase products, or whose stock they choose to invest in, based on a broader set of factors than was imaginable even ten years ago.

Today, in a world in which the market capitalization of Microsoft makes a single company worth more than many nation-states, private enterprise is increasingly being called upon to take on responsibilities commensurate with that power. Private enterprise has, at the same time, successfully challenged—particularly in the United States—the suitability of government regulation to govern corporate behavior. CSR represents the business community's response to growing demands for greater accountability in the environmental and social fields.

Compare and contrast the view of Harvard professor Lynn Sharp Payne—"As a purely pragmatic matter, a society cannot survive, let alone thrive, if it exempts its most influential and pervasive institution [the corporation] from all notions of morality"—to that of Milton Friedman. Friedman has consistently insisted that "business" cannot be said to have responsibilities, because "business" is not a person.

> What does it mean to say that "business" has responsibilities? Only people can have responsibilities. A corporation is an artificial person and in this sense may have artificial responsibilities, but "business" as a whole cannot be said to have responsibilities, even in this vague sense.

One indication of how far we have come from the Friedmanesque view of the corporation in society was brought home by a fascinating series of remarks made by Professor John G. Ruggie of Harvard's Kennedy School of Government. At a recent conference in New York sponsored by the World Business Council for Sustainable Development—a consortium of businesses dedicated to promoting and pursing market-based concepts of sustainable growth, Friedman noted:

> The role of companies in society is undergoing a profound and fundamental change. Social expectations are very different from what they

were ten or even five years ago. No longer are only products being assessed by consumers; the companies *behind* the products are being assessed as well.

Some companies have awakened public scrutiny through bad behavior, other companies have invited public praise and appreciation for good behavior. BP [British Petroleum] saw what happened to Shell in Nigeria and didn't want the same thing to happen to them in Angola. Companies are seeing a real *competitive* advantage in adopting a positive corporate social profile, not just a *marketing* advantage.

One example of just how wide a net is being cast by social activists today—and the degree to which companies are responding to this call—was cited by Ruggie:

The Coca-Cola company was targeted recently by AIDS activists for not only not doing enough for their own employees about AIDS treatment and prevention, but also for not doing enough for the employees of their bottlers and suppliers. They were cajoled and pressured into taking a stand and engaging in an issue *to which they had no intrinsic corporate connection whatsoever*.

What they did have was the money and the resources to tackle the problem because they had a bottling network. They had a distribution network that could be used as a pipeline for life-saving pharmaceuticals as for soda. This was a classic case of heightened social expectations having a direct effect on a company's operations. And lo and behold, it worked! The company took steps to meet these expectations, and ended up agreeing with the activists that they had a *responsibility* in this area because they had an *ability* in this area.

"That," he opined, "is a very different beast from the capitalism of the past."

Internalizing Your Externalities

In the opening paragraphs of *The Wealth of Nations* (1776), a young Scottish moral philosopher named Adam Smith wrote of an imaginary visit to a pin factory. The pin factory employed a staff of ten men to produce 48,000 pins a day, a rate of production that compared very favorably to the maximum of ten or twenty pins a day that a skilled pin-maker, working alone, was currently considered capable of turning out.

This extraordinary leap of productivity, Smith argued, was the logical outgrowth not just of the modern machinery employed but of a miraculous new managerial system, which he called the "division of labor." Under this remarkable system, one man—and not necessarily a highly skilled one—could draw out the wire, while another straightened it, a third cut it, a forth pointed it, a fifth ground the head, and so on through at least eighteen discrete operations.

For Smith, the pin factory was a wonderful new form of socially responsible business. The wealth and prosperity generated by it and its counterparts offered an enormous opportunity for human betterment. If the goods these new factories manufactured with such impressive dispatch could be traded freely and fairly in open markets, without mutually destructive trade wars and tariffs, the modern industrial enterprise would surely lead, he believed, to the highest form of social good.

Comparatively speaking, Adam Smith was right. The pin factory, and industrialization in general, represented an enormous improvement over mercantile trading houses and banks, on the one hand, and feudal agricultural estates on the other. The pin factory improved not just the lot of its proprietor but also of the people who worked there, not only because they earned higher wages, but because they could afford to purchase the cheaply manufactured goods that factories mass-produced.

But there are two things about Adam Smith that many of his modern disciples tend to forget. For all his enthusiasm about the "invisible hand" of market forces working without human intervention, his earlier work—*The Theory of Moral Sentiments*—laid out a comprehensive argument for morality and compassion in both commercial and governmental affairs. Smith, in short, was no hard-hearted capitalist. He would have been just as appalled at the depredations against humanity—and particularly against workers—committed in his name as Karl Marx would have been appalled at the depredations committed in his.

What Smith was rightly celebrating was a means of escaping the agricultural feudal economy, in which hereditary landowners, to the detriment of their workers, enjoyed most of the benefits. In an industrial economy, by contrast, a combination of higher wages and lower prices—the result of more efficient production—would spread wealth created far beyond the factory floor, creating a new middle class and a more prosperous working class.

Yet Smith missed out on a number of key points about the pin factory and its mechanical descendants that have since clouded the outlook for industrialization. Probably the most important omission was the possibility that the pin factory might be even more profitable if it were operated using child labor, underpaid labor, or even slave labor—although slavery throughout its modern history was almost entirely confined to agricultural economies. Smith also failed to foresee the long-term adverse effects on human health, welfare, and happiness caused by the factory's nasty outputs, ranging from air and water pollution to other forms of environmental and social degradation, including the health and safety risks, and the fatigue and monotony of a great deal of factory work. Smith also failed to foresee that while modern industrial capitalism would indeed cause a worldwide rise in wages as a result of enhanced productivity, capitalists and their senior managers would nonetheless retain the lion's share of the "surplus value" generated by their workers.

Here is where Karl Marx and his disciples stepped in. In the late 1830s, Friedrich Engels, the son of a prominent German industrialist, was sent by his father to Manchester, England, to manage one of his father's factories. The young Engels was so shocked by the squalid conditions in which the English working classes had been forced to labor and live in (the descendants of Adam Smith's pin factories, now primarily textile factories) that he wrote the *Condition of the Working Classes in Great Britain* (1844). Engels can be regarded as a classic example of a rich kid suffering from liberal guilt. He played out this role to the hilt by becoming the primary financial benefactor of a fellow German citizen exiled in England named Karl Marx. But if Adam Smith overlooked the more unsavory outputs of his pin factories, Marx and Engels can likewise be accused of ignoring the benefits generated by industrial life. The Industrial Revolution was a far more complex phenomenon than the caricatures promoted either by the anti-industrialists or the pro-industrialists.

Even in the early years of industrialization, there were a number of socially responsible enterprises established by the socially responsible entrepreneurs of their day. One of the best known was the ceramics empire founded by Josiah Wedgewood, who used his fortune and even his wares—on which he carved consciousness-raising messages just the way Stonyfield Farm conducts "campaigns" on its yogurt lids—to promote the cause of abolition and call for the destruction of slavery.

In 1799, Robert Owen took over his father's failing textile mill in New Lanark, Scotland, and by 1807 had made it so profitable that he was not only able to buy out his partners, he was able to create an idealized, progressive version of Adam Smith's pin factory. At its peak, Owen's New Lanark plants employed several thousand workers, mainly recruited from the worst slums of Edinburgh and Glasgow— itself a progressive recruitment policy, because like the underclass of today, these people were considered shiftless and unemployable. In his time, Owen was hailed for drastically curtailing the then common practice of employing child labor—he hired no one under thirteen— and for reducing the working hours for all factory hands from 13 1/2 to 10 hours a day.

But since capitalists like Wedgewood and Owen were more the exception than the rule, it's not surprising that the early decades of industrialization were dominated by controversies involving the treatment of workers in the factories. These unresolved issues would in time give rise to violent and bitter strikes, spawn a vital trades union movement, and even lead to the sparking of social revolutions engineered by activists emboldened by their interpretations of Marxist theory. The degradation to the environment caused by the expansion of industry did not go unremarked by labor advocates, but it was most acerbically noted by novelists like Charles Dickens, as well as by another early socially responsible entrepreneur, Robert Morris.

Morris was just as appalled as Marx and Engels by the degree to which industrialization fostered alienation. But while Marx and Engels focused on the degree to which capitalism denied industrial laborers the fruits of their labor, Morris was outraged by the pollution generated by factories, and by the resulting alienation of people from nature, including the decline of natural crafts and traditional forms of manufacture. Morris created a model factory that fused the best of feudal craftsmanship with the benefits of mass production. A lover of nature who abhorred industrial effluvia, he could be considered one of the first modern industrialist-capitalist-environmentalists.

What social critics like Marx, Engels, and Dickens decried about in-dustrialization—pollution, social upheaval, the decline of traditional crafts, and the tendency of wealth to become concentrated in the hands of a few controllers of capital—were only occasionally redressed by the actions of a small number of progressive and enlightened capi-talists. The overwhelming trend of the laissez-faire industrial economy was for wages to rise along with productivity, but also for a rise in lev-els of pollution, social unrest, and extreme dislocation on the part of people who lacked the skills to profit in the new economy.

All the nasty stuff that industrial processes leave in their wake are known as *externalities* by economists, because these are factors that operators *externalize*—that is, disregard, discard, and discharge into the environment. Under the neoclassical laissez-faire system champi-oned by Adam Smith and his intellectual heirs, externalities are fobbed off on the society at large, rather than being placed on the books of the producers as an expense or liability or paid for by the consumers of the product.

Of course, one person's externalities may be another person's liveli-hood. One set of externalities might be generated by the degradation of a landscape near a town where a Wal-Mart—or any other "big-box" merchant—decides to locate. Such an event may create a num-ber of low-end jobs, while simultaneously depriving locally based family businesses of their livelihoods. While some externalities are fairly easily measured and traced—such as toxic discharges—with others, the issue is more subjective. Costco recently faced strong op-position from merchants and community leaders in the city of Cuer-navaca, Mexico, when local interests accused the company of destroy-ing the historical fabric of the central city by locating one of its big-box stores in the center of downtown.

The project obviously had its supporters and detractors, but CSR might have entered the equation if Costco had deliberately cultivated a more benign social profile. What if Costco planned to foster local entrepreneurship by buying and promoting local crafts? What if Costco offered to restore a whole city block and weave its "big box" into the fabric of the neighborhood and its architecture, persuading critics that its presence downtown would be an asset, not a blight? The CSR approach might have cost more money in the short term, but in the long term, it would make more money and generate more goodwill for everyone—including the community.

Sorting out these complex issues and reaching effective compromises lies at the heart of any socially responsible enterprise. A socially responsible business owns up to its responsibility to mitigate the externalities it generates, and then sets out systematically to do something about it. You can't produce or sell anything without leaving some trace behind. But the most important thing is to fairly acknowledge and disclose the adverse effects that you do generate, and then take action to ameliorate them. A business should be willing to be held accountable to achieving measurable progress toward a predefined goal.

There is, of course, a proper sequence of steps to this process. The first is to acknowledge that you are creating a problem—first to yourself, then to the public. The next step is to do what it takes to clean up your own mess. Another step is to clearly explain to the public what steps are being taken, what steps are not being taken, what steps are likely to be taken in the future. This becomes a question of making clear commitments, setting measurable benchmarks against which progress can be determined, and then doing what it takes to stick to achieving the agreed-upon goals.

Historically, externalities have been internalized by three social mechanisms: (1) *legislation*—laws and statutes governing corporate behavior, (2) *regulation*—society's attempt to forestall having to recover damages by other means, and (3) *litigation*—what happens after laws and regulations have been violated.

A recent *New York Times* obituary of the grassroots environmentalist Fred Danback illustrates the complex intersection of legislation, regulation, and litigation as it pertains to forcing a company to live up to its obligations even under existing statutes. Danback was born and raised in Yonkers, on the banks of the Hudson River, and from an early age came to know and respect the shad fishermen who earned a decent living fishing in a once magnificent river that had long since become a toxic cesspool. As a young man, Danback took a job in Hastings-on-Hudson as a janitor at a copper cable factory owned by Anaconda Cable & Wire—a subsidiary of the notorious Anaconda Copper, then the largest employer and polluter in the state of Montana. During this time he joined the United States Volunteer Lifesaving Corps, which helped save people in danger on the river.

The most endangered species on the river, he soon found, were not careless boaters but the shad that had once thrived in its currents. The fishermen who depended upon the shad's survival started telling Danback about their dwindling shad catch, which they ascribed to the increasing pollution coming from industrial plants like Anaconda Cable & Wire. To his shock, Danback could plainly see something his employers chose to blithely ignore: daily discharges of tons of copper filings and gallons of waste oil and sulfuric acid into the river, with no one thinking anything of it. They had been doing it for years, with utter impunity. The fish were dying off, and the shad that remained could no longer be legally sold for food.

Fred Danback knew that it wasn't fair that one man's livelihood—his and his fellow workers—should depend upon the destruction of another's—the fish and the fishermen. He began drawing detailed maps of the pipes through which the company was releasing its toxic effluent. In his naiveté, he even showed them to his employers, thinking that they would be grateful to him for alerting them to a problem that was well within their capacity to fix.

But Danback didn't know from externalities. It hadn't occurred to him that in the absence of a vigorous enforcement regime, it didn't cost the company a dime to discharge its waste into the river, whereas any remediation scheme would have cost tens of thousands if not millions. In fact, under Anaconda Cable & Wire's corporate charter, the company's lawyers could easily have argued that the fiduciary responsibility of management to its shareholders was to keep on polluting, because they had no right to willfully spend their shareholders' money to unnecessarily clean up their pollution when no regulation compelled them to do so.

When Fred Danback's fellow workers elected him as union president for the plant, he tried to make the company's toxic pollution a union grievance. The company retaliated by denying him even the routine promotions he was clearly entitled to. In 1969, after being advised that his union contract forbade him from suing his own employer, Danback quit his job. He joined forces with the Hudson River Fisherman's Association to clean up the Hudson River by using a method that often precedes legislation and regulation—litigation.

Danback learned that an obscure piece of legislation already on the books—The Refuse Act of 1899—made what Anaconda was doing plainly illegal. He discovered that the venerable law had never been amended, merely forgotten. Danback and his fellow fishermen were able to persuade the U.S. District Attorney in the Southern District of New York to bring suit against Anaconda.

Anaconda ended up being charged with over 100 violations of the act, and the firm was fined $200,000—"at that time," according to the *New York Times*, "the largest fine ever imposed on an American company for polluting." Danback wasn't done fighting pollution of the Hudson River. In succeeding decades, he successfully found illegal dumping being conducted by General Motors, Ciba-Geigy, General Electric, and some of the most admired brand names in the land. By 2003, the admired and distinguished General Electric was still fighting to avoid paying the full cost of the cleanup of toxic PCB pollutants it dumped into the Hudson River decades earlier. No longer did society at large simply look the other way.

A few years back, a kindergarten teacher by the name of Robert Fulghum wrote a best-selling book called *All I Really Need to Know I Learned in Kindergarten*. I recently tracked down some of his precepts, which turn out to be exceptionally applicable to the subject of internalizing your externalities:

- Share everything.
- Play fair.
- Don't hit people.
- Put things back where you found them.
- Clean up your own mess.
- Don't take things that aren't yours.
- Say you're sorry when you hurt somebody.
- Wash your hands before you eat.

- Flush.
- Live a balanced life—learn some and think some and draw and paint and sing and dance and play and work every day some.
- Take a nap every afternoon.
- Be aware of wonder.

In the absence of a list of Ten Commandments for socially responsible enterprises, those make a pretty good start.

The Drivers

In 2000, the CIA published a report called *Global Trends 2015*, which sketched four scenarios describing the structural state of the world in fifteen year's time. One scenario was entitled "Inclusive Globalization," and described "a virtuous circle . . . among technology, economic growth, demographic factors and effective governance which enables a majority of the world's population to benefit from globalization." A second scenario, entitled "Pernicious Globalization," described a world in which global inequality widens from a chasm into an abyss. A third scenario, called "Regional Competition," saw increasingly integrated economic blocks—Europe, Asia, and the United States—engendering low-grade conflicts, primarily through commercial competition. A fourth scenario, called "Post-Polar World," described a gradual global economic and environmental breakdown brought on by a decline of the U.S. economy.

Just as Franklin Roosevelt's New Deal has been frequently described as a means of salvaging capitalism by protecting it—as well as its victims—from its own worst excesses, corporate social responsibility has lately emerged on the global stage as a way of protecting globalization—and its victims—from globalization's worst excesses. CSR is the most likely promoter of "Inclusive Globalization."

One of the most disturbing examples of globalization is the tendency of large global players to transfer manufacturing jobs from developed countries to less developed countries, where a lack of organized labor and weak government regulations reduce the costs of manufacturing. This is a very good deal for First World companies, and First World consumers, but usually a bad deal for both First World and Third World workers.

In the absence of a global regulatory framework, what would compel Nike to upgrade its contract factories in Indonesia, or Hewlett-Packard (HP) to improve the lot of workers in China assembling and disassembling components, particularly since none of these workers actually work for HP or Nike directly? A nongovernmental organization, such as the San Francisco–based Global Exchange—which helped to bring the plight of Nike contract laborers to the world's attention—can be successful in making Nike's cherished brand "synonymous with slave wages, forced overtime and arbitrary abuse"—to quote Nike CEO Phil Knight. When an NGO successfully targets a company for change, all of a sudden an interesting phenomenon occurs: Nike changes its behavior. And if a group called the Basel Action Network—another San Francisco–based group devoted to reducing global shipments of high-tech toxic waste—exposes the horrific conditions under which old computers are being "recycled" in rural China, what happens? HP, as a responsible company, responds by calling for the creation of a system to reduce the "downstream" export of toxic computer parts to less-developed countries.

Today, a new factor has become the most vulnerable corporate pressure point: *reputation*. Only relatively recently have many corporations realized that the "goodwill" often carried on their balance sheets is their most valuable asset, worth far more than a dozen factories or office buildings. In the case of Microsoft and Coca-Cola, their market capitalization vastly outweighs the value of the hard assets they carry on their books, which—comparatively speaking—are relatively worthless.

So what are those soft assets that comprise the "goodwill" that the market values so highly? First and foremost is the loyalty of its customers—a concept encompassed in the term "brand equity"—an intangible entity now widely regarded as any organization's most valuable and vulnerable asset. An organization's second most valuable asset is the human capital of the employees, particularly when those employees are motivated by a set of clearly defined core values. And if you stop to think about it, the value of the first heavily depends upon the value of the second. If your human capital, your staff, is poorly motivated and demoralized, your brand capital will quickly follow. Any behavior that sullies or compromises a company's reputation, tarnishes or reduces its brand image, or casts the company in a bad light is a serious liability. Bad corporate behavior, once exposed, is now understood to cost something. In other words, the fact that corporate social *irresponsibility* had been proven to be costly has been one of the most powerful drivers advancing the doctrine of corporate social *responsibility*.

This is where Milton Friedman gets it all wrong. What Friedman failed to foresee is the dim view with which consumers, the general public, government and nongovernment agencies alike, and even investors regard corporate culpability in its various forms. What a number of leading-edge companies have recognized is that it is worthwhile to preempt these bad brand images by not only generating good brand reputations but ensuring that they are carefully if not fanatically protected. Acting proactively to avoid and prevent public criticism from erupting in the first place is a key motivating factor behind the emergence and embrace of CSR today.

In the wake of the now legendary Tylenol crisis of 1987—when an anonymous tamperer succeeded in adulterating batches of Tylenol capsules, causing seven deaths in the Chicago area—Johnson & Johnson under then-CEO James Burke spent upward of $100 million recalling every Tylenol capsule in the country, regardless of the fact that this action was not required by law. James Burke publicly stated shortly after the fact that as far as his company was concerned, it was impossible to put a price tag on trust. "All of the previous managements who built this corporation handed us," he pointed out, "on a silver platter, the most powerful tool you could possibly have." This tool was *trust*, which he described as "real, palpable and bankable." The idea that trust is "real, palpable and bankable" forms a bedrock value of CSR. Everything that companies do, or at least should do, comes back to the preservation of that core asset—the trust of the public.

CSR is a way of internalizing best practices to prevent public outcry from bursting forth in the first place, thereby creating a deep reservoir of trust. Robert Dunn of Businesses for Social Responsibility pointed out to us the extraordinary degree to which CSR has become a self-reinforcing and self-perpetuating process: If one major company decides to clean up its act, that puts pressure on its competitors to do the same, and if that leading company also puts pressure on its suppliers and vendors to abide by the same principles, CSR becomes contagious—a genuinely "virtuous circle."

Closely related to the development and preservation of corporate trust is the notion of *risk*, which is another prime regulator of corporate behavior. For those not yet fully subscribed to the notion of doing the right thing simply because it is the right thing, risk management becomes the driver of key decisions. Risks represent potential costs and costs represent the possibility of reducing shareholder value as well as negatively affecting reputation. The Association of British Insurers, representing about 20 percent of the UK stock market, has recently asked all of the companies it insures to disclose in their quarterly and annual reports any "environmental, social and ethical risks" that might potentially affect their stock values. The Swiss Reinsurance Company recently circulated a questionnaire asking its clients to state whether they had a program in place to assess potential and future exposure to shareholder lawsuits for the company's failure to reduce greenhouse gases.

As corporations are being asked to bear responsibilities far broader than has been the historic norm, the companies that insure those businesses are demanding that their clients take affirmative steps to both disclose and avoid potential litigation related to these issues. The effect of such a requirement can be far-reaching: A business asked by its insurance company whether it has a greenhouse-reduction program in place is in effect being asked to put one in place or possibly pay an increased premium, if not forsake its insurance relationship altogether. In a broader sense, the adoption of the doctrine of CSR is an insurance policy itself—insurance against the risk of being sued, overly regulated, or regarded as a bad actor, which means that some consumers, at least, won't buy your products. That is the essence of "CSR Risk." The introduction of the insurance industry into the management of corporate risk—in areas ranging from the environment to human rights—has become a significant driver of structural change in the world of private enterprise.

A 1999 Millennium Poll conducted by Environics International (which interviewed 25,000 citizens across six continents) indicated:

- In forming impressions of companies, people around the world focus on corporate citizenship ahead of brand reputation or financial factors.
- Two out of three citizens want companies to go beyond their historical role of making a profit, paying taxes, employing people, and obeying all laws. They want companies to contribute to broader societal goals as well.
- More than one in five consumers reported either rewarding or punishing companies in the past year according to their social performance and as many again would consider doing so in the future.

Among those who expressed this view, about half defined the corporation's role as "exceeding all laws, setting a higher ethical standard, and helping build a better society for all." The remainder of this subset said companies should operate "somewhere between" the traditional definition of the corporation's role and this more demanding one.

British Telecom, according to a survey on CSR trends published by the *Financial Times*, has "calculated that its social and environmental performance accounts for more than 25 percent of its overall business and reputation—which in turn is the second biggest factor driving change in its customer satisfaction rates."

Yet another motivation for companies to behave ethically, honorably, and with the interests of stakeholders is the $13 billion currently invested in socially responsible funds, by Morningstar's reckoning. At present, this comprises only about 2 percent of total fund assets, but Barbara Krumsiek, chief executive of Wayne Silby's Calvert Group, expects this percentage to climb to 10 percent by 2012.

The nonprofit Social Investment Forum has a very different (and higher) figure for total assets being held in portfolios screened for social concerns: $2 trillion. This is said to include both socially screened mutual funds and separate accounts managed for socially conscious institutions and individual investors. Though the amounts differ, it is clear that socially responsible investing has caught on today, and investors can choose among some 230 socially responsible mutual funds, while more than 800 independent asset managers identify themselves as managers of socially responsible portfolios for institutional investors and high-net-worth individuals.

Many of these funds use indexes of social and environmental performance like the Dow Jones Sustainability World Indexes and FTSE4Good. Produced by Dow Jones and the *Financial Times*, a unit of Pearson, both indexes have become significant market factors in screening for good corporate citizenship. Both Dow Jones (DJSI) and SAM (Sustainability Asset Management), a Swiss-based asset management company that conducts the research for Dow Jones, use a best-in-class approach that identifies the top sustainability performer in all sectors, regardless of any given sector's social or environmental impact. It is possible that if no company in a given sector exceeds a defined threshold of sustainability, no company in that sector is included in the indexes. In other words, SAM and DJSI do not include a bad company just because its peers are even worse. However, they do not exclude a company simply because it operates in a so-called "sin" sector such as arms or tobacco.

Two companies that have been shunned by many social investors for years, tobacco producer British American Tobacco (BAT) and arms merchant United Technologies (UTX), are held in the DJSI index. "If you exclude them, you do not give them an appropriate incentive to improve," SAM managing director Alexander Barkawi recently responded to critics who charged that including arms manufacturers and tobacco companies in a so-called "screened" index watered down the meaning of social responsibility. "The exclusion of an industry is an ethical decision, with so many different views on what industry is considered 'sin.'" The FTSE4Good Global index, by contrast, excludes companies involved in tobacco, arms, and nuclear power.

The rise and increasing power of socially responsible investing poses great challenges for corporations hopeful of attracting these investment dollars. One of the most interesting approaches has been adopted by the New York–based socially conscious investment firm Innovest Strategic Value Advisors, which has developed its own proprietary system for analyzing a portfolio of 1500 companies with regard to their environmental and social performance. According to Frank Dixon, managing director for research, a company's environmental and social performance has become the perfect proxy for management quality in general.

If a company can deftly handle complex environmental and social issues, which require among other things "sophisticated communications skills," Dixon maintains that it can probably handle other complex issues as well, which gives CSR-savvy companies a comparatively better risk-to-return profile. Managing social and environmental risk is a pretty fair indicator of how well a company will manage risk in general.

The number of NGOs and activist groups has now risen to an estimated 28,000 worldwide. With that many NGOs out there keeping a hawk's eye on possible corporate misbehavior, the risk of one of them targeting any particular company is now higher than ever before. Every time a socially active mutual fund, public pension fund, or a religious group submits a shareholder resolution relating to some CSR issue (800 such resolutions were submitted in 2002, a number expected to rise by at least 20 percent in 2003), that costs management money and time. CSR companies, aware of this risk, make a point of regularly monitoring the NGOs known to focus on the issues affecting their company, so that they can proactively address these troublesome issues before they become the subject of shareholder resolutions and public criticism.

Yet another factor affecting companies with operations in Europe is that six European countries—the UK, France, Sweden, German, the Netherlands, Switzerland—have adopted laws requiring pension funds to consider the environmental, ethical, and social performance of companies in which they intend to invest. It is widely expected that before long the European Union as a whole will follow suit. The Paris Bourse has recently passed a resolution requiring listed companies to include clear information regarding their environmental and social performance in their quarterly and annual reports.

According to Innovest's Dixon, the most formidable barrier to implementing CSR on a broader scale—the Milton Friedman–inspired conviction that investing in social and environmental performance is a violation of management's duty to its shareholders—has been utterly shattered by the current reality, which is that any company that sticks its head in the sand and ignores these issues is in fact *betraying* its fiduciary responsibility to its shareholders.

In her book *Value Shift*, Lynne Sharp Payne notes the example of the AES Corporation, an independent power producer, which went public in 1991. In its prospectus distributed to potential investors, a passage on values apparently "set off alarm bells at the SEC." The passage described the company's commitment to four core values—integrity, fairness, fun, and social responsibility—and went on to note that "[T]he company seeks to adhere to these values not as a means to achieve economic success, but because adherence is a worthwhile goal in and of itself."

Should a conflict between these values and profits arise, the prospectus stated, the company would try to adhere to its values, even if doing so might result in "diminished profits and foregone opportunities." Alarmed by this statement, the SEC demanded that the company include its intention to adhere to those values in the section of the prospectus dealing with "risk factors."

What a difference a decade makes! Today, a company that decided *not* to adhere to a set of core values, even if doing so might result in "diminished profits and foregone opportunities," would likely be forced to put its lack of core values in the section of a prospectus outlining "risk factors."

Today, I would argue that failing to take issues of corporate responsibility into consideration when determining core values or strategic planning will subject almost any business to some level of unnecessary risk. Documentation of enhanced long-term TRS (Total Return to Shareholders) for CSR companies grows almost weekly, and it appears that the stage has been set for that evidence to continue to mount.

This is all well and good, but let's not forget that the primary reason to be good corporate citizens is not because it will help us to make more money or avoid a nasty lawsuit. It takes more than a commitment to comply with the guidelines of CSR to be a successful CSR company. It requires a commitment that is values-based and driven by a passion to use the company as an instrument to effect positive social change. To willingly, even joyfully accept the responsibility that society has rightly come to expect of its most powerful institutions.

chapter three

Risk and Reputation

For fifteen years, Royal Dutch Shell's 460-foot-tall oil storage tanker and loading platform the Brent Spar floated inconspicuously at anchor in the North Sea, 120 miles off the Shetland Islands, of no particular concern to anyone outside the company. But in 1991, having outlived its useful life, the platform was decommissioned. For the next two years, an independent committee of scientific and engineering advisors retained by Shell pondered the problem of what to do with it, which came down to how best to get rid of it.

The committee's mandate was to determine the "BPEO" ("Best Practicable Environmental Option") for the Brent Spar, an assessment that combined a weighing of environmental hazards with the degree of danger posed to the workers, while keeping a close eye on costs. After studying the problem, the committee narrowed the choice to two options: Deep Sea Disposal (DSD) and On-Shore Dismantling (OSD).

Both options had their pros and cons. DSD required towing the 4000-ton platform into the Atlantic Ocean, blowing it up with explosives, and letting the concrete and steel pieces cascade two kilometers down to the ocean floor, where they would come to rest. The liquid and solid contents of the platform included oil sludge, radioactive scale, and heavy metals. As to precisely how long this layer of toxic sludge would linger on the seabed, and to what effect, the committee's conclusion was that any adverse effects to sea life and the seabed were likely to be limited to a 500-meter circumference from the point of dispersal, and that these impacts were likely to be limited to the untimely deaths of 10,000 fish. Even these effects, the committee decided, would probably be limited to no more than fourteen months, after which the affected area could be expected to recover to a condition approaching its pristine state.

When contemplating OSD (On-Shore Dismantling), the committee could envision any number of hazards and problems. Just for starters, OSD would require the Brent Spar to be towed a considerable distance from the middle of the North Sea to some deep-harbor port where the local authorities had agreed to accept it. Once all the local environmental issues were dealt with, the platform would have to be cut up and its structure drained of toxic residue before the fuel tanks could be cut up, and the other components rendered suitable for recycling. During this complex operation, the likelihood of an oil or chemical spill could not be discounted, which made On-Shore Dismantling—according to the committee's best estimate—*six times* more dangerous to the workers involved as well as to inhabitants of the surrounding community than DSD. On a cost basis, Deep Sea Disposal won the contest hands down, with an estimated tab of £17 to £20 million compared to at least £41 million for OSD.

The data presented by the committee to Shell's senior management just about made up their minds for them. From the standpoint of protecting the wealth of Shell shareholders, there seemed to be no way to justify incurring the additional expense, danger, and potential liabilities associated with On-Shore Dismantling. After ruling unequivocally in favor of Deep Sea Disposal, Shell management submitted a comprehensive disposal plan to the environmental ministers of every country bordering on the North Sea for review. Not a single government agency objected.

In December 1994, the UK government approved Deep Sea Disposal of the Brent Spar, and by February 1995, the London office of the international environmental organization Greenpeace had been alerted to the fact that Shell intended to commence operations to scuttle the Brent Spar in the first week of May. Now, Greenpeace's executive committee had its own decision to make. Would taking on the Shell oil company over the issue of the Brent Spar be a beneficial use of the NGO's limited resources? The answer to that question largely depended upon what winning that fight—or losing that fight—entailed in terms of fulfilling the organization's larger agenda, which can be loosely characterized as saving the planet from environmental destruction.

The environmental assessment conducted by Greenpeace differed dramatically from Shell's in a number of critical ways. While Shell had accorded great weight in its analysis to the *financial* costs of the operation, Greenpeace's analysis was mainly limited to an assessment of *environmental* costs. While the Shell team focused much of its conceptual energy on determining the degree of danger to its own workers, Greenpeace focused the preponderance of its energies on the safety and health of the marine environment.

Yet another critical dimension distinguished the two teams' perspective—*time*. Shell's time horizon was almost entirely short term, driven primarily by considerations of immediate efficiency and initial cost. Greenpeace's analysis, by contrast, focused largely on the more distant future, a method of inquiry that raised to the surface one important issue that Shell seems to have overlooked in its analysis. Brent Spar was the first of nearly *four hundred* North Sea oil platforms scheduled to be decommissioned in the upcoming years. If the UK government granted Shell a permit to dispose of the Brent Spar in this fashion, what was to prevent them from granting permission for those other four hundred platforms in precisely the same fashion?

In the final analysis, this was what prompted Greenpeace to go for broke against the DSD of the Brent Spar: to prevent the setting of a precedent that, in their view, might well precipitate an environmental catastrophe. On April 30, 1995, the Greenpeace support ship *Moby Dick* slipped up to the side of the Brent Spar as she floated peacefully at anchor 118 miles northwest of the Shetlands, and a team of activists clambered aboard. On May Day morning, the world (as well as the startled security officials on the platform) awoke to a high-stakes High Noon on the high seas. Alarmed Shell officials quickly obtained a court order requiring the activists to evacuate the platform at once. But once the activists—predictably—defied the court order, Shell had the choice of physically evicting the protestors, and coming off as the heavy, or negotiating directly with what they regarded as an unruly group of fanatics who probably belonged in jail, not their boardroom.

Let's examine more closely some of the issues raised by this confrontation in the North Sea. What Shell had initiated by proceeding with its decision to deep-six the Brent Spar was what today we might describe as a nasty case of "CSR risk." This is an umbrella term that embraces the panoply of risks created by any sort of behavior *likely to exert a negative impact on a company's reputation.*

It's impossible to talk effectively about CSR risk without invoking the present-day shift from the shareholder to the stakeholder model of relationships and responsibility. The term "stakeholder" generally refers to anyone directly or even indirectly affected by a company's operations. Among a company's stakeholders are managers and employees, business partners and suppliers, in addition to people who live in the communities in which a company bases its operations. In the case of the Exxon *Valdez* oil spill, the management of Exxon (now Exxon-Mobil) learned to their astonishment that the fishermen and their families living in and around Alaska's Prince William Sound, and members of environmental groups dedicated to preserving wildlife and the environment, were actually Exxon *stakeholders*, even if they were not likely to be Exxon *stockholders*.

Not every company, nor every government, has yet bought into the validity of this concept. Asking a company to look out for its stakeholders as well as its shareholders (who are in fact important stakeholders) is a really quite radical shift in the public's expectations of a company's responsibility to society. The paradox here is that if we acknowledge that a company's reputation—and that of its brands—is often its most important asset, then any conduct that has a negative impact on a company's reputation can be a direct threat to the protection of shareholder value.

CSR risk is a real liability precisely because reputation and brand are often a company's most valuable asset. In this case, CSR risk can constitute just as much or perhaps more of a liability for Shell shareholders as the legal liability resulting from a clear-cut violation of laws or regulations. In the case of the Brent Spar, Shell had gone out of its way to ensure that it had complied with all relevant laws and regulations. Just the same, it ended up creating a genuine CSR risk because it had insufficiently evaluated the breadth of the stakeholders who felt they were entitled to voice an opinion about Shell's decision on how to decommission the Brent Spar. The prospect of suffering a blow to its reputation by coming off in the public's eyes as an environmental despoiler was outside the parameters that it considered when making its decision. This unsettling experience of being caught in a broadening circle of responsibility, one that seems at times to almost expand by the moment in unforeseen and unpredictable ways, is an experience that company after company would encounter throughout the second half of the 1990s and into the early twenty-first century.

Throughout the traditionally anti-capitalist month of May, Greenpeace skillfully guided its global publicity and media campaign into high gear. Its representatives had physically abandoned the platform, but their fighting spirit lingered on, in part because their images were so readily disseminated by the media. In Germany, consumers were so distressed by Greenpeace's prediction of an impending environmental catastrophe in the North Sea that they boycotted Shell gas stations, causing sales of Shell products in Germany to plummet by a whopping 30 percent. After a Shell gasoline station in Germany was firebombed, an irritated German chancellor Helmut Kohl raised the controversy surrounding the Brent Star at the June G–7 summit of the heads of the leading industrialized nations in Halifax, Canada. Shell's actions—and Greenpeace's reactions—had created a full-scale international incident.

Through the first weeks of controversy, the British government stood by its decision to support DSD of the Brent Spar. But in June 1995, its position was dramatically weakened by the well-timed leak of a report from the UK Ministry of Agriculture, Fisheries and Food entitled *Toxicant Levels in Ballast Water from the Brent Spar*, which turned out to agree with Greenpeace's pessimistic assessment of the long-term environmental impacts posed by the Deep Sea Disposal. The sludge emitted from the Brent Spar would be "toxic to marine organisms" and should therefore be treated as "hazardous waste," the report concluded, and in a hand-written memo attached to the body of report, Dr. John Campbell, the ministry's head scientist, stated unequivocally: "The bottom line is that the waste [from the platform] cannot be dumped at sea."

On June 20, Greenpeace followed up the release of this report by staging an aerial assault on the Brent Spar, executed with all the precision of a commando raid. With video cameras running full tilt and the world's news organizations hungry for images of confrontation, a helicopter dropped four Greenpeace activists onto the floating platform. At Shell Mex house, top management at last decided that even if the company stood a chance of ultimately prevailing on the legal and regulatory front, it was definitely losing the battle on the public relations front. The UK ministry report, combined with the negative publicity surrounding the case, had rendered DSD no longer the "Best Practicable Environmental Option" for the oil platform because the reputational risks had increased to an unacceptable level.

By evening, citing unspecified "objections by European governments," Shell announced plans to begin towing the Brent Spar to Norway in preparation for On-Shore Disposal. In a transparent bid to conduct damage control and to regain some measure of public trust, the company openly solicited suggestions from the public as to its opinion of the most environmentally benign form of disposal. Although the entire operation would take another five years, Brent Spar ultimately ended its days on land, in the Norwegian port of Mekjarvik, recycled into a new ferry terminal. Greenpeace had helped Shell to realize that its reputation was a far more valuable and perishable commodity than the Brent Spar itself.

Not that Shell was entirely out of the woods yet. In May 1995—the same month that Greenpeace activists first climbed aboard the Brent Spar—the repressive military government of Nigeria arrested Ken Saro-Wiwa, a leading environmental activist and founder of MOSOP (Movement for Survival of the Ogoni People), and charged him and seven of his colleagues with murder. Shell had been drilling for oil in the Ogoni region of Nigeria's Niger River Delta since 1958, and by

1995 had extracted an estimated $30 billion worth of oil from the country. Shell had funneled out hundreds of millions of dollars in annual profits from its operations in the troubled country, accounting for 14 percent of its total crude oil production—while the local Ogoni people, who actually lived around the oil wells, had derived little or no benefit from this bonanza, unless you counted the resulting oil spills, pipeline ruptures, and fires.

While the world watched the confrontation unfold between Greenpeace and Shell over the Brent Spar, Greenpeace simultaneously organized a massive demonstration outside Shell headquarters in London, charging it with complicity in the human rights violations and abuse being perpetrated by the government of Nigeria. As Philip Watts, the company's Regional Coordinator for Europe—later to become CEO of the global holding company—soberly observed several years later, "Brent Spar was a wake-up call for us, but Nigeria keeps us awake all the time."

Drilling for oil in Third World countries can be as much of a bane as a boon for citizens residing in those countries. But is it the company's responsibility to police the actions of the government that grants it permission to drill, or is it the responsibility of the government to police itself? Put another way, can a company be held responsible for the corruption of local officials and the likely reality that they will pocket some of the royalties that flow from the oil extracted? Is the company morally and ethically bound to ensure that at least some of the benefits from the removal and sale of the host country's own natural resources flow to its citizens and the people who live on the land from which the oil is being extracted?

In recent years, the view that companies do share some responsibility for the actions of the governments with which they do business has been gaining traction in the business community, for no other reason than dedicated NGOs have helped to raise the issue in the public consciousness, forcing companies to adopt a shift in perspective.

In the case of Shell and Nigeria, to what degree was Shell complicit in the abuses perpetrated by the government? Did it behoove Shell to be widely perceived as being "in bed" with rapacious and corrupt African dictators? Perhaps more to the point, what would incurring such a reputation end up costing the company in the long run?

Even as the company agonized over what to do with the Brent Spar, embattled Shell executives in London agreed to meet with Greenpeace representatives to discuss—as a Greenpeace press release bluntly put it—"the inextricable links between the company and with the environmental devastation in Ogoniland." At the meeting, Greenpeace confronted Shell officials with an internal Nigerian government memo strongly suggesting that the alleged atrocities and human rights abuses purportedly perpetrated by the Ogoniland activists had in fact been carefully planned by the Nigerian military.

Shell executives responded evasively—according to Greenpeace—in true Milton Friedmanesque fashion: "That they are only interested in and responsible for the business of extracting oil." To which Greenpeace reportedly responded that "it is impossible to separate business and politics" in Nigeria. At the meeting Greenpeace peppered Shell executives with questions to which they had few, if any, answers.

"Given your involvement in Nigeria, are you happy that Mr. Saro-Wiwa has been held in detention without charge since last May and may well be sentenced to death?"

"Why have you refused to allow an independent environmental inquiry surrounding Shell's activities in Ogoniland?"

Following this attempt at establishing a dialogue, Greenpeace issued a press release.

> Companies like Shell can and should be taking more positive actions in situations like Ogoni. The generation of corporate profits demands more responsible actions. If Shell worked as hard on its corporate and environmental image in Nigeria as they do in Western Europe, these problems would have been solved long ago.

"It was like being in a plane crash," commented Sir Philip Watts several years later. "You don't really know what it's like until you experience it in the first person. . . . You can't imagine the tensions inside [the company]. . . . It wasn't just losing market share in Germany. . . . Staff members were deeply affected. There were kids at home asking, *What on earth is your company doing?*"

Tom Delfgauuw, Vice President for Sustainable Development at Shell International, witnessed the plane crash from the inside. From his perspective—as a champion of change at Shell—the crisis actually could not have come at a better time. Under severe public pressure Shell management was obliged to make a critical shift in focus and behavior, from *speaking* to *listening* mode.

Tom Delfgauuw:

> Every single multinational in the world has a tendency to become too introspective, too internally focused, to take too many things for granted. Then one day you hit a brick wall and find out the world is moving much faster than you thought. We discovered there were no local issues anymore.

Delfgauuw was not alone in Shell management to conclude that, counterintuitively, as he later observed:

> [Brent Spar and Nigeria] were one of the best things that ever happened to us, first because we've come out of it much, much stronger as a company, and second because it accelerated a great many needed corporate developments.

Flash forward seven years (from "People and the Environment Report" put out by Shell Nigeria):

> How much of the profits from oil and gas are spent on the social and economic development of the Niger Delta area? Find out what our stakeholders and partners think. See how we're living up to the targets we've set and the promises we've made.
>
> Today our community development program in the Niger Delta region is based on the principles of sustainable development and best global practice. In 2001 we invested over $50 million in health, education, agriculture, job creation, women's programs, youth training and sponsorship. Everything we do is guided by expert advice from our stakeholders and strategic partners and increasingly open and honest communication with the communities. . . . (*Shell and the Community*, 2002)

On the Nigerian question, the company ultimately responded to criticism of its human rights record by engaging in a significant dialogue with a number of NGOs, several of whom had originally come to Shell's attention as mediators in the Ogoni crisis. That crisis concluded in tragedy with the execution of community leader Ken Saro-Wiwa and his seven colleagues, but it also concluded—several years later—with the deposing of the repressive military government in Nigeria and a return to civilian rule.

In 1997, Shell Petroleum Development Company of Nigeria (SPDC), the largest oil and gas company in the country, commissioned an extensive external review of the way in which it interacted with communities throughout the Niger Delta, home to more than seven million people drawn from a variety of ethnic and tribal backgrounds. This was and remains a region prone to violent ethnic conflict, exacerbated—as Shell now readily admits—by the inequities of oil revenue sharing.

Shell set up a $60 million community development fund dedicated to concrete community projects—with a year 2000 appraisal conducted by a staff of independent experts. A yearly "stake-holder consultation workshop" was convened to review the fund's projects, programs, and performance. While all this falls well short of the ultimate goal—to extract petroleum products from Nigeria in a spirit of genuine respect for Shell "stakeholders" as well as shareholders in the Niger Delta—that fact is freely conceded in its report.

"The Niger Delta continues to be a difficult place to work," the report concluded, an understatement borne out in March 2003, when oil production throughout the entire region had to be suspended for several weeks as rival tribes clashed, reportedly over the equitable sharing of oil royalties.

Nigeria remains a problem from which Shell can simply not afford to walk away. But the highly volatile relationship with Greenpeace, initially forged in confrontation, has over time evolved into an exchange of divergent views that promises a constructive outcome. In 2000, Greenpeace took a new tack in its evolving relationship with Shell by shifting its status from stakeholder to shareholder by purchasing 4400 shares of Royal Dutch Shell for 500,000 Dutch guilders. This step enabled the organization to take advantage of a rule recently passed by the Amsterdam Stock Exchange providing for the circulation of shareholder resolutions to all major shareholders once a threshold of owner participation had been reached.

Greenpeace's shareholder resolution would have required Shell to construct a solar panel factory to produce 5 million photovoltaic solar panels a year, enough to equip 250,000 homes each with a two-kilowatt solar electrical system. "Working from within the share structure of publicly owned multinational companies is one way to effectively influence their corporate agendas to include environmental objectives," commented one Greenpeace spokesperson questioned about the tactic.

Being a Shell shareholder, of course, also entailed a certain amount of risk on Greenpeace's part. "Working within the system" can easily be construed as a form of selling out. But Greenpeace had learned it was not only possible to persuade companies to improve their behavior, but to force them to establish internal systems that make better behavior the rule rather than the exception.

Intel Inside New Mexico

On a broad mesa in New Mexico overlooking the Rio Grande River, with the majestic Sandia Mountains rising directly across the river to the east, near the small municipality of Rio Rancho, a developer called the American Real Estate and Petroleum Company (AMREP) created a subdivision in the 1970s that ultimately failed after "twelve years of investigation and legal battles due to misleading advertisements, mainly in New York papers," according to a report later compiled by a local activist group.*

More than one-third of the AMREP properties in New Mexico had been acquired directly or indirectly from the King family, the scion of which, Bruce King, had been the speaker of the New Mexico House of Representatives and a state representative from Sante Fe County when the AMREP deal originally went down. In the 1970s,

---

*"Intel Inside New Mexico: A Case Study of Environmental and Economic Injustice," Southwest Organizing Project, Albuquerque, New Mexico, 1995.

King—soon to become governor of the state—appeared in a promotional film on behalf of AMREP in which he proudly announced:

> It certainly is a pleasure to appear here this morning on this beautiful spot and view the Sandia Mountains to the East. . . . I'm sure that in the next two decades, we will expand much more and the city of Albuquerque will overflow and come right in the path of where we are standing this morning.

The East Coast retirees aggressively targeted by AMREP never turned up—apparently put off by the "painted lawns and misleading claims and ultimately criminal proceedings" that contributed to AMREP's turn of fortune. What came calling instead was the Intel Corporation, which in 1980 announced plans to locate a massive new chip fabrication plant—known in the industry as a FAB—just outside Rio Rancho. The development deal had been shepherded through the state legislature by Bruce King, by then the governor, who had helped line up a series of tax incentives, including a package of Industrial Revenue Bonds, in which Sandoval County would appear to remain the owner of the real estate and would thus exempt the property from local and state property taxes, and even sales taxes.

By 1992, Rio Rancho had become Intel's largest manufacturing plant, producing approximately 50 percent of its revenue and 70 percent of its profits (according to an August 1993 internal memo). Intel and the state of New Mexico announced an enormous expansion of the Rio Rancho plant, funded by the issuance of a new $1 billion Industrial Revenue Bond, the largest such bond issue ever floated in the state. By the time the bond issue was finally approved by the state legislature, the amount had swollen to $2 billion, and by 1995 to nearly $10 billion.

From Intel's perspective, what was there not to like?

- Intel came to New Mexico in 1980, and began operations with fewer than 25 employees.
- In 2001, we employed 5,500 people.
- Our site consists of two manufacturing plants called "fabs,"

which are among the most advanced microchip-making facilities in the world. . . .

But from the more critical perspective of the Southwest Organizing Project (SWOP), based in nearby Albuquerque, there was quite a lot about the latest Intel deal not to like. New Mexico was "the 48th poorest in the U.S.," and was primarily populated by "people of color," either Chicanos or Native Americans. It has often been described—by advocates for its residents—as a "colony of the United States."

Where the famously cozy New Mexican political establishment saw a wonderful influx of new high-paying high-tech jobs and desirable economic development, SWOP recalled a darker past in which the United States military, the dominant employer in the state for years, had become a major polluter of the land, at Kirtland Air Force base, White Sands Missile Range, and the Los Alamos National Laboratories. SWOP was aware of Intel's history as a major polluter, and as the leading creator of EPA Superfund sites in California's Silicon Valley, in Santa Clara and Mountain View. As SWOP later noted, the underground plume beginning at Intel's 365 Mountain Road facility in Mountain View—plume being a technical term for toxic pollution spreading beneath the surface of the earth—was the second largest in Santa Clara County, and threatened San Francisco Bay. The address 365 East Middlefield Road in Mountain View was also significant, because that was the site of the first Intel FAB in the country. The EPA—which declared it a Superfund site in 1985—had estimated that a full cleanup of the toxic solvent trichloroethylene (TCE) underground plume spreading from it could take up to sixty years.

After obtaining a Bachelor's degree in Southwestern Studies from the University of New Mexico, SWOP executive director Jeanne Guana had spent the greater part of the next twenty years fighting for the rights of workers and low-income families in the often impoverished working-class communities of rural and urban New Mexico. One of SWOP's first projects had been to publish a history of the Chicano community in the southwest, which focused on a nearly endless litany of historical wrongs committed mainly by whites against people of color in the region dating back to Spanish colonial times.

The premise of the history was summarized in a study published in *New Mexico Business* magazine in 1971, which stressed the fact that "Spanish-Americans tend to have an emotional attachment to the land (it is part of the family) and to value intimate personal knowledge of one's own land and a continued lineal-family relationship."

"Anglos," by contrast, "tend to view land as a commodity to be bought and sold if the price is right and to stress maximum monetary income from land while they hold it." From Jeanne Guana's perspective, the looming battle with Intel was in a sense a cultural clash, exemplified by a comment made by Governor Bruce King in relationship to the Rio Rancho/Intel expansion:

> If we let the land be ruined, it's usually ruined forever. But we can't afford to forget the people who need a chance to make a living. You've got to decide how high the return has to be in terms of payroll to make it worthwhile to accept damage to the land.

Based on its experience with the electronics industry in New Mexico, SWOP had every reason to be concerned. One of the first companies to enter the New Mexico market in the early seventies had been GTE (General Telephone and Electric), which built a chip plant at Lenkurt that employed several hundred mainly Chicano and Native American women for $1.75 an hour, at the time a good rate of pay. Over a period of nearly twenty years, the women employed at the plant suffered abnormally high rates of miscarriage and other health effects directly traceable to the toxic chemicals employed in the chip fabrication process. In 1993, SWOP organized a conference on "Toxic Poisoning in Communities of Color" in Albuquerque, at which female employees from Lenkurt, Honeywell, Los Alamos Labs, and Motorola testified. The list of health effects was astounding, from adrenal gland failure to carpal tunnel syndrome, precancerous cervical tissue, sinus problems, depression, and anxiety.

From Guana and SWOP's point of view, Intel's state-of-the-art chip plant in Rio Rancho was nothing but a high-tech hacienda. The conceptual framework for SWOP's critique of the Intel Expansion had been heavily colored by the emerging Environmental Justice Movement, which holds—in her own words—that "working class people of color have paid the historical price of disproportionate and adverse affects of toxic chemicals in and around the communities where we live, work and play."

In March 1994, SWOP published a booklet entitled *Intel Inside New Mexico* that extensively and meticulously documented Intel's environmental track record in California. The booklet went on to look at Intel's successful intervention with both local and national authorities—including high-level meetings with members of both the Bush and Clinton administrations—to enable it to "streamline," that is, evade, the environmental review process. SWOP contended that the true costs associated with the Industrial Revenue Bond's financed handouts and tax breaks to Intel was so enormous that it made the cost of jobs being created by Intel a burden for the taxpayers of the county. The report also raised serious questions about the amount of water that would be used in the manufacturing process, the quantity and character of the toxic emissions likely to be released into the air and water, the identity and quality of the jobs that Intel promised to create, and whether they truly would end up being given primarily to New Mexicans, as the backers of the bond and Intel had promised.

Only after local news organizations reported that Intel was stonewalling SWOP's request for a meeting with its representatives to discuss these issues did Intel grudgingly offer to meet with Jeanne Guana—alone. But after turning down Intel's request, on the principled grounds that its identity and mandate of a "participatory, constituency-based organization" contraindicated any such many-to-one meeting, Guana picked up the phone and called her friend and supporter Stephen Viederman, president of the Jessie Smith Noyes Foundation in New York, for advice on what step to take next.

The Jessie Smith Noyes Foundation had been established in 1947 as the beneficiary of a bequest left by the New York realtor and developer Charles Noyes, who "at one point owned a good deal of Lower Manhattan," according to Viederman. As he recently recalled over breakfast at his favorite landmark coffee shop on New York's Upper East Side:

Noyes took over the Empire State Building when it was a white elephant in the depths of the Depression, and turned it into a premier address. He was a passionate opera buff, and one evening he invited Marian Anderson [the black opera singer] out to his house in Connecticut, and had the naïve inspiration to encourage her to buy property in the neighborhood. Needless to say, that didn't work out, but many of his other progressive initiatives did. . . .

By the mid-1980s, the foundation had shifted its focus to family planning and environmentalism, with the majority of its grantees being the larger, mainstream environmental organizations like the National Resources Defense Council and the Environmental Defense Fund (now called Environmental Defense). In Viederman's view, when he came aboard in 1986, this was anything but a growth path, philanthropically speaking. "We had no competitive advantage in that area, given our size."

Viederman was looking for a new programmatic strategy that might yield "the biggest bang for our philanthropic buck" when it occurred to him that very few foundations, particularly those based in the elite philanthropic corridor of the East Coast, were funding real-honest-to-goodness grassroots organizations. These organizations, Viederman felt, were primed "to put pressure on business to move in the direction of participatory democracy," a direction in which—he knew from experience—very few businesses were eager to be pushed.

From Viederman's perspective, SWOP was the ideal Jessie Smith Noyes grantee. It was a relatively new organization, relatively obscure (outside its own district), but very well organized and managed. "These grassroots organizations run on fumes," Viederman says, "but I can say from experience that such organizations can often be remarkably well informed, even about the most sophisticated environmental subjects." He was impressed by the quality of the environmental reporting reflected in *Intel Inside New Mexico*, and realized that working with SWOP would further the goal he had recently articulated for the foundation to legitimize and increase the impact of these community organizations.

Steve Viederman, whom I have known for many years and consider a good friend, is no fan of big business, and a confirmed skeptic with regard to the ethical and moral conduct of most businesses. "The more pressure we put on big corporations to become better social actors the better," he insisted, "because I don't believe that they will do anything that they don't have to do. You have to make it worth their while to do the right thing, which in our case mainly involves creating strong disincentives to do the wrong thing."

According to the *New York Times*, the Jessie Smith Noyes Foundation happened to already hold three thousand shares of Intel stock in its portfolio. But as Viederman pointed out, the true departure for the foundation in its partnership with SWOP was to use that stock portfolio as a vehicle for social action. "Taking an active role as a shareholder in the company would be a new role for the foundation," he later wrote in an article published in a philanthropic journal, "but it would be a role consistent with our goal of reducing the dissonance between the way we managed our endowment and our grant making values."

As Viederman saw it, he had three choices as to what to do about Jeanne's request and the foundation's possession of Intel stock. He could (1) write a letter threatening to sell the shares unless Intel changed its community relations practices. He could (2) sell the stock, "after sending a strongly worded letter to Intel explaining the circumstances." Or he could (3) file a shareholder resolution. After thinking about those three choices for a few minutes, he made up his mind.

In May 1994, Viederman and Guana turned up at Intel's annual shareholders' meeting in Albuquerque and asked, from the floor, when Intel would respond to SWOP's *Intel Inside New Mexico* report. Then chief operating officer (later chief executive officer) Andrew S. Grove gruffly replied from the podium, "We at Intel do not deal with vocal minorities."

Viederman was perplexed by this statement of rebuff on a number of counts, not the least of which was that he couldn't be at all sure that this wasn't a reference to Jeanne Guana's Chicano heritage. But even after giving Grove the benefit of the doubt on that count, if he meant "minority shareholders" it seemed like the height of arrogance. Thinking quickly on his feet, Viederman replied to Andy Grove—himself an immigrant from Eastern Europe—"If we didn't have vocal minorities we wouldn't have a United States."

This elicited nothing more than a huff from the platform.

As Viederman later explained it to us, "These annual shareholder meetings are like the meetings of the Supreme Soviet. Everything has been figured out beforehand, and they have the meeting mostly for show. The audience was made up almost entirely of Intel employees and money managers who couldn't have cared less about what we were doing, except that they considered it a nuisance."

On June 13, 1994, an article appeared in the Metro section of the *New York Times* describing the confrontation between two "curiously matched adversaries"—the Jesse Smith Noyes Foundation and Intel—at the shareholders' meeting. It quoted Peter Goldmark, the president of the Rockefeller Foundation, as being impressed with Viederman's chutzpah. "We're following it with interest," Goldmark told the *Times*, "because I've always had grave doubts that passive ownership of stock is an effective lever for change, but maybe Steve [Viederman] can prove otherwise."

The *Times* went on to quote Timothy Smith, director of the Interfaith Center on Corporate Responsibility (ICCR) in Manhattan and a pioneer of the effective use of the shareholder resolution to bring about corporate change, hailing Viederman's gutsy decision to step forward as an advocate for change, which was not at all typical for foundations at the time. "The Noyes Foundation's appearance at the Intel stockholder's meeting is the first time a foundation executive has ever taken such a step and raised tough questions with corporate management," Smith contended. In the genteel world of philanthropy, the Noyes Foundation was very deliberately rocking the boat, and according to Smith, had put itself "on the cutting edge of a new trend."

Be that as it may, Intel had thus far failed to respond to SWOP and Viederman's challenge. In the fall of 1994, Noyes filed a shareholder resolution to be voted on at Intel's 1995 annual meeting asking the company to revise its Environmental, Health and Safety (EHS) policy to include language that would—in Viederman's words—"commit the company to sharing information with community-based organizations."

That doesn't sound like a dramatic change, but Viederman understood just how dramatic it could be. At the time, Intel's EHS policy committed the company to share the knowledge that they gained with employees, customers, the scientific community, and the government, but not the community, which it clearly did not regard as a legitimate party.

Viederman's shareholder resolution was an attempt to force Intel to shift from a *shareholder* to a *stakeholder* model of corporate responsibility. The community may not have been a shareholder, but it was certainly a stakeholder. The irony of the situation was that it took a shareholder like the Jessie Smith Noyes Foundation to provide a stakeholder with a voice. As Viederman later recalled, "A year into the process we included funds in our grant to SWOP so that they could purchase Intel stock, making them shareholders as well as stakeholders."

Filing the resolution, as Viederman anticipated, quickly put SWOP on Intel's agenda. In December 1994 an Intel corporate vice president and the manager of the New Mexico site traveled to New York to meet with Viederman—and only with Viederman. But just as Guana had not felt comfortable meeting with Intel without her own partners present, Viederman felt strongly that the meeting should be with SWOP and not with him filling in as SWOP's surrogate.

As the gentlemen from Intel "pulled thick notebooks from their briefcases, filled with data on water usage, air emissions, and the like, as the basis for a discussion of the issues raised by SWOP," Viederman said, "I absolutely refused to enter into a discussion with them. I observed that our concern was Intel's accountability and transparency to its community constituents, and that as a representative of the community, they should be talking to SWOP, not to us."

Viederman did, on the other hand, sense that the men from Intel were searching for a way to resolve this impasse, which was beginning to be embarrassing for Intel and was hardly enhancing its reputation. Viederman recalled:

We actually had an interesting discussion about corporate cultures. There is a culture at your place, I said, that says you shouldn't talk to these people in the community, and it is that culture that you need to change, and we'd like to help. There is a culture in our place that says we need to go to the annual meetings and speak up, engage in a dialogue, exert shareholder pressure for change, advocate on behalf of community groups. We were proposing a new model to the community groups, which don't tend to have the money to buy shares.

As a result of that conversation, in January 1995 Intel initiated a series of facilitated discussions with SWOP on a range of issues. The Foundation did not participate. The SWOP–Intel discussions focused on specific issues detailed in SWOP's report, and continued for most of the year. "SWOP and Intel learned more about each other's cultures," Viederman later explained, with evident satisfaction at the outcome. "A continuing issue was Intel's culture of secrecy concerning such things as their suppliers and subcontractors. At one point, with a smile on his face, Intel's staffperson had said he was 'unable to affirm or deny' that Taco Bell, whose trucks had been seen coming to the plant, was the supplier to their commissary." (A year later, when chair Andrew Grove's autobiography, *Only the Paranoid Survive*, was published by Grove Press, Viederman developed his own personal take on the title.)

In partnership with the thirty-year-old ICCR, a coalition of religious institutions committed to progressive shareholder activity, the Noyes Foundation filed a second shareholder resolution calling upon Intel management to revise the company's Environmental, Health and Safety policy to include information-sharing with communities. At Intel's 1995 annual meeting in April, the resolution received support from almost 5 percent of the shareholders voting, with another 8 percent abstaining.

By the early fall of 1995, as new resolutions had to be filed with Intel for the 1996 annual meeting, Viederman and ICCR's Smith simply re-filed their resolution from the prior year. In December 1995, Viederman was "pleasantly surprised to receive a draft of a revised EHS policy that included the community language that we had requested." After checking with SWOP, Viederman withdrew its resolution for the 1996 meeting.

Viederman and SWOP had taken on the giant Intel and won something important—not just a change of wording in the company's EHS policy, but a concrete concession that the community counted for something, and that it was indeed a legitimate party, a stakeholder of Intel.

"To their credit," Viederman recently acknowledged, "Intel became much more open with us on a number of issues of accountability and transparency. They have been more receptive to SWOP and other communities' approaches to them, and have often provided information before SWOP had to request it. Intel, however, still has a distance to travel. Sharing information is not yet intuitive for them."

But let's let Intel speak for itself. In a letter to *Foundation News* in response to an article on the shareholder process, an Intel spokesperson wrote:

> The experiences we have shared with the Jessie Smith Noyes Foundation illustrate the value of establishing a dialogue with the company where an investor concern exists. We at Intel welcome constructive dialogue with our stockholders.

Ever the editor, and a stickler for precision of language and definition of terms, Viederman would have made only one small change to that last sentence. Given his druthers, he would have changed the last word from "stockholders" to "stakeholders."

———

Not long after the imbroglio at Rio Rancho, and the Noyes/SWOP/ICCR battle with Intel management, a young EHS officer at Intel, Dave Stangis, sent his superiors a memorandum that was basically a pitch for the creation of a new position. Stangis had started out at Intel in 1996 in the Environmental, Health and Safety area before going to work for External Affairs, where he managed the editorial production of the company's annual Environmental, Health and Safety Report. He had observed the fight over Rio Rancho from the inside, and he had a pretty good idea of how he might be able to prevent such incidents from occurring in the future. In a fifteen-point memorandum, Stangis created his own title and function, "Manager/Director, Corporate Responsibility," and pointedly suggested that he could be the company's "single point of contact on Corporate Accountability and Social Responsibility (CA/SR) Issues for Intel."

He proposed to "lead response to or initiation of stakeholder engagements on CSR issues." He would be the project manager for Intel's CSR reporting, and would "manage with Investor Relations relationships with Socially Responsible stock indices and holdings (DJ/Sustainability, KLD, Citizens, Wall Street houses, etc.)" He would "watch, monitor for impact to Intel reputation and disseminate news on strategic external issues on the CSR front."

The main barrier to the creation of this new position was Stangis's superiors' belief, as he later put it to us, "that we were doing all this stuff already."

To which Stangis invariably replied, "What about your relationships with NGOs?"

He knew he had his work cut out for him when the person shot back: "NGO—is that some new sort of toxic chemical?"

Stangis's superiors ultimately bought his pitch, and gave him his position. They did, however, impose one condition: that he not go out and create a whole new bureaucracy to manage this new function. As a simple means of enforcing this prohibition, they refused to provide him with a department, a staff, or much of a budget. He was cordially advised that he had now become the head of a "virtual network," or "ad hoc CSR committee."

At first Stangis was mildly disappointed with this decision, but he also realized that this cultural abhorrence of bureaucracy at Intel was one of the main reasons he liked working at the company. He also realized that by being forced to make a virtue of necessity, this stripped-down style could be an asset, not a liability. In practice, whenever he needed to mount a new program or a new initiative, he had to pull people in from all over the company who might be right for that particular program or initiative.

As Stangis told us over lunch at his hotel in Portland, Oregon— where he was scheduled to lecture a class at Portland State University on CSR issues—"If I was part of some big CSR unit reporting directly to the CEO, we might be able to tell a great story and look good at conferences, but I don't think we'd be even halfway as effective."

Corporate social responsibility, Stangis ultimately decided, is a function not necessarily best managed "at a corporate level," at least not at Intel. Despite its size (80,000 employees worldwide) Intel tries very hard to maintain the can-do spirit of a small company by pushing as much decision-making as possible out from the center in Santa Clara to the business units. To gain support for any decision, any would-be change agent needs to gain the support of the leaders of those units who are doing the work in the field.

"Of the 80,000 people at Intel worldwide," Stangis told us, "even though I haven't met every one of them in person, I can say with some confidence that everyone I've ever met inside Intel sincerely *wants* to do the right thing. They just don't necessarily know what that is. I see my job as helping them to figure that out. We found that a lot of people in the company cared deeply about this stuff, but had nowhere to go until we gave them an outlet."

In his first months of the job, Stangis set out on a fact-finding expedition. Instead of trying to tour every one of Intel's fifteen major manufacturing centers in seven countries—"our factories look precisely the same all over the world, so if you're inside one, judging by the way that it looks you could be anywhere in the world"—he decided to see if it might be possible to let the NGO community, and in particular the socially responsible investing community, do some of his research for him.

As he knew from the intense ICCR interaction over Rio Rancho, the SRI community had been studying Intel closely for years. Stangis took a few exploratory trips to the eastern establishment media corridor running from Boston south to New York and Washington to find out what Intel issues were appearing on their radar screens. He talked to people at the Interfaith Council on Corporate Responsibility and to the analysts at all the leading socially responsible funds, including Dreyfus, Calvert, Neuberger-Berman and Kinder, Lydenburg, and Domini. He met with the Pension Fund of New York City and with the SRI arm of the Presbyterian Church. He invited Vicky Cummings, executive director of the Sisters of Mercy—a major force on the spiritual side of the SRI community—to take a personal tour of one of Intel's sites. On a western tour, he met with PETA—the nation's leading animal rights group—and even the Silicone Valley

Toxics Coalition, one of the most persistent and aggressive watchdogs over the entire high-tech manufacturing sector.

The point of this exercise—which he religiously repeats several times a year—was to proactively get out in front of the issues disturbing the NGOs about Intel *before* they turn into shareholder resolutions. The secret to successful NGO engagement, in Stangis's view, was simple: "Knowing that it's a process with no end." Every year, it's something different on the agenda, but one measure of his success was a negative one: "Every year since 1998, the first year I started doing this stuff, we haven't had a social [or environmental] shareholder resolution in our proxy statement."

But then he paused, his mouth forming a wry smile. "Okay, this year, we have seven, so there you go. We're always going to get dinged about something," he admitted cheerfully, "it's all just part of the process."

Stangis is doing a sophisticated and highly personalized form of risk management. He represents Intel's first line of defense against CSR risk. He talks to the NGOs, the people who are really tracking the problem areas, and he communicates those insights to the areas at Intel where the improvements are most needed. He gains grassroots support within Intel because—as he says—99 percent of the people inside Intel are dying to do the right thing, but don't necessarily know where to start.

It's a simple system, an inexpensive system, an extremely nimble system, and a highly effective system. It's not just that Intel now dodges shareholder resolutions before they arise, or that they're just being clever about keeping the NGOs off their backs. The real moral of the story is that by opening up this channel of communication, in a consistently proactive manner—to the NGOs who represent a significant group of the company's stakeholders—Intel is now not only "talking to vocal minorities," to quote Andy Grove, but actively listening to them, and learning from them as well. NGOs are the canaries in the coal mine for a company, in the sense that they give advance warning of trouble afoot. A good CSR structure, even of the ad hoc informal sort that Intel has in Dave Stangis, a one-man CSR band, has been proven to be the best insurance policy against CSR risk.

The pace of change, however, is never fast enough, far-reaching enough, or deep enough to satisfy the NGOs, Stangis insisted, and he readily conceded "that I can give you the URLs of six Web sites right now that will swear up and down that we do the work of the devil." But he credited the NGO community and the SRI community with starting Intel on the right path.

If you were to ask where we thought we would find the most innovative, proactive, and forward-thinking approach to relationships with NGOs, and to a certain extent CSR in general, Intel would not have been high on the list. It might not have even been on the list. But we came away from lunch very impressed with David Stangis. We had not a doubt that he was the real thing.

Standing back and thinking about Stangis and Intel in the context of other businesses facing similar challenges, it seems truly remarkable that in the space of just a few years, Intel—with a little help from NGOs like SWOP and the Noyes Foundation—has transformed its posture from the typical head-in-the-sand corporate stance of reflexive defensiveness to an open and proactive role. Stangis actually goes out looking for areas of potential confrontation; he travels the country seeking them out, in the knowledge that this sort of investigation can pay enormous dividends for his company, and its reputation. Stangis's fearless approach—and insistence that there's no organization he's afraid to talk to—struck us as verging on the visionary and certainly a model worth emulating.

Jonathan Wootliff, who has a big beard and a strong British accent, spent a few years as the communications director for Greenpeace International in Amsterdam before going into consulting with business on how best to engage with NGOs like Greenpeace. After directing a department of forty communications professionals at Greenpeace, he is now managing director of the Global Stakeholder Relations Practice for the international public relations agency Edelman Worldwide, with clients including Pepsi-Cola International, Kellog's cereals, Texas Instruments, and the British Post Office.

According to Wootliff, the growth of NGO and activist groups is a fact of life for business today, and rather than try to duck the threat, it makes more sense to see the NGOs as presenting business with an opportunity to positively transform themselves. "Too many people in business still see NGOs as hippies or anarchists throwing rocks at the Battle at Seattle," Wootliff says, but that caricature overlooks the fact that the ranks of certified NGOs range "from the Vatican to the NRA." They also range all over the map and encompass virtually every field of human endeavor from environmental affairs and poverty alleviation to human rights monitoring and advocacy, animal rights, labor relations, health issues like HIV/AIDS, and an astounding array of diversity, ethnic, and racial advocacy groups.

"Meeting with these people can be a much-needed reality check," Wootliff insists. "It's also a way of confronting some of those people who, rightly or wrongly, have become deeply involved with your brand. Engaging with NGOs can provide you with valuable insights into the way people think, in a very different way—quite possibly—from the way that you think."

"Our crisis management practice," he laughs, "might not be quite so lucrative if stakeholders relations were taken more seriously." Engaging with NGOs is perhaps the key element in the insurance policy against the risk of ruining a corporate or brand image that might have taken decades and hundreds of millions of dollars to create. "It has to do with reputation management, but not in a cynical or arrogant sort of way." Wootliff counsels clients to view the engagement far more positively, "as a kind of trend spotting."

It's also a fact that some NGOs can use better reputation management themselves. "Greenpeace is seen in the U.S. as extremely radical," Wootliff points out, "but very few people realize that in Europe it is frequently called upon by major companies to help them with technical solutions to a wide variety of environmental problems. Did you know that Greenpeace scientists have been working with Monsanto scientists on developing a new biodegradable plastic?"

I didn't. What I do know is that you can learn a lot by going outside the internal view held within your organization—and finding out what other people think of you. It's like a 360-degree peer review, except that it's for an entire company.

Bob Dunn, the executive director of Businesses for Social Responsibility, presents the problem succinctly: "Our starting point in counseling companies is the following question: 'If you were told that you had five minutes before *Sixty Minutes* was going to come barging in the door, what is the subject you would least like them to ask you about?'"

With five minutes to go before Mike Wallace pops in, if you don't know the answer already, you can call up the NGO most likely to attack you, and they'll be happy to tell you.

chapter four

Sustainability

Ray Anderson's first epiphany occurred on a sunny day in June 1969 in the showroom of Carpets International, a company based in Kidderminster, England. He was staring down at a sample of a carpet tile, a new product that CI was touting. The product came in 18-inch squares for the U.S. market and 50-centimeter squares for the UK and European markets. Its big selling point was that it was easy to install, without adhesive, and easy to repair or replace.

"The timing and the product concept were perfect," recalled Anderson in a speech many years after. At the time he was unhappily employed as the director of the floor coverings division of the Georgia-based Deering-Milliken textile company. The "office of the future" was just coming into its own, and the new computerized offices had electrical wiring installed not just in the walls, but under the floors. With carpet tiles, a maintenance person only needed to pull up a couple of tiles, attend to the wiring, and put the tiles back. Unlike conventional wall-to-wall carpet, there was nothing that had to be ripped out and repaired. That carpet tiles dramatically reduced the level of waste powerfully appealed to Anderson. Standing in the showroom of CI, fixating on his first carpet tile, he realized that this 18-inch square—which came in assorted textures and colors—might be his ticket out of Deering-Milliken into a company of his own.

Not long after that, Anderson contacted Carpets International and proposed a joint venture to bring the company's proprietary carpet tile technology to the United States, with himself as an equal partner. After some wrangling with Milliken over a noncompete clause in his contract, Anderson and CI launched Interface in 1974 with a small manufacturing and distributing facility in La Grange, Georgia. Interface grew rapidly, through internal growth and by strategic acquisition. Over a twenty-year period, Anderson took over more than fifty carpet companies, including Carpets International, which it quickly sold off to make a more strategic acquisition in the United States.

By 1994, Interface was the largest producer and distributor of carpet tiles—"soft modular flooring systems"—with 29 factories in the United States, Canada, the UK, Holland, Australia, Thailand, and China, and sales offices in more than a hundred countries. Its annual sales topped $800 million, and it had captured a nearly 40 percent share of the world carpet tile market. In the midst of the 1990s business boom, Interface was poised for another decade of progress. Ray Anderson had lived the American dream, a self-starter who became an enormous worldwide success, and he had every reason to look forward to a prosperous and fulfilling future.

Until he had his second epiphany.

During the summer of 1994, a group of employees at Interface Research, the company's product development arm, decided to organize an Environmental Task Force. An increasing number of questions had come into Interface's headquarters over the previous few years inquiring about the company's environmental practices and policies, putting the company in an awkward position. Interface had no environmental policy to speak of, and its philosophy, as Anderson later put it, was to "comply, comply, comply."

However, there were no new regulations with which to comply, there was no litigation in the hopper, no bad publicity to dispel, and no crisis to contain. When this newly formed task force asked Anderson to deliver the keynote address, he found that he had less than three weeks to prepare a speech in which he would lay out his vision for the company.

Ray Anderson was utterly stumped, unable to get any sort of handle on the topic. Then he serendipitously came across a remark former secretary of state Henry Kissinger had made during a speech two years earlier. Kissinger had observed that "sustainable development" was likely to replace the Cold War as the defining paradigm of our age. "I had no idea what the phrase meant," Anderson later recalled. "I seriously wondered if [Kissinger] knew what it meant either." But being curious and not wanting to let his own people down, he set about finding out.

The Sustainability Paradigm

Dr. Kissinger got the phrase, Anderson learned, from Dr. Gro Harlem Brundtland, a Harvard-trained public health expert from Norway. In 1985, Brundtland had been asked by the United Nations General Assembly to chair the World Commission on Environment and Development (WCED), whose mandate was to suggest ways to resolve the apparently irreconcilable conflict between the imperatives of economic growth and environmental and social protection. Many observers considered the 1987 report that they produced, *Our Common Future*, the public policy equivalent of Rachel Carson's influential *Silent Spring*.

Brundtland started out by making a huge leap of faith. She cogently argued that adopting a "low growth" or "no growth" economic policy for a world experiencing a population explosion would result in a full-scale economic and social disaster. While governments, she believed, could and would play a useful role in providing guidelines, frameworks, and regulatory regimes for economic growth—as well as appropriate forums in which to resolve disputes—she came down emphatically on the side of those who contended that the primary engines of growth and opportunity in the late twentieth and twenty-first century were likely to be private enterprises, not public sector concerns.

Coming two years before the fall of the Berlin wall, and speaking from a perspective informed by the European tradition of social democracy, this was a courageous, unconventional, and, to some minds, politically dubious position. But Brundtland insisted that "far from requiring the cessation of economic growth . . . the problems of poverty and underdevelopment cannot be solved unless we have a new era of growth in which developing countries play a large role and reap large benefits."

What was most urgently required, Brundtland maintained, was a radically revised model for global economic development that she referred to as "sustainable," and defined efficiently as follows:

Sustainable development seeks to meet the needs and aspirations of the present without compromising the ability to meet those of the future.

After reading *Our Common Future*, it began to dawn upon Ray Anderson that the world economic system of which he was proudly a part was failing on both counts: It wasn't meeting the needs of the present and yet it was compromising the ability to meet those of the future.

Meanwhile, a friend sent Anderson a copy of Paul Hawken's 1993 book on sustainability and business, *The Ecology of Commerce*. Hawken is probably best known as the founder of the high-end gardener's supply company Smith & Hawken as well as the host of an acclaimed PBS series called "Growing a Business." To advocates of the doctrine and culture of sustainable business, Paul Hawken is a prophet and a sage. To many of the businesses he regularly attacks, he is—not without reason—regarded as a sanctimonious pain in the ass.

Just as most Biblical prophets offer doom as well as hope—doom if you don't follow the message, hope and salvation if you do—Hawken insists (with more than enough evidence) that apocalypse is near unless we as a species embrace the doctrine of sustainability, get religion, and start cleaning up our act in ways that many citizens have never dreamed of.

Many people, and even some experts, question the assumptions on which the doctrine of sustainability is based. Sustainability advocates are essentially proceeding from a set of convictions—once again, based on very strong evidence—that the world's natural systems are in a state of serious decline, that we cannot continue to extract and wastefully consume our limited, nonrenewable resources, that toxic chemicals cannot continue to be manufactured and dumped into the environment, and that it is simply impossible to continue doing business as we have been doing it without incurring dire consequences. The underlying premise of the doctrine of sustainability, in short, is that the status quo system is unsustainable.

Reading *The Ecology of Commerce*—subtitled *A Declaration of Sustainability*—made Anderson see his accomplishments in an entirely new light. From the point of view espoused by Hawken, Anderson's life was not the simple story of innovation, growth, prosperity, and progress he had always thought it was. Interface Carpet was not a success story, but had abysmally failed to conduct its operations in a way that could be sustained into the future.

Sustainability advocate William McDonough, dean of the School of Architecture at the University of Virginia, has called our present economic system a form of "intergenerational tyranny," because it takes the ill effects of all of our waste, profligacy, and consumption and throws it onto the backs of the next generation. According to this point of view, Ray Anderson, carpet-tile entrepreneur, was no hero. Instead, he could fairly be branded—and indeed, branded himself—an environmental criminal.

Anderson, the president of one of the biggest carpet companies in the world, has said that "in the future people like me should go to prison." While Interface was breaking no environmental laws then on the books—its philosophy was, after all, "comply, comply, comply"—it was breaking an unspoken moral contract with the members of the next generation, and the next generation after that. The entire economic system, and its "perverse tax laws," Anderson insisted, were his "accomplices in crime," because they failed to force companies to "internalize" their "externalities."

That terminology—central to the thesis of sustainability—was first advanced by the environmental economists Herman Daly and John Cobb, who in a steady stream of books and articles over several decades laid out a cogent argument—long ridiculed by mainstream economists—that an economic system that placed a fictional "self-interested" individual at its center should be replaced by an economic system in which the "common good" was assigned the highest value. Rather than the "invisible hand" celebrated by Adam Smith—a force that comes into play in human affairs as the result of the self-interested acts of millions of individuals competing in a free market—the true costs of manufacturing a product or making a purchase should not be "externalized" as a burden to be borne by the society at large, but should be paid by the producers and consumers of those products, in the form of a tax. According to a system now referred to as "full-cost accounting," those "externalities" would be "internalized," providing self-interested organizations and individuals with a strong incentive to produce more efficiently, and with less waste.

The simplest form of internalizing an externality would be for a government to levy a tax on pollution and waste, or charge a fee for it to be disposed of. If Shell had been forced to pay a very high tax to dispose of the Brent Spar in the North Sea, advocates of "full-cost accounting" insist, it would never have considered dumping it into the ocean as a cost-effective means of disposal. And as a sign of how far we have come in a fairly short time, one of the more influential advocates of "full-cost accounting" today is Sir Philip Watts, coauthor of a recent book on sustainability, *Walking the Talk*, whose day job happens to be chairman of Royal Dutch Shell.

The dramatic language that Anderson employed to describe his conversion to Paul Hawken's doctrine and philosophy of life is rather religious in tone, a tone that is appropriate when you take into account that advocates of the doctrine of sustainability are very clearly latter-day prophets. "It was an epiphany," Anderson later wrote, in reference to his reading of Hawken's *The Ecology of Commerce*, like "a spear in my chest." The doctrine of sustainability structures its arguments in terms of sin and redemption. Ray Anderson was a sinner in need of redemption, and Paul Hawken was the prophet of doom who helped him to see the light.

"Since business in its myriad forms," notes Hawken in *The Ecology of Commerce*, "is primarily responsible for" global climate change, species depletion, ozone depletion, dwindling natural resources, and environmental degradation, "it is appropriate that a growing number of companies ask themselves: How do we conduct business honorably in the latter days of industrialism and the beginning of an ecological age?" In his speech to the Interface Research Environmental Task Force, Anderson revealed that for the first time in his life, he was actively in search of an answer to that question. He "borrowed shamelessly" from Hawken's ideas, he said, but he had already internalized those ideas with the ardor of the convert. "Business," he preached from his CEO's bully pulpit, "is the largest, wealthiest, most pervasive institution on earth, and responsible for most of the damage. It must take the lead in directing the earth away from collapse, and toward sustainability and restoration." Anderson concluded his 1994 speech by setting his task force, and his company, a very specific and daunting challenge:

> To be the first company that by its deeds shows the entire industrial world what sustainability is in all its dimensions: People, process, product, place and profits—by 2020—and in doing so we will become restorative through the power of influence.

We should note that the concept of being "restorative" is the ultimate objective in a situation of serious environmental degradation. Beyond being sustainable, restorative means to repair the damage we and others have done. This notion is clearly one that would be considered far-fetched by many, especially when approached as part of the mission of a business.

———————

Interface began its journey to sustainability by zeroing in on the elimination of waste, which the company defines economically—"anything that does not provide value to the customer." This includes traditional forms of waste such as off-quality product and scrap, as well as nontraditional forms of waste such as overuse of materials, inventory losses, wasted human effort, and opportunity loss. One of the first pieces of raw data that Ray Anderson asked his new Environmental Task Force to come up with was a hard number for how much raw material his company consumed to make its products in a given year. What he learned absolutely appalled him.

> We found that in 1995 our factories and our suppliers extracted from the earth and processed 1.224 billion pounds of material so that we

could produce $802 million worth of products. I had asked for that calculation, and when the answer came back, I was staggered.

Of the more than 1.2 billion pounds of raw material that Interface consumed in a year, approximately 400 million pounds—or roughly one-third—was composed of relatively abundant and environmentally benign inorganic material, mainly mined from the earth's lithosphere, or crust. But some 800 million pounds—or roughly two-thirds—of the raw material Interface consumed was petroleum-based, derived from oil, coal, or natural gas, including the synthetic materials used in the carpet tile and backing, as well as the fuel used to transport it. Interface had to find some way to cut back on the unaccounted-for externalities, or remain—in Anderson's eyes—a criminal enterprise.

How are Ray Anderson and Interface Carpet faring nearly a decade after he first laid out his challenge? At the Businesses for Social Responsibility 2002 conference held in Miami, Joe Foye, a vice president of Interface Research Group (the organization that first started Anderson climbing "Mount Sustainability"), presented a timely update. Foye had helped to create and manage Interface Recycling, the company's ambitious and innovative carpet leasing program. This program pioneered one of the more powerful "best practices" of sustainable business: the idea of converting a product into a service.

Interface decided that rather than define itself as being in the business of selling carpet tiles, they were really in the business of selling a service—that of providing floor covering, over time. Interface's contract with clients included regular and frequent replacement of old carpet tile with new carpet tile, and the recycling—"carpet takeback"—of the old product, which the company recycles insofar as it is feasible into new product. The service is a perfect example of the "closed-loop system" that sustainability advocates recommend.

"Sustainability is part of our culture at Interface," Joe Foye began, "and by that, I mean that we try to push it all the way down and out to every employee. Our overriding goal is to take that carpet and keep it out of the landfill, and through our comprehensive waste-management program, we've saved $165 million since 1994."

Interface has saved itself $165 million in part by reducing the packaging materials used when they ship their products. They used to ship carpet tiles, twenty at a time, in a cardboard box. But now they shrink-wrap the tiles and stack them in the trucks, reducing the weight of the product to be shipped, reducing the packaging, and eliminating the materials that went into that packaging and the energy used to produce it and then ship it to the landfill, and even reducing harmful emissions from the truck doing the shipping.

At Interface's 26 manufacturing plants around the world, Foye reported, they've closed 27 percent of the pipes emitting heat and gas through a carbon-offset emissions program called Cool Fuel. The program was set up in partnership with British Petroleum, now one of the largest providers of renewable energy in the world as a manufacturer of solar panels. Every Interface manufacturing plant in the world boasts an array of solar panels on its roof, supplemented by wind power and passive solar designed to let in a maximum amount of daylight into their buildings, reducing the energy needed to run lighting devices. In their never-ending quest to create closed-loop processes and products, Interface's goal, according to Foye, "is to stop buying new petrochemicals and to recycle old ones. The cheapest reservoir of petrochemicals for us is the carpeting we produce and it's sitting right on the floor," he said, "and we do everything that we can do to mine that reservoir for oil, and leave the rest of the stuff in the ground."

"This is Ray Anderson's life," Foye declared, "and it has become a way of life for all of us—from customers to carpet installers."

All told, since 1995, Interface's cumulative savings from the elimination of waste have totaled $209 million, including an additional nearly $50 million in savings accrued outside the packaging reduction program. That's more than $200 million going straight to Interface's bottom line, concrete confirmation that sustainability as a concept is a financial winner.

———————

Although we call ourselves a post-industrial society, we still continue to work in buildings, make things, buy things, and throw things away, and generate waste while we do it. We can outsource manufacturing and ship it overseas, and we can certainly make it more efficient and eco-friendly, but in the absence of some magical transformation, our dependence upon tangible stuff is not likely to disappear any time soon. In fact, our gains in efficiency seldom go toward conservation; they are usually turned into more and bigger stuff.

The doctrine of sustainability, however, with its emphasis on dramatically reducing industrial waste and pollution, and the introduction of new processes and new innovations, can be regarded as a conceptual bridge to a more truly post-industrial society. Every time a property manager or builder shifts to wind power or energy-efficient windows, the cause of sustainability is incrementally advanced.

The doctrine that is emerging, contrary to many characterizations, is not one of denial or monkish austerity, but one that promotes a new sense of awareness and responsibility for the impacts we have on the natural world and the idea of defining wealth by a new set of measurements, including greater leisure time, getting greater pleasure out of life, living in a clean environment with water that's safe to drink and air that's safe to breathe, doing creative and satisfying work, and leaving as few problems as possible to following generations.

"We see a world of abundance, not limits," write William McDonough and Michael Braungart in *Cradle to Cradle: Remaking the Way We Make Things*, the pages of which are made of a plastic from which the ink can be easily washed and captured for reuse. *Cradle to Cradle* builds on the work of Amory Lovins, founder of the Rocky Mountain Institute (and an original advisor to Seventh Generation), who during the 1970s launched an entirely new way of addressing the ongoing energy debate by focusing on issues of intelligent product redesign as a way of cutting back on energy consumption, as opposed to cutting back on creature comforts. Lovins painstakingly calculated that we waste more than half the energy we consume, a fact that is still true today, and proposed better designs that employed existing technology to improve the efficiency of a wide range of products, from lightbulbs to electric motors and automobiles. McDonough and Braungart, cofounders of the cutting-edge green design firm McDonough + Partners, have refined that principle into a vision of sustainable abundance, not constraint. "What if humans design products and systems that celebrate an abundance of human creativity, culture, and productivity?

That are so intelligent and safe that our species leaves an ecological footprint to delight in, not lament?"

Braungart is a chemist who led Greenpeace's chemical division before founding the German Environmental Protection Encouragement Agency, which helps companies design products with an eye to their entire life cycles. Bill Ford, chairman of the Ford Motor Company, was sufficiently impressed by McDonough and Braungart's ideas that he handed the firm $2 billion to turn the original Ford factory outside Detroit, the famous River Rouge plant, into a green manufacturing facility.

Defining "sustainability" is a little like defining CSR: It tends to morph a little bit in the mind of the beholder. In Brundtland's *Our Common Future*, the term was defined economically, as living off the earth's interest, not its capital. The original sustainability advocates largely understood and used the concept as an environmental term. As the doctrine has evolved, it has increasingly incorporated a social component. Activists have understood that a socially unbalanced system that mercilessly exploits underprivileged and underdeveloped countries, or exploits the rights of individuals in places with deficient labor laws and human rights statutes, is as inherently unsustainable as an environmentally unbalanced ecosystem.

Today, sustainability can be seen as a three-legged stool, comprising economic prosperity, environmental stewardship, and social responsibility. This foundation was first proposed by the British writer and business consultant John Elkington, founder and principal of the London-based consulting firm Sustainability, in his influential 1997 book *Cannibals with Forks: The Triple Bottom Line of 21st Century Business*. Elkington's "triple bottom line" has formed the conceptual basis for much CSR reporting today.

In their wonderful 2002 book *Dancing with the Tiger*, Brian Nattrass and Mary Altomare recount sustainable practices as applied by a number of leading companies, including Starbucks and Nike. The authors came up with the tongue-twisting formulation that says sustainability is "an emergent property of a nested hierarchy of socioeconomic and ecological systems."

These ideas come from the field of complexity theory, which envisions a hierarchy of different kinds of order—starting with fundamental physics at the bottom, moving up through chemistry and biology to very complex systems like ecologies and the wind—in which each level shows new and essentially unexpected ("emergent") properties. The laws that govern the living cell, for instance, are not entirely deducible from the laws of chemistry. Nattrass and Altomare are saying that sustainability is not an inherent property of either ecology or socioeconomics, but that it emerges from the two systems' interaction.

In the end, sustainability focuses our eyes on the future while providing a critical lens through which we can view virtually all human activity. Although conventional business pays lip service to the idea of the future, with all its endless focus on strategic planning, long-range thinking, and scenario development, most business decisions are based on short-term thinking, which can often be self-defeatingly reactive, and myopic. All of Western society has tended to think in much the same way, except—ironically—when it comes to war planning and defense. In just about every other arena, short-term thinking rules. The doctrine of sustainability tries to shift our radar screen into a new dimension, that of time. And that is probably its most critical contribution to the ongoing debate about the role of business in society.

Walking the Talk: The Business Case for Sustainable Development (2002), by Charles O. Holliday Jr., CEO of DuPont, Stephan Schmidheiny, chairman of Anova Holdings, and Philip Watts, chairman of the Shell Group of oil companies, offers a remarkable example of the degree to which the thinking (if not necessarily the actions) underlying the doctrine of sustainability has been embraced by mainstream business. Whatever you think of their basic arguments—which among other things strongly favor voluntary shifts in corporate behavior over new regulatory regimes, and offer some pretty meager examples that they define as significant progress—the simple fact that the sitting chairmen of DuPont and Shell have signed their names to a book on the subject is surely significant. Both were brought into the sustainability tent by the third author, Stephen Schmidheiny.

Shortly before the Rio Earth Summit of 1992—convened in direct response to a challenge raised by Gro Brundtland in *Our Common Future* for a global forum to begin confronting these issues—Schmidheiny delivered a speech "in the L-shaped hold of a noisy, creaking wooden ship tied up in Bergen, Norway"—as he later recalled—that posed an excellent question: "Was it possible to create a world in which what was good for the planet was good for business, and vice versa?" Sitting in the audience on that leaky boat—an appropriate symbol for our stressed-out planet—was Maurice Strong, Secretary General of the Rio Earth Summit, who after the speech beseeched Schmidheiny to help spread the message of sustainability among international business leaders. Schmidheiny responded by organizing a working group of business leaders called the World Business Council for Sustainable Development (WBCSD), which he originally thought might come together for six months, issue a report, and disband.

A decade later, WBCSD has grown into a blue chip coalition of 160 major international companies, including Time Warner, AT&T, Bayer, BP, Coca-Cola, Dow Chemical, and many other global brand names, drawn from more than thirty countries and twenty major industrial sectors. They say they are united—so the organization's literature puts it—"by a shared commitment to sustainable development via the three pillars of economic growth, ecological balance, and social progress." WBCSD insists that the best long-term solution to transforming society "is to mobilize . . . and leverage the power of innovation and global markets for the benefits of everyone, not just the developed world." The emphasis here is very definitely on "market forces" doing the driving.

What sustainability truly requires, this group argues, is further liberalization of the world's trade market and an even more fervent embrace of globalization. The group maintains that business cannot succeed over the long haul by failing societies, in either the developing nations or the developed ones, and that "when the global market fails poor countries, where most of the world's people live, it will also eventually fail business." It is therefore in the self-interest of business to mobilize itself to help society. This puts them directly at odds, of course, with the anti-globalization movement. Critics contend that WBCSD is merely a sham designed to forestall the inevitable re-regulation of business and the dismantling of the free-market Washington Model—promoted by the Americans—of globalization according to Big Business.

But Watts, Schmidheiny, and Holliday are not blind defenders of the status quo, and are not at all persuaded that the present system constitutes a truly free market. They vigorously contend that providing subsidies for rich countries' products and tariffs against poor countries' products—as both the European Union and the United States do, for political reasons—is entirely contrary not just to the interests of less developed and poorer countries, but also to market-based solutions to global problems.

In *Walking the Talk*, the authors quote the Columbia University economist Jagdish Bhagwati to the effect that Adam Smith needs a little radical updating for our present era:

> Adam Smith's invisible hand will guide you to an efficient allocation of resources only if markets yield prices that reflect the "true" social costs. If there are market failures, as when a producer pollutes the air but does not have to pay for this pollution, then the invisible hand can lead you in the wrong direction. Or to put it in flamboyant terms, it can immiserize [impoverish] you.

That the CEOs of DuPont and Royal Dutch Shell have come out in favor of companies *paying for externalized costs* is a noteworthy shift, a sign of how far even big business appears to have traveled in a remarkably short period of time. Is this mere window dressing and greenwashing? Only time will tell. So much of the legislation their lobbyists are fighting for takes place behind closed doors, evading scrutiny. More transparency is clearly needed. But I believe that these well-intentioned gentlemen might not fully grasp the extent to which fairly radical solutions are required to address the daunting global challenges they so admirably recognize.

Among the market-based measures the authors call for are the use of tradeable permits for pollution rather that command-and-control regulations, the phasing out of perverse subsidies, and, perhaps most important, a move toward full-cost accounting for externalities. They define "full-cost accounting" in fairly unstinting terms:

> The prices of goods ought to reflect *all* of the costs—financial, environmental, and social—involved in making them, using them, disposing of them or recycling them. The prices of services ought also to reflect their full costs. That way the market reflects environmental and

social as well as financial realities. It reflects scarcities. It requires less government tinkering. Leadership companies would be happy with full-cost pricing because, being cleaner and more efficient than other companies, they would be producing goods and services for less.

People like Herman Daly had been saying the same thing for years, but his ideas had been dismissed by mainstream economists as fringe and even socialistic. Then in 2002, the CEOs of DuPont and Royal Dutch Shell were saying it. As to their credibility and the commitment that lies behind their proposals, I remain skeptical. Equally important is how quickly they are willing to make these changes to create the internal corporate culture that these changes will require. It's fair to assume they don't want to make these changes if other businesses don't willingly or aren't compelled to change along with them. One wonders how they expect this will all happen.

One of the more vocal opponents of what might be termed the "pro-globalization" school of sustainability is John Cavanaugh, vice president of the International Forum and editor of *Alternatives to Economic Globalization*, a collection of essays critiquing, or rather attacking, globalization. Cavanaugh recently debated Chad Holliday, chairman of DuPont and one of the authors of *Walking the Talk*, on these issues.

This intellectual wrestling match was held at Freedom House in New York, an elegant townhouse in Murray Hill built according to strict ecological principles by the late labor mediator Theodore Kheel—a perfect place in which to mediate the arguments over sustainability. Cavanaugh kicked off the debate provocatively, asking why DuPont continued to produce a gasoline additive that he maintained has been proven to be a terrible toxin and probable cause of cancer in humans. "The scientific consensus is unassailable," he maintained, "and there is no confusion in the scientific community. Yet DuPont consistently fails to acknowledge the harm that this toxic chemical causes to the world and to our communities."

Needless to say, the guests sipping chilled Pellegrino and chopping off thin slices of brie held their breath as they awaited Chad Holliday's response. There was none, in part because the format of the "conversation" prevented it. So Cavanaugh proceeded to answer his own question by citing a book by Ralph Eskes called *The Tyranny of the Bottom Line: Why Corporations Make Good People Do Bad Things.*

Summarizing Eskes, Cavanaugh maintained that corporate charters lie at the root of the problem. Until corporate charters are comprehensively revised to reflect changing priorities, Eskes and Cavanaugh maintain, companies will continue to be bad social actors because they are, in effect, mandated to act that way by their narrowly defined fiduciary duty to their shareholders.

As examples of this phenomenon, Cavanaugh cited the peculiar and certainly inconsistent behavior displayed by the CEOs of Exxon and Union Carbide in the wake of the two worst corporate-sponsored environmental disasters of recent decades, the Exxon *Valdez* oil spill of 1989 and the toxic cloud that enveloped Bhopal, India, in 1984. "Shortly after both incidents," Cavanaugh insisted, "the CEOs of both companies openly expressed contrition, regret, compassion for the victims, and a deep sense of personal grief. They reacted to these disasters as human beings." But within a matter of weeks, both men had been "forced" by a variety of pressures to put on their CEO hats and to callously disregard everything they had been saying before. This 180-degree turnaround in their public presentations was intended to minimize their liability and protect their corporate image.

The implication of this story was clear to the audience. Though a vast oversimplification, and an argument that flies in the face of many of the positive examples cited in this book, Cavanaugh's point was that while Chad Holliday was undoubtedly a very nice guy, as the loyal upholder of his corporate charter and corporate agenda, he was honor-bound as well as legally straitjacketed to do bad things to the environment, because otherwise he wouldn't make enough money for his stockholders and he would find himself out of a job.

Of course, Cavanaugh did not mention a contrary case, the Brent Spar incident, which just happened to have been presided over by Philip Watts, Chad Holliday's coauthor of *Walking the Talk.* While Exxon and its corporate successor Exxon-Mobil continue, to their everlasting dishonor, to fight damage awards in court more than a decade after the disaster, the shareholders and management of Royal Dutch Shell took a very different view of a similar situation. They clearly decided—under pressure from Greenpeace—that the company's reputation for responsibility was worth more to its share-holders than endlessly litigating its "legal" right to dump the Brent Spar into the North Sea.

As for the environment, Cavanaugh argued that climate change is scientifically undeniable, yet the primary emphasis in *Walking the Talk* has been on using market forces to drive the required change in business practices. On this, Cavanaugh was skeptical. He contended that "during the disastrous Depression that followed the boom of the Twenties, a fundamental rethinking of corporate behavior was enforced by the government on behalf of enraged people who had lost their life savings. A regime of useful regulation was established, including the FDIC [Federal Deposit Insurance Corporation] and the SEC [Securities and Exchange Commission], to name just a few of the integral parts of the New Deal. Today, it's more like the S&L scandal of the Eighties, a sweep-it-under-the-rug scenario, combined with a hope that the public will forget because everyone knows the public has a short memory."

This is absolutely dead on the mark. "Market-based reform" is often a code phrase for doing nothing until the issue goes away—at least in the public's mind. But it is also the case that much government regulation has been demonstrated to have perverse effects unintended by its drafters. Government agencies like the EPA and the SEC do provide companies with a much-needed level playing field with regard to compliance, which leading-edge companies can then transcend, if they choose, in forging their own strategies. But most advocates of corporate social responsibility and sustainability rightly contend that while there are valid market forces inducing companies to be better corporate citizens, those market forces alone are rarely adequate to effect necessary change. Market forces, when they work, often produce cheaper and more innovative solutions to social and environmental problems, but that in and of itself will not provide an acceptable solution to the challenges we face.

At present, our society provides two primary methods of inducing companies to internalize some of their externalities and to help ensure that they behave reasonably: regulation and litigation. Both are imperfect. Sustainability advocates see those two methods being rapidly supplemented in part with a growing market force that can provide equally effective incentives for corporate behavior modification: the need for a good reputation, a strong brand, and a reduced risk of liability, not just legal liability, but moral liability.

Sustainability advocates further contend that pursuing sustainability has its own rewards. Reduction of waste brings significant cost savings. 3M's Pollution Prevention Pays program has saved close to $1 billion, while Interface Carpet has saved upward of $200 million through a comprehensive waste reduction program. The introduction of a more environmentally sound and values-based work environment boosts productivity and reduces health care costs; more efficient production and distribution processes reduce pollution while they save money; sustainable product designs reduce material intensity, which saves money. All of this needs to be supported by a culture in alignment with these values, and that enables a business to attract and keep a more loyal, committed workforce.

But "purely voluntary efforts," Cavanaugh insisted, only go so far—presumably not far enough—in advancing the twin agendas of social justice and environmental stewardship. "They can create a dynamic and creative tension in combination with a useful regime of regulation, but they are no substitute for regulation." Externalized costs, for example, will never be significantly internalized unless regulation forces business to reflect those costs and does so on a level playing field, which forcefully and dramatically creates incentives for sustainable business behavior.

To which Chad Holliday, not surprisingly, responded cordially:

Will voluntary efforts be enough? Absolutely not. But our position is this: Tell us what you want from us, tell us where to go, and let us figure out how to get there. Give us a deadline, hold us accountable, but let us find the way. Don't tell us how to do it and don't lead us by the nose to the stream.

The Natural Step

In 1989, a Swedish oncologist named Karl-Henrik Robèrt observed a significant increase in childhood leukemia cases in his practice, as well as in the Swedish population at large. After studying the available evidence and literature, he traced this alarming upsurge of child leukemia to one cause: a significant increase in the level of environmental toxins generated by industry.

In the early 1990s, Robèrt collaborated with physicist John Holmberg to define a set of guiding principles for a sustainable society, which evolved into a framework and a practice they dubbed the Natural Step. Their work gained the ringing endorsement of the country's environmentally conscious King Carl Gustav, who wrote the introduction to a package of educational materials about environmental sustainability sent to virtually every household in Sweden.

The idea behind the Natural Step can be summarized as follows: Human behavior needs to be altered to reflect our now greater understanding of nature's cyclical processes. A number of Swedish companies—IKEA, Electrolux, McDonald's Sweden, and Scandic Hotels—initially commissioned the Natural Step to help them climb "Mount Sustainability," as Ray Anderson calls it, and by 1995, the Natural Step had established itself in the United States with a headquarters in Cambridge, Massachusetts. The board of advisors originally included Paul Hawken—who has since disassociated himself from the organization, reportedly out of unhappiness over its relationship with companies of which Hawken does not approve. In 1996, the organization relocated to downtown San Francisco, where it inhabits what might be considered a corporate sustainability quadrant along with its neighbors the Social Venture Network and Businesses for Social Responsibility.

The Natural Step compares our current planetary predicament to a funnel, where the walls are nearing intersection and there is diminishing room to maneuver. From this decidedly ominous (sometimes called "declinist") point of view, all of the natural mechanisms and supporting resources essential to our continued life on this planet—clean air, clean water, productive topsoil—are threatened by overconsumption. At the same time, society's demands on these resources are increasing. How do we escape from this predicament? The solution advocated by all sustainability proponents in its most simplistic form is to re-engineer processes to form a "closed loop," in which nonrenewable resources are replaced by renewable ones and all material formerly discarded as waste is re-utilized as a resource.

The Natural Step Web site carries some impressive endorsements, from such luminaries of the corporate sustainability movement as Ray Anderson, Amory Lovins, and executives at Home Depot, Starbucks, and Nike. And then there is this:

> *The Natural Step has some unique characteristics: It's based on science. It's also based on collaboration and cooperation. I have found in my career that many NGOs are more committed to making a point, maybe pontificating, than making a difference. This is not the case with the Natural Step.*
>
> —Mats Lederheusen, Executive Vice President,
> McDonald's Corporation

At this, I confess, I experienced an involuntary shudder, followed by the thought: *They've got to be kidding.*

Can McDonald's—any McDonald's—ever be considered a sustainable enterprise? If you're still wondering why Paul Hawken is no longer associated with the Natural Step, wonder no more.

McSustainability

As of the middle of 2003 McDonald's worldwide was in deep trouble. Its stock price, growth rate, revenues per store, and, most significantly, its reputation were all deep in the dumps. The business model that McDonald's and the other fast-food chains rode to worldwide prosperity during the decades after World War II is badly broken— one might say, unsustainable—and to give McDonald's credit, senior management appears to know it.

One of the many reasons that McDonald's is struggling not just with its business but with its corporate image is that the journalist Eric Schlosser was commissioned some years back by *Rolling Stone* to write a piece on the slaughterhouses of Colorado. Researching this article provided Schlosser with much of his background for a best-selling exposé of the entire fast-food industry, in the great tradition of Upton Sinclair's muckraking classic *The Jungle*, on the meatpacking houses of Chicago.

"The profits of the fast food chains have been made possible by losses imposed on the rest of society," Schlosser writes, including widespread obesity, food poisoning, rural poverty, and environmental degradation. Although Schlosser does not use the term, McDonald's and its fellow fast-food companies have been busily and merrily externalizing their costs, and he was not the first to catch them at it.

> This industry has been driven by a lack of awareness of its practices, as well as an absence of values. Culturally, the essence of this industry is uniformity and conformity. The key to the success has been recreating identical restaurants that serve identical food. In a different era, with different values, that might not succeed as well as it has over the last 20 years. I may be a deluded optimist . . . but I would argue that that might be one of the downfalls of this industry.

In summary, the fast-food industry, as presently constituted, might not be sustainable as either a business model or an environmental and social proposition. In a country like the United States, born and bred on beef, burgers, and everything fat and fried, this is rank heresy, but it has struck a powerful chord in the public consciousness. The book lingered on the best-seller lists for months.

Schlosser points out, to our collective disgust, some ugly facts about McDonald's and the other fast-food chains:

- The cattle the fast-food chains grind up into their products spend their last days packed in feedlots full of pools of manure.
- Poor hygiene practices in abattoirs (slaughterhouses) have led to a sharp rise in the spread of the pathogen *E. coli* 0157.
- A typical artificial strawberry flavoring found in McDonald's milkshakes is a cocktail of more than 50 different synthetic chemicals.
- Every day in America 200,000 people get food poisoning, 900 are hospitalized, and 14 die from fast-food poisoning.

- Americans spend $120 billion a year on fast food, more than on higher education, PCs, computer software, new cars, magazines, films, recorded music, newspapers, videos, and books combined.
- Out of every $1.50 spent on a large order of fries at a fast-food restaurant, just two cents goes to the farmer who grew the potatoes.
- Ninety-six percent of American schoolchildren can identify Ronald McDonald, more than recognize Jesus on the crucifix.
- Giant agribusiness and slaughterhouse chains that supply fast-food chains are driving America's small farmers off the land and out of business.
- The stores themselves are notoriously hostile to workers' rights and have bitterly resisted minimum-wage laws.
- They invest large sums of money designing equipment so streamlined that it requires as little skill as possible to operate, while accepting vast U.S. government subsidies for teaching job skills to the poor!

Schlosser quotes Ray Kroc, the founder of McDonald's, to devastating effect:

> We have found we . . . cannot trust some people who are non-conformists. We will make conformists out of them in a hurry. . . . The organization cannot trust the individual; the individual must trust the organization.

Let's look at the other side of the coin for a moment. McDonald's has long been a leader in corporate philanthropy. I can tell you this, on good authority, because it's printed in McDonald's first Corporate Social Responsibility Report, which specifically pointed out that more than 3 million families, most of them with very sick and often terminally ill children, have stayed in the Ronald McDonald Houses—at an average rate of 100,000 families per year, for the past thirty years.

The report delves into considerable detail about all the things that McDonald's has done right while pursuing the path to sustainability, including retaining the Natural Step to help it negotiate the often painful "transition from a traditional approach of environmental responsibility, embodied by the practical philosophy of 'reduce, reuse, recycle,' to a broader sustainable framework." The Natural Step is helping McDonald's realize a "vision for the environment, [which] is now entering a new stage of development within the framework of a 'sustainable' society." The report notes, "achieving deeper levels of environmental stewardship is consistent with our business needs as well. For example, we depend upon a food supply that is sustainable."

Making matters even more complicated for those inclined to be reflexively dismissive of McDonald's efforts, the company has very definitely begun to walk the talk. In 2002, McDonald's startled environmentalists by opening the world's first (and only) CFC-free restaurant in Vejle, Denmark, eliminating the use of the chlorofluorocarbons long contained in aerosol sprays and many refrigerants that combine to devastating effect in our upper atmosphere to deplete the ozone layer. The Danish Minister for the Environment hailed the opening as "a good day for the environment." A spokesperson for Greenpeace International, on hand for the opening, jubilantly characterized the event as a "bold step" for the emerging corporate sustainability movement.

McDonald's CFC-free refrigeration and ventilation systems technology were developed by McDonald's scientists and engineers and presented at an international Refrigeration Summit cohosted by the company, in conjunction with the United Nations Environmental Programme and the U.S. Environmental Protection Agency.

Here are a few facts about McDonald's Sweden worth noting:

- Seventy-five percent of its 160 stores serve organic ice cream.
- Fifty percent of its stores run on renewable energy.
- All new McDonald's in Sweden have water pipes made of recycled plastic, not copper, wood window frames instead of steel ones, and wooden foundations as opposed to concrete.
- All McDonald's in Sweden serve organic milk, recycle 97 percent of their solid waste, and meet the strict ISO 14001 standards of environmental integrity.

Even more recently, McDonald's announced a plan to open biodiesel stations—an environmentally friendly vegetable-based alternative to diesel fuel—adjacent to its burger franchises. Biodiesel fuel, which comes from recycling the cooking oil used by McDonald's, cuts down on the use of diesel fuel and recycles the oil used to fry fries. A company spokesperson called the filling stations "a natural extension" of the company's business and mission. To which Lila Cousins, an alternative fuels expert at the Natural Resources Defense Council, memorably responded much as I did to this news. She described it as "pleasantly flabbergasting."

What are we to make of the fact that McDonald's has hired Dr. Temple Grandin, the leading U.S. expert on humane methods of slaughtering cattle, as its outside animal welfare consultant? "McDonald's integrating social animal welfare into its quality assurance program has made a huge difference," Dr. Grandin tells us in McDonald's first CSR report. "I have been in this business for more than 25 years, and I have never seen such a transformation." She is probably the most respected person in her field. Would she risk her own reputation for a pot of gold—or a Happy Meal—if she didn't believe it? One must conclude that either Dr. Temple Grandin has been corrupted, or that McDonald's seriously intends to improve its animal welfare practices.

In response to the criticisms that it serves unhealthy food and is contributing to worldwide epidemics of obesity and Type 2 diabetes, McDonald's in the UK has begun offering its customers sliced fruit. McDonald's France provides low-fat yogurt, and many countries (including the United States) have begun to offer beverage choices other than sugary soda pop, whether it be low-fat milk, bottled water, juices, or noncarbonated drinks. McDonald's Australia serves a Happy Meal with a toasted cheese and tomato sandwich, raisins, and orange juice. McDonald's Spain permits customers to create their own Happy Meals. McDonald's Japan offers a tofu burger with soy sauce. In 2003, McDonald's introduced a new line of salads topped by dressing provided by one of the world's best-known socially responsible companies, Newman's Own, in a brilliant stroke of cobranding.

McDonald's has recently announced the creation of an "Advisory

Council on Healthy Lifestyles," composed of some of the world's leading experts on nutrition and healthy lifestyles "to help guide the company on activities that address the need for balanced, healthy lifestyles." It has also begun working with the U.S. Department of Health and Human Services and the World Health Organization in a collaborative effort to help educate consumers about the role nutrition and fitness play in maintaining healthy lifestyles.

"McDonald's endeavors to do the right thing for our customers and the communities we serve," said Jim Cantalupo, McDonald's CEO, who no doubt believes every word he says. "This is a principle that guides our decision-making in all aspects of our business. Our customers take their family's health and fitness very seriously, and so do we."

Is McDonald's truly turning over a new leaf? Paul Hawken doesn't buy it one bit, and dismisses all this as greenwashing. Writing in the *San Francisco Chronicle*, Hawken—a third-party evaluator on Ben & Jerry's first CSR report—blasted McDonald's highly touted CSR efforts as a pious-sounding fraud.

> McDonald's "Report on Corporate Social Responsibility" is a low-water mark for the concept of sustainability and the promise of corporate social responsibility. It is a melange of generalities and soft assurances that do not provide hard metrics of the company, its activities or its impacts on society and the environment. While movements toward corporate transparency and disclosure are to be applauded, there is little of either in the report.

Hold on—the man's just warming up.

> The McDonald's Social Responsibility Report presupposes that we can continue to have a global chain of restaurants that serves fried, sugary junk food produced by an agricultural system of monocultures, monopolies, standardization and destruction, and at the same time find a path to sustainability. Having worked in the field of sustainability and business for three decades, I can reasonably say that nothing could be further from the idea of sustainability than the McDonald's Corp.
>
> The report carefully avoids the corporation's real environmental

impacts. It talked about water use at the outlets, but failed to note that every quarter-pounder requires 600 gallons of water. It talked about energy use in the restaurants, but not in the unsustainable food system McDonald's relies on that uses 10 calories of energy for every calorie of food produced.

McDonald's and other chains are aiming for automated equipment that will require zero training and are nearly there. Nevertheless, they fight hard to retain hundreds of millions of dollars of government subsidies for "training" their workers. A worker has only to work for 400 hours for the chain to receive its $2,400 subsidy. In essence, the American taxpayer subsidizes low wages, automation and turnover at fast-food chains.

In light of that well-grounded criticism, what then do we say to the good folks at Ben & Jerry's (now owned by Anglo-Dutch food giant Unilever), whose core product, in strictly health terms, could hardly be considered "socially responsible"? Setting aside their social and environmental leadership, Ben & Jerry's ice cream, mostly nonorganic and with super-high fat content (so critical to its taste and texture, not to mention its brand positioning), can lead its eager consumers unable to moderate their consumption down the slippery slope to disease and obesity just as surely as a Big Mac and fries.

"A foolish consistency is the hobgoblin of little minds, adored by little statesmen and philosophers and divines," Ralph Waldo Emerson wrote in *Self-Reliance*. Yet Paul Hawken never got on Ben & Jerry's case about the health effects of its core product while auditing its CSR reports. He never complained about their failure to go organic. So why jump all over McDonald's?

To their credit, Ben & Jerry's, before they were a Unilever brand, spent a great deal of time and money struggling to remove the chlorine from their packaging, and to their regret never managed the conversion to 100 percent organic ingredients. In fact, only under Unilever's deep-pocketed auspices did the company succeed in introducing an organic line of ice cream in the summer of 2003. When Ben & Jerry's finally did manage to pull most of the chlorine-bleached, and potentially dioxin-releasing materials out of their cardboard containers, a reporter had the bad taste to claim that the high fat content of the product inside the container provided a safe haven for more dioxin—right there in the ice cream itself—than they even came close to removing from the carton!

But that person was not Paul Hawken. He didn't even ask the question, let alone come to a conclusion on this complex and misunderstood subject.

Let's imagine that every McDonald's in the world served organic food and veggieburgers—and provided fair wages and benefits, even to its part-time workers. Let's say that like McDonald's of Sweden and Denmark, every McDonald's in the world recycled nearly all of its waste material and was a CFC-free (as well as smoke-free) zone. Let's say the company became known for treating its workers with respect, and that even its least healthy entries were as healthy as they could possibly be. It would still be a chain, and it could still serve fast food. Is there something inherent in this business model that prevents a company from ever acting responsibly? Let's also ask that question in light of the fact that Gary Hirshberg of Stonyfield Yogurt has recently established a chain of organic fast-food restaurants.

What would the verdict be? Can McDonald's be socially responsible and sustainable? Certainly it's possible, but only if its business model was convincingly committed to the type of fundamental change that Ray Anderson has achieved at Interface Carpet, or British Petroleum is attempting to achieve in its celebrated move "Beyond Petroleum." Such fundamental change has not yet occurred at McDonald's. But that real and rapid change is afoot is undeniable. The challenge for all businesses that venture down this path is at least threefold, and embraces pace, scope, and depth:

1. Are they moving quickly enough?
2. Are they committed to applying these values broadly across all aspects of their business?
3. Have they drilled down to integrate these values into their corporate culture?

The only way for us to answer these questions with any degree of reliability is if these companies are also committed to enough disclosure and transparency for those of us standing on the sidelines to venture an informed opinion.

McDonald's conversion to sustainability is clearly a work in progress, albeit an important one. If McDonald's can truly transform itself into a sustainable business, that would be a remarkable achievement, one potentially replicable on a worldwide scale. What matters most for our world is not really whether Seventh Generation is able to add more post-consumer recycled plastic to the composition of its laundry bottles, but whether those industries that are most responsible for getting us into this mess in the first place will take the responsibility to help us all find a way out. Will the critical and major players in forging the destiny of our civilization wake up to the urgency of these problems soon enough to help lead us all away from the brink of disaster? Or will they only change reluctantly, kicking and screaming, as the earth dances with a destiny that none of us wants to contemplate?

chapter five

Accountability

On August 18, 1987, thirty-four-year-old Howard Schultz called all of his employees into one room and laid out his vision for the new Starbucks. The original Starbucks had been established in 1971 as a retail coffee store in Seattle's Pike Place Market, modeled after Peet's Coffee & Tea in Berkeley, California, a purveyor of high-quality *arabica* coffee, dark-roasted in the European style. After buying their beans from Peet's for a few years, the three founding Starbucks partners—Jerry Baldwin, Zev Siegel, Gordon Bowker—began to emulate their mentor by purchasing their own beans on the open market, and blending and roasting them to their own specifications. Starbucks quickly developed a cult following in Seattle, opening a second store, a third, and a fourth, practically single-handedly launching a boom in coffee connoisseurship that earned the city the nickname "Brewtopia."

In 1981, Schultz—then vice president and general manager of the United States operations of Hammerplast, a large Swedish housewares company—was going over his retail accounts one day when he was struck by the fact that a small coffee chain in Seattle was ordering significant volumes of a Hammerplast drip coffeemaker designed to appeal to hard-core coffee connoisseurs. On his next trip to Seattle, Schultz dropped in on this little company, which seemed to be launching its own coffee revolution in the Pacific Northwest, met with the partners, and toured their roasting operation. He came away so impressed by "the magic and passion and authenticity" he found there that he decided to move to the Pacific Northwest to help Starbucks build up its fledgling retail operation.

In 1983, after working for Starbucks for about a year, Schultz attended a housewares show in Milan. He found himself sipping a cup of espresso in one of that city's innumerable coffee bars, an experience far different from what Starbucks had managed to create in Seattle. Schultz came away so impressed by the light, the cleanliness of the place, the friendliness of the staff, the speed and efficiency of the operation, the quality of the coffee, and the *barista*, who expertly crafted customized drinks for a devoted following of fanatically loyal customers. Schultz returned to Seattle hoping America was ready for a national chain of Milanese-style cafés.

The senior partners had recently extended themselves to the limit in buying out Peet's Coffee & Tea, so they were in no position to embark in a new strategic direction. Schultz persuaded them to let him open an espresso bar in one of Starbucks retail stores in downtown Seattle, but even after the café was a confirmed success, the partners refused to regard the project as validation of Schultz's long-term vision for Starbucks. "We're coffee roasters," Jerry Baldwin told Schultz without apology, "I don't want to be in the restaurant business."

Undaunted, by 1986, Schultz had scraped together enough capital—including $150,000 from Starbucks—to launch a Milanese-style coffee chain called Il Giornale, which quickly grew to three cafés. In the spring of 1987, he was surprised to hear that Bowker and Baldwin—Zev Siegel had since left the company—had decided to put the entire Starbucks operation (stores, roasting plant, trademark) on the block. While Bowker and Baldwin concentrated on building up the Peet's brand, Schultz acquired Starbucks for $3.8 million in cash in August 1987, and immediately merged his three existing Il Giornale cafés with the six Starbucks stores to create the nucleus of the new Starbucks.

Addressing his anxious employees on August 18, 1987—their first day of working for this new entity—Schultz made it clear that he intended to maintain the traditions that had drawn him—and them—to Starbucks in the first place. "I want to assure you that I'm not here to do anything to dilute the integrity of the company," he told them, but his goal was "to build a national company we all could be proud of."

In five years, he continued, he wanted all of them to be able to look back on this day and say, "I was there when it started. I helped build this company into something *great.*"

His employees had reason for skepticism—no one in the American food and beverage industry had ever pulled off anything even remotely like it. History seemed to dictate that there was an inverse relationship between quality and scale at practically every level of the food-service business. But Schultz radiated such evident sincerity, and was equally passionate that he intended to launch a company that would "leave no one behind."

Most of these employees had never been treated as important or held in as high a regard as the way the coffee tasted and how much money was made. The new Starbucks, Schultz insisted, could become a national beverage-and-food chain without creating a pool of dead-end service jobs lacking in security, benefits, or opportunities. He persuaded his board that it made sound strategic sense to grant full health care and other benefits to all Starbucks employees who worked for the company at least twenty hours a week. He justified this costly measure on two complementary grounds: On the one hand, it was the *right* thing to do, and on the other hand, the plan would retain talent, reduce turnover, heighten morale, and improve service to customers, the last of which he regarded as the cornerstone of the company's future.

Even if Schultz didn't know exactly what it meant to "leave no one behind," when the words first left his mouth, from its inception, Starbucks set out to be a socially responsible enterprise. Employee relations and personnel management were clearly two of Schultz's strong suits, but in 1990, three years into the new operation and two years before going public, Schultz drafted a team of senior executives to craft a mission statement that was designed to crystallize and codify the values he had worked hard to instill in Starbucks' DNA. The mission team ended up with a list of six Core Principles that still guide the company's operations:

1. Provide a great work environment and treat each other with respect and dignity.

2. Embrace diversity as an essential component in the way we do business.
3. Apply the highest standards of excellence to the purchasing, roasting, and fresh delivery of our coffee.
4. Develop enthusiastically satisfied customers all of the time.
5. Contribute positively to our communities and our environment.
6. Recognize that profitability is essential to our future success.

Insofar as we know, Starbucks has never been faced with a shareholder resolution questioning its decision to put profitability last on that list.

———————

By 2002, Starbucks' international empire had grown to 6000 stores serving 20 million customers a week, generating annual revenues of $3.3 billion. Starbucks had escaped some of the most scathing criticisms leveled at the fast-food industry by NGOs and other social critics, in part because it had eschewed the franchise model, giving it greater control over its stores. In addition, the company had split from the industry pack in making visible commitments to improving the lives of its employees—by then known as partners—as well as the communities in which it operated.

Still, as a consumer brand that was willing to label itself as "responsible," it could not escape criticism altogether. One point of criticism leveled at Starbucks by community groups, which did hit home, was that its spectacular growth siphoned opportunities away from small-scale retailers. Yet few of the small, locally based competitors from whom this criticism often originated could compete with Starbucks on employee benefits. Starbucks' image got a further boost from consumer research showing that the presence of a Starbucks store in most neighborhoods tended to build traffic for all coffee retailers in the area, including smaller competitors. Even the more curmudgeonly critics conceded that in contrast to other chains, the opening of a Starbucks in a neighborhood was usually a sign that it was on its way up, not on its way down.

To Starbucks' credit, the benefits also appeared to improve over time. By 2000, the company's health care coverage had been extended from partners to the partners of partners, provided that the couple was in a committed relationship. The company's CUP ("Caring Unites Partners") Fund (contributed to by partners and the company) had provided substantial amounts of financial aid to partners confronted by extraordinary needs not covered by insurance. The Bean Stock program, which provided stock options for all employees working twenty hours a week or more, had been combined with an ambitious employee stock purchase plan that gave even part-time employees a chance to own a piece of the action. Starbucks had been featured in *Fortune*'s "Best Places To Work" issue so many times running that most people inside the company had lost count.

CSR issues had played a defining role in the company. In the fall of 2001, all that passionate conviction was put to the test. When the price of coffee on the world's commodity markets dropped to a level not seen for decades—sinking to under 50 cents per pound by the spring of 2003—some large coffee companies initially greeted this development as a boon to their bottom line. But Starbucks knew better. If the world coffee crisis kept up unabated or was left to the markets to solve, the hardship it was causing the world's coffee growers threatened the sustainability of the entire enterprise.

How well they responded to this crisis is open to debate. Yes, you will find coffee labeled "fair trade" (meaning a fair price as determined by an independent third party was paid for the coffee) together with "organic" and "shade grown" in almost every store, as part of the company's "Commitment to Origins" program. While some are impressed, "fair trade," "organic," and "conservation" coffee still represents less than 2 percent of all the coffee Starbucks sells, though all the coffee they purchase is of the highest quality *arabica* beans, which cost more than twice as much as commodity beans.

Is Starbucks responsible for the impossibly hardworking conditions suffered by some coffee farmers, or for the fact that the economics of coffee farming are forcing many long-time growers out of business? Were some of the beans you drank in your last 1 percent decaf, hold the foam *latte grandé* grown by farmers who unsafely applied pesticides to the crop, exposed themselves and their workers to unsafe working conditions, and were paid too little to afford a doctor for their children? Starbucks, for all its good intentions, is unable, unwilling, or just not quite ready to tell you. By reading the company's 2001 CSR report you get part but not all of the story.

One of the most sweeping changes on today's corporate scene noted by Robert Dunn, executive director of Businesses for Social Responsibility, has been the "strong tendency on the part of some global companies to start putting pressure on their value-chain partners to comply with new standards, in both the environmental and social arenas." A company's "value chain" was once more simply known as its "supply chain," but the notion has been updated with a contemporary stakeholder twist. "Supply chain" generally refers exclusively to the economic relationships with vendors and suppliers, but "value chain" encompasses the social, environmental, and economic relationships with *all* of its stakeholders, including relationships with suppliers, vendors, wholesalers, retailers, and customers, but also with neighbors, partners, competitors, and contract workers not necessarily employed by the company. The value chain also covers the entire life cycle of a product, from birth to use to disposal by whatever means. If a product or an ingredient is toxic or harmful in any way, that's part of the value chain. If it has good long-term environmental effects, that's part of the value chain, too.

Value-chain and product life-cycle analysis obliges companies to ask—and answer—questions that they would have had no reason to think about in the past. Does the miner who dug the ore out of the vein that went into your car get paid a living wage? What about the process by which they extract the ore? Is it sustainable? Is it toxic? Is it environmentally and socially benign, or does it have detrimental consequences? Is it an energy-efficient process, and where did the energy come from? Does the miner work under conditions designed to protect his or her health? Does the miner's salary allow their children to have a decent place to live? Is health care provided and, if not, is the employee paid enough to purchase it? Does the community in which employees live have access to clean water and safe schools and decent roads and medical care? These are but a few of the literally thousands of questions that must be asked as the circle within which one is held accountable—the value chain—widens or lengthens.

The premise supporting value-chain analysis is that it doesn't matter if people work for you directly; if you are using their product to make one of your products—such as a raw coffee bean that you grind and mix with hot water and sell as a decaf, skinny latte—you have some responsibility to ensure that they make a decent living. Why? Because your customers and maybe even your shareholders are likely to ask, and even demand that these workers are well treated. From a purely pragmatic perspective, you are in the best position and have the most leverage to ensure that things are done "right" or at least to know how they're done, and to ensure that you've done your best to positively impact the process.

The concept of the value chain is simply the logical extension of the idea of sustainability into the nuts-and-bolts transactions that define all commercial activity. With value-chain responsibility, the social and environmental costs of products and services are theoretically more fairly distributed to specific suppliers and consumers, as opposed to the society at large. Externalities can be, if such analysis is properly applied, fairly internalized.

Today, few international protocols govern these issues. Most governments have neither the power nor the political will to control, let alone understand, how corporate behavior is affecting the often precarious livelihoods of all of their citizens. In some cases, nations and regions and municipalities have excellent laws on the books but little means to enforce them. And this is where NGOs and the media come into play, to exert sufficient pressure on governments to hold companies accountable for their behavior, particularly when government finds it more convenient (or lucrative) to ignore the problem. When that fails, NGOs appeal to the media or directly to the consumer or shareholder for help in redressing these inequities.

Business must also be conducted on a level playing field with a consistent and fair set of rules applied to all competitors. Today, not only is the field not level when it comes to ensuring that all companies pay the real costs of doing business, but the legal system, the system of subsidies, and the tax code all too often encourage anti-environmental corporate behavior. Why, for instance, does the U.S. government, promote clean air, but encourage the production of virgin rather than recycled paper—with a $1 billion-a-year subsidy, which includes the cost of building and maintaining logging roads in national forests? Producing recycled paper consumes significantly less water and energy, creates less pollution, and keeps the air cleaner. Under the guise of protecting jobs, the federal government helps a small handful of producers avoid not only the externalities but some of the ordinary costs of doing business.

A few incipient regulatory regimes like NAFTA, or the European Union's social and environmental regulations, or the voluntary CERES principles (more on these later) combined with a few other emerging nonmandatory codes of corporate conduct like the UN's Global Compact, have attempted to bridge the widening gap between globe-straddling international enterprises and the capacity of national governments to control their behavior. But in the absence of a truly global regulatory apparatus, the social and environmental police force of our planet—our collective conscience, if you will—resides collectively in the NGOs, whose numbers range into the tens of thousands worldwide—28,000 by one count.

Globalization and its discontents—to borrow the title of former World Bank economist Joseph Stiglitz's recent book—is the primary reason the value chain has become such a critical concept over the past decade, a period of unprecedented deregulation coupled with unprecedented global growth in transnational business. If consumers in the United States and Europe can trust that the coffee they drink is fairly sourced or that the sneakers they buy are produced under safe conditions by workers earning a living wage, it's because of rigorous monitoring by NGOs and the media, not government intervention. Until a regulatory regime is put into place that crosses national borders and has the teeth to back up its statutes, no company is legally obligated to take responsibility for its value chain. Until a global system of reporting is put into place to monitor compliance with some mutually agreed-upon set of social and environmental principles at every stage of a product's evolution, we must rely on information gathered primarily by NGOs and their allies in the media for knowledge of abuses. That obviously imperfect information is all that we as consumers, shareholders, and opinion leaders have to make decisions and take action on.

As we cobble together a patchwork quilt of shareholder resolutions, media exposés, boycotts, Internet research, and more sophisticated NGOs, there remain many who believe that no system of regulations, monitoring, and disclosure will ever tame the voracious pursuit of profits and market share. That may be so, but as we have said before, however imperfect this path may be, there is simply no other realistic path at this point. Probably the most important thing is to not let the perfect become the enemy of the good.

From Bean to Cup

Starbucks buys and sells a commodity that is the second most valuable in the world after oil. More than seventy countries grow coffee—in 2002, an estimated $6.5 billion worth. The value-chain problem is this: A surprisingly small amount of that money makes its way into the pockets of the estimated 25 million small-scale farmers who grow the crop. Yet the social and environmental consequences of that farming—depletion of natural resources, toxic pollution from pesticides, and impoverishment of people's lives—are growing as fast or faster than the CSR movement's attempts to alleviate them.

Nearly all of the world's coffee is produced between the Tropics of Cancer and Capricorn but consumed in the rich Northern Hemisphere. Today's global coffee glut originates in some of the more pernicious effects of rampant globalization. As a direct result of the widespread acceptance of the so-called "Washington Model" for a world economy—undoubtedly the United States' most influential global export—a long-standing trade agreement known as the International Coffee Agreement (ICA) was dismantled in the early 1990s.

The often harsh—although theoretically liberating—economic regime known as the Washington Model is largely defined by "free" trade, although exactly how free is a subject of heated debate. It is characterized by minimal government regulation, unbridled competition, and export-driven national economies, and it tends to pile up profits for those entities—typically based in the more developed countries—that are closest to the consumer and farthest from the producer. The regime underserves the people who grow or dig or mine or cut down the raw materials, who live in some of the world's poorest areas, and overserves the middlemen, shippers, and packagers of finished product and, yes, in most cases the consumers.

After the United States withdrew its support of the International Coffee Agreement (originally negotiated between producer companies in 1962) in 1989, the London-based International Coffee Organization lost its capacity to regulate coffee prices, which have since plummeted by 70 percent, to a level not seen since the Great Depression.

After the ICA was scuttled on ideological grounds as a classic anti-competitive cartel, international institutions like the World Bank responded to this new "opening up" of the international coffee market by encouraging new entrants such as Vietnam to plant coffee. Many Asian producers quickly and efficiently flooded the market with low-quality *robusta* beans, and just as quickly surpassed one of the two largest traditional producers, Columbia, and began closing in on the largest, Brazil. At the same time, the unfettered reliance on market forces has resulted in an enormous expansion in volume of so-called "technified" coffee, grown with the intensive use of highly toxic chemical fertilizers and with the extensive destruction of tropical rain forests as traditional "shade-grown" coffee was replaced by high-yield "sun-grown" coffee. There is a major difference: "shade-grown" coffee is planted under the forest canopy, preserving the rain forest, whereas the cultivation of "sun-grown" coffee often exacerbates already rampant rain forest destruction, leading to soil erosion, loss of biodiversity, and other long-term ill effects.

Who were the true beneficiaries of the breakdown of the coffee cartel? Not the growers in the poor regions, but the big coffee companies like Procter & Gamble (Folgers), Altria (formerly Philip Morris, of which Kraft is the food subsidiary), which owns Gevalia, Maxim, and Maxwell House, Sara Lee (Chock Full O' Nuts, Hills Brothers), and Nestlé (Nescafe). All but Nestlé, which is Swiss, are based in the United States. Together, these four companies account for an estimated 40 percent of worldwide consumption of low-price *robusta* beans. As prices fell, their gross margins rose. And by not passing on those savings to their customers, their business has become significantly more profitable. Coffee brokers and other intermediaries have also benefited, as volumes rose to record levels; they simply adjusted their cut to maintain their old profit margins as prices dropped, squeezing the farmers.

According to the international relief agency Oxfam, one decade ago developing countries received thirty cents out of every $1 spent on a cup of coffee. Now Oxfam calculates they get less than ten cents a cup. The unknown farmer who grew the beans for our espresso gets only two cents out of the $1.71 we now pay, on average, for an espresso served in a café. Ten years ago, according to the nonprofit Café Direct, the world coffee economy was worth $30 billion, with $12 billion going back to the growers. Today the coffee market value stands at $50 billion, with only $8 billion going back to the growers.

As is the case with a variety of imported agricultural products, those with no clout to change the system, the growers, have no "market mechanism" available to them to tighten up the market, raising prices in the process, and thus no incentive to reduce production. Recall that the market mechanism previously in place to benefit producers, the ICA, was scrapped as a "cartel." The result of free trade was thousands upon thousands of people leaving the land and an agricultural way of life throughout Latin America, flooding into already unsustainable cities, looking for jobs that did not exist. Many in the coffee industry did not see this as their problem. According to a Web site that promotes Fair Trade Coffee (Peacecoffee.com): "In 1994 a Nestlé coffee executive was asked for an opinion on sun- vs. shade-grown coffee. The executive had never heard of the issue and responded, 'Price and quality are our two determinants—we have NO relationship with coffee growers.'"

Of the total worldwide coffee market, about 10 percent is made up of "specialty" coffees, of which Starbucks purchases about a tenth, or 1 percent of the world harvest. Starbucks pays a steep premium to obtain the highest-quality beans—paying on average $1.20 per pound ($2.64 per kilo) for top-quality *arabica* beans, some grades of which sell on the open market today for as little as thirty cents per pound. Starbucks pays that premium to ensure that it gets the best coffee available, which by itself is beneficial, as more of that purchase price inevitably reaches the producers.

On a recent visit to the Starbucks Support Center in Seattle we met with Sue Mecklenburg, the company's Vice President for Corporate Social Responsibility and Business Practices, who had just returned from two weeks of meetings in Guatemala and Costa Rica with growers and NGOs, trying to hash out a set of Coffee Sourcing Guidelines for the company.

"We are a coffee company," Sue began, "so we have no choice but to source and serve in significant volume a product that lies at the root of a genuine human crisis. Our business bridges the north–south divide, which is also a divide between the haves and have-nots, and as a company—and as an industry—we're sincerely struggling with what sustainability means when it comes to coffee. What we do know is that when your core product is agricultural, that the farmers who grow the crop need to be sustained. And that, during a global glut like the one we're currently facing, is itself a challenge."

The most sensible starting point for Starbucks to enhance its value chain, Mecklenburg believed, is for the company to enter into as many long-term purchase contracts as possible with responsible coffee producers, effectively eliminating the middlemen wherever and whenever possible and ensuring that more money ends up in the hands of the farmer. Entering into these relationships provides several benefits for the producers as well as for the company. For farmers, long-term contracts are a means of hedging their risk in a time of falling prices and ensuring a more stable and certain market. Starbucks, in turn, advances its stated goal "to establish more direct relationships with farms and co-ops we know and trust," to quote from its most recent CSR report. In 2002, 36 percent of the company's coffee purchases were covered by long-term contracts, a substantial jump from just 3 percent in 2001.

"We need to be able to say to our prospective suppliers," Sue Mecklenburg said, "'If you want to be a Starbucks Preferred Provider, you need to pay your workers fair wages, you need to have environmental guidelines in place, you need to do nothing less than utterly transform a centuries-old supply chain.' We feel the same sense of urgency about this that the NGOs feel, except that with us it's a sense of *business* urgency."

Prospective Starbucks suppliers submit an application to the program extensively documenting the environmental and social measures they are taking to produce coffee in a sustainable and responsible fashion. By the end of fiscal year 2002, Starbucks had received 50 applications from growers hoping to become Preferred Providers, signifying that they are willing to abide by a series of principles known as the Conservation Principles for Coffee Production. This production code was developed by a consortium of NGOs, including Conservation International, the Rainforest Alliance, and the Smithsonian Migratory Bird Center. The government of Costa Rica has also recently agreed to adopt these conservation principles as a national standard, lending them additional legitimacy as an effective path toward growing coffee sustainably worldwide.

In the El Triunfo Biosphere Reserve in Chiapas, Mexico, Starbucks has been providing financial support—admittedly on a fairly small scale—to farmers to grow coffee in the traditional style, which means "shade-grown" beans grown on shrubs beneath the protection of the rain forest canopy, as opposed to high-yield "sun-grown" or "technified" coffee, which often requires the destruction of that canopy. Conservation International (CI) also certifies Shade Grown Coffee grown according to sustainable methods it pioneered in the El Triunfo Biosphere Reserve, of which Starbucks purchased 1.8 million pounds in fiscal 2002, while adding Decaf Shade Grown Mexico to its line of conservation coffees.

Because small coffee farmers often experience significant cash shortfalls well before the harvest, the only time in the year they make any money, Starbucks has gotten into the business of extending low-interest micro-credit loans to a number of farmers in Latin America through Ecologic Enterprise Ventures (EEV) and Conservation International. The $500,000 extended so far through the program may sound like a drop in the bucket, but micro-credit functions on comparatively small loans, so that half a million was able to help over 200 farmers receive pre-harvest financing and 691 farmers receive post-harvest financing in 2002.

Starbucks has also formed a strategic alliance with TransFair USA, an independent organization devoted to increasing the availability of Fair Trade certified products in the United States. Fair Trade Coffee is mainly grown on cooperatives that agree to abide by guidelines issued by the FLO (Fair Trade Labeling Organizations International), but this is not quite the same thing as a certificate of environmental or social responsibility, although it represents an alternative to patronizing agribusiness.

Organic coffee, as the label implies, is grown without synthetic pesticides, herbicides, or chemical fertilizers and is sold by Starbucks in small quantities. In 2002, Starbucks purchased 1.7 million pounds of certified organic coffee, once again a drop in the bucket but certainly a step in the right direction.

This is, as so often is the case with larger companies, obviously a work in progress. But when we inquire as to why these good efforts seem to represent such a small portion of Starbucks' overall purchases, or why the CSR report doesn't really make clear what percentage of all purchases these programs actually represent, Mecklenburg sounds a tad defensive: "The certification systems developed in the developing countries are not market based, and do not begin to meet the needs of Starbucks. They are specialty products, which do not necessarily provide us with the range of criteria we need."

> It is a complex global market, and when people suggest simplistic solutions to deal with a complex issue it can get frustrating. There's certified coffee and free trade coffee and shade grown and all of these categories, all of them quite useful, which at the same time do not begin to address the complexities of what we are grappling with as a buyer in this marketplace.

"What the consumer wants of course is that seal of approval." She sighed, betraying a trace of exasperation at the impatience of some NGOs. "We are moving through the first phases of what we believe to be a three-step process: (1) have the program in place, (2) communicate it effectively, (3) put into place some form of NGO certification." Beyond that, she will not commit herself or the company.

"Most NGOs have a specific issue or viewpoint, while what we need is an all-embracing program. But I think it's more important for a company like us to figure out what we want to do and stay on that path than follow somebody else's guidelines, and not get distracted by special interests. Just for example, coffee in Africa is grown in savanna, so the term shade-grown is simply not applicable there."

Mecklenburg's tone and language show that Starbucks is still in the early stages of working through "what it means to grow coffee sustainably." But just as clearly, despite pressure from many in the NGO community, Starbucks is determined to create a solution that feels like its own.

A self-styled socially responsible company, Starbucks has made it publicly clear that it recognizes its responsibility to sustain the producers of the commodity that keeps it in business, and that it justifies its investments in coffee sustainability—however small, at this point—not on the basis of an abstract moral principle but on the grounds that it makes sound business sense to help keep its suppliers in business.

This would seem like a no-brainer, except that—as Mecklenburg pointed out—even these tentative steps toward a new definition of corporate accountability represent a profound departure from the way the commodities markets have functioned in the past, when all that ever mattered was price. Now what matters is that the appreciation for good coffee quality that Starbucks has cultivated in its customers is joined by a new appreciation, on the corporate level, of the efforts and hardships that go into making and growing it.

Yet a higher level of transparency is within easy reach. Starbucks does not disclose or take responsibility for the tons of pesticides still used, the workers' injuries sustained, and the loss of habitat suffered as more coffee has been planted to satisfy the demand that it has helped to create. We all like to point out our progress, but without a more complete context, the picture we are permitted to see is limited at best and at worst distorted.

Does that distortion justify the target that Starbucks has become from the more radical elements of the anti-globalization movement? Like so much of this unfolding story, the answer must be yes and no. Starbucks certainly receives more than its fair share of attention because it is a highly visible consumer brand with a strong retail presence. Take note if either of these describes your business, let alone both. To even talk about social responsibility as a consumer brand often feels like walking down the street with a target on your back.

A Better Banana

I'm Chiquita banana and I've come to say
Bananas have to ripen in a certain way
When they are flecked with brown and have a golden hue
Bananas taste the best and are best for you
You can put them in a salad
You can put them in a pie-aye
Any way you want to eat them
It's impossible to beat them
But, bananas like the climate of the very, very tropical equator
So you should never put bananas in the refrigerator.

© 1945 Shawnee Press Inc.

In 1870, an American ship's captain and merchant named Lorenzo Dow Baker bought 160 bunches of bananas—an exotic fruit originally imported from Asia—in Jamaica for a shilling per bunch. After sailing to Jersey City in eleven days, he managed to sell his cargo for $2 a bunch—a hefty profit. Flush with this windfall, Baker and a Boston entrepreneur named Andrew Preston joined forces to develop a banana market in Boston.

The following year, a wealthy young New Yorker named Minor C. Keith, the son of a prosperous timber merchant, traveled to Costa Rica to help his uncle, the railroad magnate Henry Meiggs, build a national railroad. The contract from the Costa Rican government stipulated that the railroad was to run from San Jose, the capital, in the center of the country, to Puerto Limón on the Caribbean coast. But building a railroad through the dense tropical jungle turned out to be a more arduous undertaking than anyone had anticipated, and during the first twenty-five miles of construction, which took nearly three years, nearly 5000 workers died. One of the victims of tropical disease was Henry Meiggs. His intrepid nephew was left to finish the job.

It took Keith nearly twenty years to complete the link from San Jose to Puerto Limón, and by then he and his company were deeply in debt. Keith soon discovered, moreover, that not enough paying passengers wanted to take his railroad to make it a going concern. In desperation, he turned to transporting freight, and fortunately he had just the right cargo in mind. In 1873 he had planted bananas as an experiment beside the railroad tracks to provide a cheap source of food for his workers.

Meanwhile, Baker and Preston's Boston Fruit Company had prospered, and they had the capital in 1889 to merge their company with Keith's railroad to form the United Fruit Company. Ownership of the means of transportation, the means of production, and the means of domestic distribution gave the firm a foundation for a sweet monopoly.

By the early 1900s United Fruit had pioneered a number of technological innovations that enhanced its capacity to ship fresh fruit over long distances, including painting all of the company's ships white to reflect the tropical sun (as well as to maintain the optimum temperature for the perishable cargo inside the ships), introducing the world's first refrigerated oceangoing cargo vessels in 1903, and bringing wireless communication (later known as "radio") from the United States to South America in 1904. But for all its technological sophistication, the company operated under labor policies that were positively feudal. Its vast banana plantations operated much like the colonial haciendas of old, with thousands of workers kept in virtual involuntary servitude on the farm, living in company housing with their children attending company schools, buying high-priced goods on company credit in company stores. Much of this was a direct extension of the appalling conditions under which Minor Keith had built his railway.

This was the era that gave rise to the ripe phrase "Banana Republic." In Guatemala, Honduras, and Costa Rica, United Fruit's will was law, and local governments were little more than wholly owned subsidiaries. The company was known as *el pulpo*, "the octopus," for the degree to which its tentacles reached into every cranny of life. If any politician dared to defy the company line, on wages, on unions, on working conditions, United Fruit could count on the United States government to intervene and install a candidate or a politician more to its liking. Labor organizers, invariably branded as outside agitators and Communist sympathizers, were physically intimidated, often brutally.

By World War II, United Fruit owned some 3.5 million acres of land in Jamaica, Cuba, the Dominican Republic, Panama, Honduras, Nicaragua, and Colombia. Throughout these banana-growing regions, human and workers' rights were routinely violated, and environmental and social degradation became the accepted way of life.

In 1900, Panama disease had struck banana crops throughout the Central American region, followed in the early 1930s by black sigatoka, a devastating leaf fungus that arrived from the western Pacific and spread all over the tropics. Efforts to eradicate these diseases ushered in a new era of "scientific" cultivation featuring modern chemical controls. Herbicides, pesticides, and fungicides were sprayed indiscriminately on people and crops, on neighboring villages, on workers' homes—anywhere—so long as the pests and fungi were kept down and the bananas kept growing.

During the Depression, United Fruit, then teetering on the brink of bankruptcy due to the global collapse in commodities prices, was taken over by an American immigrant, originally from the Russian province of Besarabia, named Samuel Zemurray. Zemurray had settled in Selma, Alabama, in the early 1890s and built a profitable banana business in Mobile. After becoming one of United Fruit's few serious competitors, Zemurray succeeded in gaining a controlling share of United Fruit in 1933. Although as a young banana importer and producer he had been directly involved in the overthrow of several Central American governments not to his liking, he took the company in a new, somewhat more socially responsible direction, deploying his fortune to finance a Child Guidance Clinic in New Orleans, back the foundation of the liberal magazine *The Nation*, and establish an agricultural institute in Honduras that pioneered new pest- and fungus-resistant breeds of banana. In 1948 he even provided one of his ships—rechristened *Exodus*—to the first wave of Jewish immigrants entering Palestine to found the state of Israel.

World War II brought the banana industry to a virtual standstill as the Great White Fleet was requisitioned by British and American governments for troop and cargo transport, and the Caribbean teemed with German U-boats. But after the war, determined to improve his firm's corporate image, Zemurray hired the legendary public relations man Edward Bernays, who encouraged United Fruit to put a new face on the octopus. Zemurray and Bernays introduced the name Chiquita to the American public, suavely embodied by Miss Chiquita Banana, swaying in her tropical dress, who familiarized Americans with the still fairly exotic fruit with her famous jingle.

By the early 1990s, the banana industry was once again thriving, but had also come under increasing criticism from environmental and human rights groups over a massive expansion of banana cultivation in Guatemala and Costa Rica in preparation for a move into the European market. The fall of the Iron Curtain had created a hope among the banana companies that Eastern Europe would become an enormous market. During the decades of isolation, one of the commodities that East Germans and other Eastern Europeans had most prized had been fresh bananas, still considered something of a delicacy throughout much of Europe.

In 1990, plans were laid by the banana industry to expand the total acreage devoted to banana production in Costa Rica by nearly 160 percent. This was the work not just of Chiquita (United Fruit's corporate successor) but also of the two other major players in the region, Del Monte and Dole. This dramatic expansion, inevitably coupled with increased pesticide use and extensive defoliation, attracted the attention of the New York–based Rainforest Alliance.

With nearly one billion people living in or near the world's biodiverse tropical forests, the Rainforest Alliance believes that these regions must be managed as places in which people can live and work while conserving the natural environment that sustains them. A comprehensive solution to the long-term problem of sustaining people in their habitat while sustaining the habitat as well, needed to go beyond the traditional answer of wildlife sanctuaries.

This philosophy focused on promoting sustainable agriculture in the world's tropical biodiversity "hot spots"—those often small areas within a rain forest where a high proportion of native species may be found, sometimes right in the path of the banana industry's planned expansion. Ironically, the European market for Latin American bananas never fully materialized, because in the early nineties, the European Common Market—the precursor to the EU—passed a set of protective tariffs designed to favor their former banana-growing colonies in Africa and the Caribbean.

"The Europeans tried to dress these protective measures up as so-cially responsible pressure points, because of all the bad press that the banana industry had generated over the years," explains Chris Wille, the Costa Rica–based head of sustainable agriculture for the Rainfor-est Alliance. "But the reality was that since banana-growing practices were no more environmentally or socially sound in Africa or the Caribbean than in Latin America, there was definitely a degree of hypocrisy to their position." Hypocritical or not, the European tariffs helped motivate Chiquita to begin cleaning up its act, as Europeans were not about to let a product into their market that activists could target as leading to the destruction of the rain forest.

In cooperation with several Costa Rican conservation groups, the Rainforest Alliance organized a cluster of study teams comprising ex-perts in soil erosion, water pollution, worker safety, and deforestation. The ultimate goal was the creation of a set of guidelines for a sustain-able banana agriculture modeled on the Alliance's successful Smart-Wood program, which had been developed in collaboration with forestry companies to aid forest managers in instituting sustainable and responsible timber practices.

SmartWood and its client companies rely on a conservation tool known as "independent third-party certification." Under this system, companies agree to abide by a rigorous set of environmental and so-cial guidelines and are "certified" by an independent third party, which ensures that their actual business practices follow those guide-lines. The primary benefit to companies from certification is that it permits them to market their products at a higher price because cus-tomers are assured that they are not contributing to environmental or social devastation.

"We decided to add our voice to the chorus of critics of banana cul-tivation as currently practiced," Wille recalls, "at a point of maximum polarization between the two sides. The environmentalists were pushing the companies to institute changes, but the banana compa-nies were digging their heels in. These were companies, after all, which had grown accustomed to rolling over whole governments. What were a bunch of NGOs to them?" They would soon find out.

The NGO coalition's first task was to convince the banana compa-nies that they weren't going to support a boycott, yet at the same time weren't going away until they had accomplished their goal. "We had studied boycotts as they related to forestry," Wille says, "and had concluded that for the most part, they tend to be counterproductive. Boycotts rarely solve problems but tend to simply shift difficult problems from one place to another. At worst, they can create more problems. So we made a conscious decision to check our emotional baggage at the door, which certainly facilitated the dialogue."

Over a period of two years the NGOs created a set of nine principles and guidelines.

1. ECOSYSTEM CONSERVATION: Farmers should promote the conservation and recuperation of ecosystems within and around production areas.
2. WILDLIFE CONSERVATION: Concrete and constant measures must be taken to protect biodiversity, especially endangered species and their habitats.
3. FAIR TREATMENT AND GOOD CONDITIONS FOR WORKERS: Agriculture should improve the well-being and standard of living for farmers, workers and their families.
4. COMMUNITY RELATIONS: Farms must be "good neighbors" to nearby communities and a positive part of their economic and social development.
5. INTEGRATED PEST MANAGEMENT: Farmers should enlist nature and diversity as an ally in maintaining a healthy farm. Pesticides may only be used as a last resort and must be strictly controlled to protect the health and safety of workers, communities and the environment.
6. COMPLETE, INTEGRATED MANAGEMENT OF WASTES: Farmers must have a waste management plan to reduce, reuse and recycle wherever possible and properly manage all wastes.
7. CONSERVATION OF WATER RESOURCES: All pollution and contamination must be controlled and waterways must be protected with vegetative barriers.
8. SOIL CONSERVATION: Erosion must be controlled and soil health and fertility should be maintained and enriched where possible.

9. ENVIRONMENTAL PLANNING AND MONITORING: Agricultural activities should be planned, monitored and evaluated, considering economic, social and environmental aspects.

In 1992, with the standards complete, the NGO coalition invited a number of small independent producers to begin testing them on their farms. They initially selected small independent farms first to avoid creating the impression that the program was tailored only to large agribusiness. Despite the fact that the code is not easily implemented, the small producers were persuaded that in the long run, they would be good for business.

The following year, two independent producers in Hawaii and Costa Rica became the world's first growers to earn certification from the Better Banana Project. This earned them the right to label their products with the label "ECO-O.K." Shortly thereafter, the Costa Rican subsidiary of Chiquita Brands, under the leadership of local manager David McLaughlin, began to actively pursue certification as a means of improving the health and safety records, yields, employee relations and morale, image, and productivity of their wholly owned properties.

McLaughlin's results so impressed corporate headquarters in Cincinnati that the company made a decision to begin implementing them as soon as practicably possible throughout its extensive Latin American holdings, numbering 127 farms and plantations. Unlike many of the other companies that have recently adopted CSR programs, Chiquita took around $20 million off its bottom line to improve its farms throughout Latin America during a period of terrible turbulence in the global commodities markets, which contributed to forcing the company into bankruptcy in 2001.

But even while operating under severe financial stress, Chiquita's commitment to promoting sustainable practices on all of its farms, and even throughout its Great White Fleet, never slackened. The improvements involved can be quite capital-intensive, including installing waste management systems, water management systems, improved chemical storage methods and facilities, soil erosion and reforestation, new programs and protocols for the reduction of toxic chemicals use, training programs for worker safety, environmental education, and improved schools for the children of workers.

"In some ways," Wille contends, "I think one of the most important developments that arose out of the banana certification program with Chiquita was that the company began documenting everything that went on at their farms, from the number of trees planted to the number of accidents that occurred, to the number of pounds of pesticides sprayed, to the number of pounds of pesticides and other chemicals they have eliminated through improved technology, improved practices, and improved chemical compounds."

Here's an example from the company's 2001 CSR report:

> Although we reduced our total agrichemical usage in 2001, all of the reduction came from the least toxic products. Our use of Class 1 products, the most toxic, increased in Guatemala and Bocas, in an attempt to control higher populations of nematode worms, which attack the roots of banana plants. We are actively searching for ways to reduce nematicide usage. As an example, to replace manual application of nematicides on the soil surface, we have developed a prototype applicator that injects nematicide directly into the soil.

And here is an intentionally revealing footnote that provides a sense of the level of detail and degree of self-criticism apparent throughout the report:

> Agrichemical products without proper labels were found in a shed in Santa Marta, Colombia, along with soft drinks that workers were storing there improperly.

Beyond this there are independent third-party critiques of the report, details of accidents by farm, details on the use of toxic pesticides listed by farm and sorted on the degree of toxicity, and no shortage of reflection on where they see specific opportunities to improve. This level of documentation, disclosure, and transparency—in combination with a proactive and deep commitment from all levels of the company—when compared to most of the companies we've discussed, and hundreds of others that produce some sort of CSR report, is rare, if not unique. It presents a window into the future of what is possible with social and environmental reporting, as well as tangible evidence to those who say this level of openness and honesty simply isn't possible for a public company.

Pursuing sustainability has meant that Chiquita scientists and engineers have developed new technologies to reduce pesticide, fungicide, and herbicide use, including a new "fungicide chamber" that replaces the barrels of liquid fungicide typically kept at the packing stations, into which bananas were dipped by hand before being dumped into boxes. According to Wille, "the fungicide wasn't harmful in small doses, but prolonged exposure did have an adverse cumulative effect, so Chiquita developed a special spray chamber through which the bananas are passed, which sprays an infinitesimally small dose of fungicide over the banana electrostatically, leaving practically no residue on the banana peel."

To reduce the deleterious effects of aerial pesticide spraying, Chiquita scientists have designed a spray nozzle that sprays a finer mist with greater accuracy, greatly reducing pesticide use. The spray itself is based on a vegetable as opposed to petroleum compound and permits only a tiny amount of pesticide residue to cling to the banana.

In the bad old days, "flag men" would stand in the fields where the bugs were and wave their red flags at the pilots flying overhead, indicating when and where they should dive and start spraying. The flag men were then supposed to scatter, but of course most of them got sprayed, and few ever wore protective coating. Today, Chiquita employs a GPS navigational system, which tells the planes precisely where they need to spray, and accurately records where they sprayed and how much.

Fully organic banana farming—without any pesticides, fungicides, or herbicides except for biological controls (releasing wasps to control nematodes, for example)—represents a long-term but elusive goal for the industry. According to Wille, as long as black sigatoka continues to infest nearly every banana-growing region in the Western Hemisphere, some chemical controls will be necessary, until a reliable biological method of fungus control is developed.

Costa Ricans who have lived near the banana plantations for their entire lives tell Wille that the changes they see on the farms amount to a transformation "from black to white." They can remember when the rivers ran blue from discarded plastic banana wrappers, while the farms themselves were once knee-deep in assorted plastic and other junk. Now all that plastic is recycled, and much less of it is used in the first place. Certified farms are beginning to resemble parks, with tree buffers to protect the workers from the spraying, native trees, not exotic species, planted along the riverbanks, with these and other forbidden zones kept free from banana cultivation, and the careful preservation of what little native forest they have left.

In 1999, as Europe kept its markets closed to nearly all Latin American bananas, banana prices collapsed—no doubt as a consequence of the massive expansion in the early 1990s. Though Chiquita Brands International was forced into bankruptcy in late 2001, its 2002 Social Responsibility Report notes that the recent restructuring "brought a change in our ownership structure, a new board of directors, and [the appointment of] Cyrus Friedheim as chairman and chief executive officer." But according to the company, "what remains unchanged is our commitment to corporate responsibility."

"We have answered two vital questions many stakeholders have about corporate responsibility efforts at leading companies," Friedheim writes: "'Will the company stick with [CSR] when times get tough?' and 'What will happen when there is a change in the CEO?'"

The company's commitment to social and environmental justice "motivated employees and helped us emerge from the reorganization without a single formal objection to our restructuring plan and without losing any major customers or suppliers," Friedheim insists. CSR provided a bottom line benefit even to a company in very tough straits. But why should we believe Cyrus Friedheim? Third-party verification comes from Stephen Coats of the U.S. Labor Education in the Americas Project:

> Chiquita continues to impress. The transparency of its corporate responsibility reporting and the use of highly respected independent observers combined with some real progress on the ground is a track

record which is unmatched in our work in Latin America. While the road is long, Chiquita has traveled far in a few short years.

Where the Value Chain Ends: Toxic E-Trash

The television set you're watching right now may be one of the most toxic things in your home.

—Bill Moyers, *Now* PBS Series,
"Toxic E-Trash," July 19, 2002

The toxicity Bill Moyers spoke of was not metaphorical but literal. In a small city called Guiyu ("Gwee-you") in the Guangdong Province of China, bordering Hong Kong, investigators working for the Basel Action Network (BAN) and the Silicon Valley Toxics Coalition had shot a video depicting nineteenth-century methods being employed to clean up twenty-first-century high-tech trash. Young Chinese women, primarily migrant workers from poor agricultural provinces, could be seen grilling motherboards over open charcoal fires to extract the chips and trace amounts of gold and other metals. Like any other scavengers, they wore no protective gear. In one disturbing sequence a group of them could be seen melting the carcinogenic PVC off the computers' copper cables, creating dense clouds of black toxic smoke.

Since 1995, Guiyu had rapidly been transformed from a rural farming community by the once-pastoral Lianjiang River into a high-tech-waste boomtown. Rice is still grown in the outlying fields, but the city's center is almost entirely taken up by hundreds of small electronic waste shelters, most of which are devoted to "recycling" computers shipped illicitly into the country from the United States.

According to a recent joint report by BAN and the Silicon Valley Toxics Coalition,* types of waste and processing are segregated within the city, with one neighborhood involved in dismantling old printers while another might process recovered plastics. As recently as 1995,

---

Exporting Harm: The High-Tech Trashing of Asia, February 25, 2002, Basel Action Network and Silicon Valley Toxics Coalition.

the Lianjiang was the source of all drinking and bathing water for the villages lining its banks. Today, a sample drawn from the river's tea-colored waters reveals levels of lead, cadmium, zinc, and chromium 190 times higher than the threshold set by the World Health Organization for drinking water. Today the residents of Guiyu drink water shipped in orange plastic tanks from Ninjing, thirty kilometers away.

Guiyu is one of a number of places in Asia where old computers come to die. According to BAN, "The village exists in a landscape of black ash residue which covers the ground and the houses of the village. The burning always takes place in the middle of the night, indicating that local authorities have likely frowned upon the black smoke plumes."

Western observers decry the pollution in Guiyu, but when reporters and investigators from Greenpeace China, the Basel Action Network, and the *San Jose Mercury News* arrived in the town in the fall of 2002 to further document the flagrant pattern of abuse, the "recyclers" they spoke to begged them to go away and leave them alone. At least one threatened them with bodily harm if they continued. These investigations, the recyclers complained, simply stirred up the Chinese authorities to crack down on their activities, depriving them of jobs and much-needed income.

The situation in Guiyu, and its gruesome counterparts all over Asia, represents one of the most flagrant cases of environmental injustice on the planet, and is yet another example of the bad things that happen when costs are externalized. Not only computers but all sorts of toxic materials are exported from rich countries, well protected by environmental regulations, and shipped to poor countries, where environmental regulations tend to be minimal or unenforced. "Rather than having to face the problem squarely," writes BAN in *Exporting Harm: The High-Tech Trashing of Asia*, "the United States and other rich economies . . . have made use of a convenient and, until now, hidden escape valve." The "escape valve" is the shipping of old computer parts and other equipment to "recycling" places like Guiyu. It may be decades until the adverse health effects of this toxic exposure can be evaluated let alone quantified. The citizens of Guiyu and other small villages are paying the price for our unwillingness to clean up our own mess.

In 1998, an estimated 21 million PCs became obsolete, according to the National Recycling Coalition, which also predicts that as many as 500 million computers will become obsolete by 2007. Only about 10 percent of those computers are currently recycled in America, and as the scene in Guiyu all too vividly illustrates, "recycling" in China is not necessarily what we associate with the term. CPUs (central processing units) contain chromium, which damages DNA, and mercury, which harms the nervous system and kidneys. A typical CRT monitor contains five to eight pounds of lead. While you're using the monitor, as with TVs, the lead inside shields you from radiation. But once that lead gets into the ground or water, it can cause developmental problems in children who are exposed to it.

In 2001, when California passed a well-intentioned law banning the disposal of lead-containing TVs and computer monitors in landfills—mandating a fine of up to $1000 per instance for improper disposal of used computer equipment—Susan Katchee, recycling supervisor for the city of Oakland, told Bill Moyers's *Now* reporter Emily Harris what happened next:

> When TVs and monitors got banned, one of the things that we noticed here in Oakland is that they started showing up on our streets . . . as illegally disposed of materials and something the city now had to deal with. We now have to send an additional crew out with a separate truck because the TVs and monitors have to be specially handled on the streets. They can't just be picked up and thrown in a regular garbage truck. Then they have to be off-loaded and handled appropriately at that point. And then again, there's the cost of disposal. . . .

There's a long-term solution!

Katchee has a better idea: "The cost for disposal needs to be built into the product itself, so that whoever buys or wants to use that product pays for the cost of disposal at the time they purchase it."

That's certainly the direction in which Europe is moving, and much of Asia, but not yet in the United States, where the computer industry for a long time has fought the idea tooth-and-nail. Renee St. Denis, business manager for Hewlett-Packard's Product Recycling Unit, defined her company's position as of July 2002, before HP had fully come to grips with the problem:

I think we have as much responsibility as anybody in the value chain. What isn't possible is for us to dictate what the consumer's behavior is going to be at the end of the product's life. I can't go into somebody's house and take their old PC away. So we have to rely on them to have the responsibility to actually make sure these things get into the right system for recycling and disposal.

In August 2002, California governor Gray Davis vetoed a bill that would have imposed a $10 fee on the sales of all new computers, to pay for a statewide recycling program. The bill would have required hardware manufacturers and retailers to begin collecting the fee on new purchases by January 2004, but Davis insisted that he could not support the bill because it threatened to expand government bureaucracy. But according to the *San Jose Mercury News*, the bill was scuttled in part because Hewlett-Packard chief executive Carly Fiorina made a personal appeal to him insisting that the bill "would do more harm than good." In his veto letter to California legislators, Davis explained that he would be willing to sign similar legislation based on the "European model," although precisely what he meant by that phrase was left a little vague.

Solutions other than a specific fee tied to the product place the burden broadly on the public, as is the case today when a local municipality must handle the waste and pay for it through taxes. This removes the responsibility for the manufacturers and users. Why should my mother-in-law, who has never owned, let alone used, a computer be responsible for disposing of the new equipment I seem to feel I need to purchase every 18 months?

In other words, in California disposing of the toxic TV or CRT remains largely the buyer's headache, not the manufacturer's. Still, HP has consistently stood on the cutting edge of industry efforts to create a responsible product stewardship program that would share the cost burdens among three groups: the hardware manufacturers, the consumers, and the government.

In 1995, in response to the first worldwide airing of some of the footage later shown on Bill Moyers's PBS show, HP spent $10 million building two state-of-the-art computer recycling facilities, one in Roseville, California, and a twin in Nashville, Tennessee, each capable of processing up to 4 million pounds of used computer equipment per month. HP sorts out still-functional devices and donates them to charitable organizations, while the remaining equipment is devoured by the machine in an operation HP likens to other forms of precious metals mining.

As St. Denis recently recalled at a Businesses for Social Responsibility conference in Miami:

> We spent nine years following that waste stream, and I've got to say, there was no economic model we had to go on to turn that stream of material into anything useful at all. It's easy for people to say, "Okay, let's not ship to China." But what we said instead was, "Why don't we figure out some way to mine computers for valuable materials? Instead of mining below the ground, why not mine above ground?"

It's a laudable start but by no means a comprehensive solution to the high-tech trash problem. Ninety-five percent of the computers and other peripheral devices processed at HP's Roseville and Nashville facilities are the company's own factory discards, and only around 5 percent are equipment sent in by corporations and consumers. A broader solution to the problem demands precisely the sort of infrastructural framework for which government regulations are a prerequisite. Judging by current global trends and a variety of state initiatives, a federal program in the United States is only a matter of time.

"Who is responsible? Who's going to pay?" asked St. Denis.

> HP doesn't have fleets of trucks to take the stuff back, but local governments do, in the form of garbage trucks. No matter how you cut it, the consumer is going to pay in the end. Whether it's at the point of sale, or by paying their tax bills, or paying someone to take the stuff off their hands, the consumer is ultimately going to pick up the tab.

Fair enough, but until recently HP and the other OEMs (Original Equipment Manufacturers) have been fighting against any solution that would impose an up-front fee on electronics purchases fearing that the resulting higher prices would reduce sales. Instead, HP's voluntary Planet Partners program accepts any manufacturer's obsolete equipment from any consumer for a fee ranging from $13 to $34. HP launched its product take-back service in Europe on June 1, 2001, in response to mandates in Norway, Sweden, the Netherlands, Switzerland, and Italy requiring that manufacturers finance such programs. IBM has launched a system similar to HP's, in which consumers can get rid of any manufacturer's computer equipment for a flat fee of $29.99. Sony Electronics introduced a free drop-off program, but limited its reach to its own products and to the state of Minnesota. This certainly is not an effective way to ensure that manufacturers or consumers take responsibility for their toxic waste. We already know that too few consumers will take up the opportunity to pack up and ship off old computers along with the privilege of writing a check for $13 to $34—certainly not unless they have to.

At the 2001 BSR conference in Miami, Robert Houghton, CEO of the product stewardship company Redemtech, observed the problem from a broader perspective. Providing "end-of-life product services" to large corporations has become a big business—for him. "Making responsible end-of-life choices has become part of the IT strategy for every company," he argued, adding that the best way for companies to keep their products out of the waste stream was to be less intent on building obsolescence into their equipment to begin with.

But as the system stands now, there is no incentive for manufacturers who have legally been allowed to avoid the full product life-cycle responsibility (having externalized their costs) to accept that responsibility, except as a reputation-enhancing exercise. Ultimately, Houghton insists, OEMs will be obliged to create a global recycling infrastructure in the United States as they have had to throughout much of Asia and Europe. "Until regulations are in place and a fee schedule is set up, people will only pay for what they have to pay for." Not surprisingly, the United States lags behind both Europe and Asia in taking serious regulatory steps to cope with this mounting problem. The Basel Action Network, which is based in San Francisco, derives its name from the reprehensible failure of the U.S. government to ratify the 1992 Basel Convention banning the shipment of toxic waste from one country to another.

With the exceptions of Massachusetts and California, it's still legal to toss toxic TVs and monitors into landfills. Contrast that with

Japan, where Asako Nagai, a corporate environmental affairs officer for Sony, describes the April 2001 Home Appliance Recycling Law, which mandates that washing machines, TVs, air conditioners, and computers all be recycled by manufacturers. "In the U.S.," she said, "while a debate is still going on over who should pay the bill, in Japan, the Home Appliance Recycling Law has established that producers must pick up part of the tab."

Sony built its first recycling center in Japan in 1990 and recycled around 1.7 billion tons of material in fiscal year 2001, representing 8 percent of the total tonnage generated by the company in its home country. Japanese law mandates that producers recycle 55 percent of the weight of each product; Sony is exceeding that goal by successfully recycling 78 percent. As for lead, "we take it out of our old Sony products, and put it back into our new Sony products."

Often well-meaning CSR efforts simply cannot take the place of a clear-cut regulatory regime and mandate. Properly crafted regulations create a level playing field on which companies need not worry that expensive environmental measures put them at a competitive disadvantage. In the United States, where the regulatory fabric is spotty, Sony's product take-back program exists only in Minnesota, while in Japan, the same company proudly discusses the tonnage it recycles, and even competes to go beyond compliance to higher levels of environmental performance.

In the spring of 2002, Wayne Silby's Calvert Group began pressuring manufacturers to assume more social responsibility for their discarded products. Working with As You Sow, a group that promotes corporate accountability through shareholder activism, Calvert pressed the management at a variety of the larger OEMs to initiate feasibility studies to reduce toxins in PCs, and for more rigorous recycling programs.

"I don't think any of these CEOs wake up in the morning and say, 'How can I trash the planet today?'" said Julie Gorte, Calvert's director of social research. The issue becomes: How to help them find the way to stop trashing the planet today in a way that doesn't piss off shareholders.

In November of 2002, a few weeks after a three-part series ran in the *San Jose Mercury News* revealing that computer equipment bearing

HP labels continued to turn up in Guiyu's waste stream, something changed. Now there was a very visual and visceral connection between HP's discarded products and the dumping of this toxic waste halfway around the world into the hands of rural Chinese villagers who would one day exhibit the ill health effects of HP's failure to support a proactive solution. HP—which had been lobbying against the new and innovative e-waste take-back bill just introduced into the California state legislature—abruptly switched its position. At a hearing in Sacramento held by the California Environmental Protection Agency on e-waste regulation, California EPA secretary Winston Hickox kicked off the session by waving the front page of the *Mercury News*, featuring a dramatic photograph of a Chinese man scavenging for computer plastic near the bank of a polluted river. HP's Renee St. Denis then stunned the audience by announcing her company's decision to break with the industry pack and support state legislation to require PC makers to bear the cost of disposing of discarded computers. Under the plan, manufacturers would share the cost of recycling based on their market share in California.

"It seems that California is going to set the agenda for the country on this issue," she said, "so we thought it was important for us to put our cards on the table, to say what kind of role we would play in the solution." Ted Smith, director of the Silicon Valley Toxics Coalition, called HP's shift a significant breakthrough: "The combined HP-Compaq company is the single largest manufacturer of PCs in the world. They are the linchpin for producer responsibility. The fact that they have changed their position vastly improves the likelihood we'll get a very good e-waste bill in the new session."

Walt Rosenberg, HP's Vice President for Social and Environmental Responsibility, noted in a subsequent conversation with us:

> We got out in front of the industry on product take-back because we basically are in favor of a national solution, even a mandate to take back equipment, because what's most important to us is regulation that creates a level playing field. When the state of California began moving in the direction of a mandated take-back regime, we saw the writing on the wall. Our greatest desire is to avoid a patchwork quilt situation of conflicting laws and regulations. We took a lot of flak from our com-

petitors but this is one bus that we felt that we should be driving, as opposed to being driven—into a corner. We also saw it as a means of differentiating between ourselves and our competitors.

While HP doesn't want to come out and say so, its executives must have felt that televised images of underpaid workers being exposed to carcinogenic fumes while handling products that visibly bear the HP brand name wasn't exactly the best way to burnish their corporate image. Beyond that, however, they seem to have concluded that either being on the wrong side of this issue was in some fundamental way in conflict with their corporate values, or, as Walt Rosenberg told us, "the writing was on the wall" so why not get credit for leading the pack rather than end up being dragged along kicking and screaming as a follower? In July 2003, this full-page ad appeared in the *New York Times*:

TODAY'S COMPUTERS, TOMORROW'S TRICYCLES

By 2010, an estimated 350 million outdated computers will end up in landfills worldwide. HP began its first PC recycling program 11 years ago. Today, we process 6.5 million pounds of high-tech product each month globally, turning old PC's into material that can be used to make new PC's, car parts, and even bright red tricycles. . . .

Credit for this transformation must go to the Basel Action Network, Silicon Valley Toxics Coalition, Greenpeace China, As You Sow, the Calvert Group, and their allies in the new media like Bill Moyers and the *San Jose Mercury News* for putting an issue on the national and corporate radar screens that had formerly been utterly ignored, to our collective peril. But it is equally important to recognize the limits of CSR to make the requisite changes. When the largest PC maker in the United States—which like all corporations reflexively tends to oppose any new government regulation on philosophical grounds—positively *begs* for the government to step in and regulate, that's saying something that Chad Holliday, chairman of DuPont, and all the other free-market deregulation advocates need to sit up and pay attention to.

This winding tale again highlights the fact that the future of corporate social responsibility will not follow a straight and narrow path. There is almost never one solution to a problem. Our society, led by private enterprise, must find the solution to the myriad problems we face. Sometimes, the solution will be a media exposé that sends a corporation running for cover to protect the value of its brand. Other times the solution will come from the hard work of NGOs behind the scenes or pressure exerted upon a company from its own employees, a shareholder resolution sponsored by a religious group, a consumer boycott, or even the leadership of a committed and visionary management team that understands that we are all living in a new and different world.

chapter **six**

Transparency

Sunlight is the best disinfectant.
—Louis Brandeis

One spring day in 2001, a customer called the Seventh Generation 800 number to say that our new dish liquid smelled like rotten eggs. Our customer-service people are well trained, so the woman who fielded the call asked the customer to send the bottle back to us so that we could run a few tests on it. We volunteered our Fed Ex account number so that the shipping would be at our expense, shipped her a replacement along with $10.00 of coupons, and thanked her profusely for helping us identify a quality control problem.

After receiving the offending dish liquid, we discovered that a small amount of bacteria was growing inside the bottle, despite what we believed to be an adequate level of preservative in the formula. When reformulating our old product, we had used a new sugar-based surfactant—a substance that lowers the surface tension of the medium in which it is dissolved, and an essential ingredient in all cleaning products. To prevent bacteria from feasting on the surfactant—since bacteria like sugar even more than they like the oil-based surfactants used in traditional cleaning products—we had to add a nontoxic preservative.

141

Further analysis showed that the preservative we had chosen was effective only at much higher levels than we were using. We decided to put a new dish liquid formula containing higher levels of preservative into immediate production, pull all the old liquid off the shelves of thousands of stores and warehouses before we turned off more customers, and hoped not to lose too many sales during the transition.

After notifying our employees that we had a problem—and believed we had a solution—I wrote a detailed letter to our distributors, retailers, brokers, and shareholders explaining the our reasons for the product withdrawal. We also notified consumers via our Web site, e-newsletter, and consumer relations department.

While this may sound like a smooth and rapid process, it was actually painful, complex, and confusing. How serious does a quality problem have to be before you spend the money and resources to take the most extreme action you can by withdrawing the product from the marketplace? There were no health risks, and most of the product on store shelves was unlikely to ever develop an unpleasant odor. There are no absolute answers or guidelines. Our sales, financial, and operations staff didn't necessarily see the problem through the same lens as our marketing, customer service, and product development groups. Would the lost sales jeopardize bonuses, or cause us to lose valuable shelf space we might not be able to get back? In the end, two sentences from our mission statement—which we meet monthly to discuss—helped clarify our decision.

> Trust & Authenticity: We are committed to becoming the world's most trusted brand of authentic, safe, and environmentally responsible products for a healthy home.
> Service & Inspiration: We are dedicated to setting the standard for superior service.

Having controlled that crisis, we were tempted to relax; but bad luck, as they say, comes in threes. A couple of months later, we began receiving phone calls from customers complaining that the spray mechanism on our newly released hydrogen-peroxide-based spray sanitizers wasn't functioning properly. Once again, we asked our customers to return the three products (a kitchen, shower, and bathroom cleaner) to us free of charge, and soon learned that the ball bearing inside the sprayer—made by the same manufacturer that supplies similar spray bottles to other leading household product companies—was defective. After replacing the sprayer with an improved and cost-lier version, we paid our brokers and retailers to replace all the sprayers still on the shelves with the new product, swapped the prod-uct in our distributor warehouses, and absorbed the extra expense, which significantly reduced our gross margins on the entire line.

But we were not out of the woods yet. Our new nontoxic hydrogen-peroxide-based cleaners did such a great job killing germs—which is, after all, the main job of a disinfectant—that we (and anyone who sells a product that claims to kill germs) were obliged to obtain federal EPA approval and classification for its use. But only after we had released the new product into the marketplace were we advised that a recent change in the state product labeling law permitted individual states to request modifications in the standard federal FDA-approved label, if they felt the product failed to comply with certain state mandates.

And only after we had gone to the trouble and expense of replacing all the old sprayers with the new bottles did three states notify us that if we wanted to sell our new germ-killing cleaners within their bor-ders, we would have to add an off-putting "handle with severe cau-tion" statement to our label. The most frustrating part of this exercise was that our primary reason for developing this new product was that, unlike all the traditional disinfectants on the market, it did *not* need to be handled with caution. But in our brush with the new laws on prod-uct disclosure—a principle with which I fully concur—we had run afoul of the Law of Unintended Consequences, a constant companion of government regulation.

Transparency is a fundamental value of all socially responsible companies. The first episode—the rotten egg smell and our response to it—represents one form of transparency, namely *accessibility*. We not only keep an 800 number with which our customers can easily contact us, but we have gone to some lengths to create a brand profile that encourages customers to get in touch with us and to expect a friendly, reasonable, and effective response when they do.

Our response to the calls on the offending odor and the defective spray cap brought yet another facet of transparency into play: rapid and candid disclosure that there is a problem and that the problem is our fault—an important first step toward defining a solution. In order to be effective as a strategy, disclosure must be combined with rapid, decisive, and effective measures to rectify or ameliorate the situation, regardless of cost.

The template for this method of crisis control was pioneered by Johnson & Johnson during its 1982 Tylenol-tampering scare. J&J's response is now regarded as a model of corporate responsibility and transparency under pressure. On September 30, 1982, Johnson & Johnson and its McNeil Consumer Products unit, manufacturers of Tylenol, were notified by authorities in Cook County, Illinois, that cyanide-laced Tylenol capsules had killed three people in the Chicago area. By the end of the day, the death toll had risen to seven, and it was apparent that a mad tamperer was on the loose.

Panicky telephone calls swamped the company's switchboards. The incident threatened to undermine the reputation and brand value of by far the most popular over-the-counter painkiller in the United States, with about 35 percent share of the $1 billion annual market. "We didn't care what it cost to fix the problem," J&J CEO James Burke later recalled; the point was to fix it, by whatever means necessary. When Burke initially suggested recalling every bottle of Tylenol capsules in the country, the EPA and the FBI resisted, arguing that such a massive recall might trigger a public panic and possibly inspire the poisoner to increase his efforts. Instead, they advised a recall strictly limited to particular lots they believed could have been accessible to tampering.

Burke said no. J&J voluntarily recalled 31 million bottles of Tylenol capsules, and stopped making capsules for two months until tamper-resistant packaging could be developed and distributed, at an estimated cost of more than $100 million. That sum came straight off the bottom line, which some stingy shareholders might have argued represented an unnecessary and excessive expenditure of their money, since it was an extreme step that even the relevant government agencies had not advised.

According to Burke, the company's rapid response to the worst public relations crisis in its history was guided by close consultation with the company credo, a one-page statement of principles originally drafted in 1943 by longtime CEO Robert Wood Johnson Jr. (son of the founder of the same name), which explicitly stated that the firm's first responsibility was to its customers, second to its employees and the communities in which it operated, and last to its shareholders. It was strictly fortuitous that a few weeks before the crisis, Burke had called his twenty-eight senior managers together to study the credo in light of recent developments that might require revision. These wide-ranging discussions had been fresh in the minds of senior management when the crisis hit, and when they formulated their response.

Technological advances have made one aspect of transparency—timely disclosure—immeasurably easier for companies to handle. The Internet provides an instantaneous communications link from companies to the outside world. During our rotten-eggs and spray-bottle problems, we could quickly, broadly, and cheaply transmit the essential facts—that we had a problem, that it was our fault, that we were implementing a solution—without having to resort to costly and clumsy mass mailings, telephone appeals, or advertising to reach the public.

Once we applied for EPA approval for our hydrogen-peroxide-based disinfectant, we encountered yet another aspect of corporate transparency: factual disclosure mandated by government regulation. Here, like thousands of other complainants, we ran into a lick of trouble. We had no problem gaining EPA approval for use of our product as a disinfectant. But we did have a problem when the federal government abdicated its regulatory authority in favor of a states-rights provision, which created an inconsistent hodgepodge of regulations, and confusion and needless cost in the marketplace.

The disclosure itself would have posed no problem for us either. We have a clear policy on transparency that says, among other things, "Stakeholder need-to-know takes precedence over inconvenience and cost to the corporation." But in this case, what we were made to "disclose" was not only untrue, it contradicted the very reason someone might want to use the product in the first place.

We took our dilemma to the EPA, which listened sympathetically before replying that this was an issue to be resolved between us and the three states. When we brought the matter up with the states, they could see no way to revise their protocols. In the end, we had no choice but to redesign and reprint the label, removing the germ-killing claim—which was its primary unique selling benefit. This confused just about everyone involved, from our own sales force to retailers and customers. Try as we might to explain the situation, our predicament just didn't make sense. The EPA did suggest we resume the original application process (which should have taken 90 days, but took over a year) and apply for a different category of registration that they believed the states were likely to find acceptable. There was just one catch: We had to conduct animal testing to obtain the reclassification.

This we categorically refused to do, because as a company policy we do not do animal testing. We have a written agreement with PETA (People for the Ethical Treatment of Animals) that we will neither conduct animal testing nor purchase ingredients from suppliers who do. In time, it became clear that our only option was to attempt to use an unprecedented animal testing waiver in the new application, created for chemicals that were known to be safe and thus did not require additional testing.

One of the things that really frustrated PETA, we later learned, was that no one else had ever tried to use this exemption. Instead, whatever the chemical in question, a new battery of animal tests would be conducted. Now we were using hydrogen peroxide at a lower concentration than people were buying in drug stores to gargle with when they had a sore throat. Yet because the FDA regulates gargling and the EPA regulates household disinfectants, no one at the higher reaches of government seemed bothered by the fundamental absurdity that a solution that one government agency says is safe to put in our mouths is not considered safe to use to kill mold in your shower, unless someone in a lab somewhere first tried it out on several hundred rabbits. Just to complicate the story, if you didn't want to *claim* that you were killing germs, you could put whatever chemicals you wanted to use in your products. No testing at all was required.

One year after their mandatory deadline for responding to such applications, we had still not received a decision from the EPA. The conventional wisdom is that if you hassle government bureaucrats, they just shove your application deeper in the pile, so we haven't lodged a protest but have simply waited patiently. We are still waiting.

Having survived the rotten-egg crisis and its defective spray bottle encore, followed by the product labeling imbroglio, we voluntarily decided to tackle yet another problem that only we knew about, which raised in our eyes yet another issue of transparency. Are there limits to reasonable and timely disclosure?

For several years, we had known that our baby wipes had a trace amount of chlorine in them. The amount was infinitesimal, but the amount didn't matter. What mattered was that we knew it was in there, and our customers did not. They could reasonably assume that Seventh Generation, a company that had educated them about the dangers of chlorine and proudly announced on all its other products that they were "chlorine-free," simply wouldn't use chlorine, especially in a baby wipe. Right? Wrong.

Our rationale for not fixing this problem had always been that since our product was far and away the best in its category from a health and environmental standpoint, it did not need to achieve total environmental purity. Additionally, no matter how hard we searched, we simply couldn't find a manufacturer that could or would make a totally chlorine-free wipe. But in thinking this way we were ignoring expectations, assumptions, and the nature of our bond with our customers, let alone our public stance on the dangers of chlorine. That we did not explicitly advertise that our baby wipes were 100 percent chlorine-free and instead emphasized that the wipes were soaked in a wonderful all-natural solution (while the wipe itself was "slightly" compromised) was irrelevant. It bugged me that we as a company were unable to make a hard and fast commitment to ourselves as to how long we would be willing to accept this lack of undisclosed inauthenticity and continue to collectively rationalize that it was okay to do so.

At some point during the long wait between thought and action, it occurred to me that this was as much a problem of policy as principle. The incentive system we had in place gave our sales, product development, and marketing people little reason to be obsessed with such a minor problem, and little reason to go out on a limb—or lose valuable sales and personal compensation—to adhere to an abstract moral and social principle.

This is where I confess, I suffered something of a leadership lag. There were always plenty of very good reasons why it made sense not to tackle the problem, not the least of which was that no one was getting on our case about it. And in fairness, it wasn't for lack of trying, we just weren't succeeding. Tackling the problem uncompromisingly could leave us with no product to sell. I wasn't willing to do this until, at a certain point in 2001, I said to myself that we simply had to stop kidding ourselves. We had to start asking, how long can we permit this to go on? When I said precisely that at a senior management meeting, our team swung into motion.

Bad Chemistry

Before I am accused of overreacting, let me tell you a little bit about chlorine. In 1890, a young graduate of the Case School of Applied Science in Cleveland, Ohio—the predecessor to Case Western Reserve University—arrived in the declining lumber town of Midland, Michigan, hoping to make his fortune. His name was Herbert Dow. As a chemistry student, Dow had participated in a college project in which he had analyzed samples of brine from the oil wells around Midland, which contained small amounts of the chemical bromine, used in those days in medicines—"bromides"—as well as photographic chemicals. While standing at the well site, he noticed that the brine had oozed up to the surface, which the oil men regarded as a nuisance. One of them asked Dow to taste it. Both men agreed that the brine from the well was unusually bitter.

"I wonder why that brine is so bitter," the driller asked Dow.

"I don't know," Dow replied, "but I'd like to find out."

When Dow brought the sample of brine back to his lab for testing, he found that it contained the element lithium (which caused the bitterness) as well as a startlingly high level of valuable bromine. The standard method of extracting bromine was to evaporate the liquid using leftover wood scraps from nearby lumber mills, and remove the sodium chloride, which crystallized first. Chemists would then add an oxidizing agent to the remaining liquid, which contained bromine ions, and finally distill the bromine.

By the time Herbert Dow set up shop in a rented barn on the outskirts of Midland, the city had fourteen saloons but not much of a future. Nearly all of the woods surrounding the town had been cut down, drastically reducing the amount of sawdust and chips available to power the bromide-extraction plants. Herbert Dow solved that problem by hooking a homemade rope up to the steam engine of a nearby flour mill, powering a 15-volt generator that sent powerful jolts of electricity through buckets of brine obtained from a disused brine well.

The bromine market had potential, but for his first several years, Dow struggled to survive. His brine cells, for one thing, were too small, while the current he passed through the brine was too weak to free all the bromine. When he strengthened the current, he freed the bromine, but significant amounts of a greenish gas called chlorine were produced. After struggling for several years, "Crazy Dow," as the people of Midland had begun to call him, realized that he might be able to turn a profit selling chlorine as a disinfectant.

By 1895, Dow had constructed an electrolytic plant devoted exclusively to the production of chlorine extracted from brine. An hour after it went into operation, it exploded. Undeterred by that accident, two years later Dow founded the Dow Chemical Company—after raising most of his working capital from Case faculty members—and over the succeeding years parlayed escalating sales of various chlorine compounds—used primarily as the basis for bleach, fertilizers, and pesticides—into a booming global empire. Today, Dow Chemical boasts annual sales of $28 billion in more than 170 countries, and is better known as a manufacturer of plastic products than chlorinated compounds.

Although Dow has successfully diversified out of the chlorine business, the effects of the branch of industrial chemistry it pioneered linger in our environment. One of the main reasons chlorine makes such a good building block for new chemical compounds is that chlorine atoms create unusually strong bonds with other elements. Nearly all of the roughly 15,000 chlorine compounds in commercial use today share a tendency, as a consequence of these strong bonds, not to easily break down in the environment. Chlorine compounds tend to hang around for years and even decades in the water, the air, and the bodies of living things, causing problems long after their additional usefulness has ended.

Some of those compounds are infamous.

1. PCBs (poly-chlorinated biphenyls), once used in electrical transformers to replace flammable petroleum-based oils, were for years dumped by General Electric into the Hudson River. For nearly as many years as GE dumped these dangerous PCBs, the company has waged a tooth-and-nail court battle to evade responsibility for permanently purging them from the river, a case that the Bush administration's former EPA chief Christie Whitman settled against GE shortly before retiring from office.

2. Perchloroethylene ("perc"), a chlorinated compound used extensively as a degreaser for cleaning dirty automobile parts and as the fluid in dry cleaning, has been implicated as a carcinogen and hormone disrupter in mammals.

3. DDT, a chlorinated compound developed in 1939 as an insecticide, nearly eradicated the insidious disease malaria by killing the mosquitoes that carried it, but not without consequences. By the 1950s, DDT was discovered to lead to adverse mutations and disruption in the reproductive systems of animals. Its insidious effects were extensively documented by Rachel Carson in *Silent Spring*.

4. CFCs, organic compounds composed of carbon, fluorine, chlorine, and hydrogen, are used as aerosol-spray propellants, refrigerants, solvents, and foam-blowing agents. In the 1970s CFCs released into the atmosphere were found to accumulate in the stratosphere, where they steadily broke down the protective ozone layer, exposing the surface of the earth to the harmful effects of the sun's ultraviolet radiation.

In the 1980s, a growing body of evidence surfaced indicating that chlorinated hydrocarbons are harmful not only to fish and birds, but to mammals (including humans). Volatile organic halides (VOXs), like chloroform and trichloroethane, were found to be carcinogenic in small animals. In the 1990s, evidence continued to accumulate that many chlorinated hydrocarbons disrupt human reproduction, much as DDT disrupted reproduction in birds and fish. A 50 percent decline in the male sperm counts of some species, as well as a host of other developmental disorders, has been traced to the lingering effects of chlorine-based compounds pumped indiscriminately into our environment.

The most insidious chlorine derivative of all is dioxin, considered by many to be the most dangerous chemical compound on earth—300 times more toxic than the defoliant Agent Orange used in the Vietnam War. Dioxin, aside from being carcinogenic, has been estimated by the EPA to cause severe immune system malfunctions, alter endocrine hormone activity—including those regulating sex steroids and growth—and cause inheritable and irreversible genetic changes in humans and animals, with even the most minimal exposure. The U.S. EPA estimates that the maximum acceptable safe level of lifetime dioxin exposure is just .006 picograms per kilogram per body weight per day, equivalent to just one drop in a train of railroad tank cars 10,000 miles long. The reason this mattered to us as a producer and distributor of environmentally safe paper products is that one of the largest sources of dioxin in our environment is the process used by mills to bleach paper. Paper mills use an average of 110 to 176 pounds of chlorine to bleach every ton of wood pulp, about 10 percent of which ends up combining with organic molecules naturally present in the wood to create a nasty series of compounds known collectively as organochlorines.

In spite of all this, most people were unaware of the dangers of chlorine and simple knew or at least believed that it kept their water safe, removed nasty stains from their clothes, and killed germs and removed mold from their shower. In many cases Seventh Generation was the primary source of information to the contrary.

On the corporate transparency front, we considered circulating a statement to our customers that there were trace amounts of chlorine in our baby wipes, that we were aware of the problem, and that we were actively in search of a solution. But we didn't do that, partly because we didn't want to cause a level of alarm in our customers that the reality didn't justify, and partly because—to be perfectly frank—we didn't have to. I preferred to find a solution before transmitting to the world the message that we had a problem without a solution. This, I have subsequently learned, is not only wrong but a fundamental part of the reason so many people don't trust business.

By late 2002, we had managed to locate a new supplier willing to work with us to fabricate a rayon-based wipe that is totally chlorine-free, though it was combined with a polyester fiber derived from petroleum. Not perfect—but much better, and consistent with our mission and quest for authenticity. We spent quite a bit of time and effort and money formulating this new product, which we extensively promoted as the first all-natural totally chlorine-free baby wipe in the United States. Amid general euphoria, with prototype products proudly sitting in their newly designed box on my desk, I sent out an e-mail asking our staff to make sure not to place any new purchase orders for the old wipes because our new product was ready to roll.

In the jewelry business, transparency—the technical term is *diaphaneity*—is a function of the way a beam of light interacts with the surface of a given substance. A beam of light shined at a perfectly transparent substance enters and exits undisturbed, which means that the signal doesn't bounce around or get distorted or degraded by interaction with the substance. What goes in is what comes out. What you see is what you get.

But if that same beam of light is distorted or degraded as a result of its passage through the material, the substance is considered translucent. And if that same beam of light cannot penetrate the substance at all, that substance is considered opaque.

When you think of transparency as a moral value, you tend to associate it with frank and honest people, with open societies and democracies, and most of all with trust. Opacity, by contrast, one associates with closed, hierarchical, elitist, and authoritarian societies. Many elite institutions, such as the Federal Reserve Bank in New York, exhibit fortresslike architectural styles, with conspicuously thick walls and virtually no windows, which reflect a tendency to keep the outside at bay and to protect the weighty deliberations occurring within—which would be "polluted" by sunlight. When Supreme Court justice Louis Brandeis famously opined that "sunlight is the best disinfectant," he was speaking from the perspective of an outsider, a Jew who had penetrated through the intervention of the Theodore Roosevelt administration into the most secret and solemn sanctum of American society.

One reason opacity remains the default position for so many institutions is that from time immemorial knowledge has been power, and the willful withholding of knowledge a particularly potent form of power. Whether the knowledge is possessed by a company that owns a portfolio of trade secrets, a group of people who know where a valuable mine is, or insider traders who know whether a company's stock is going to rise or fall, secrecy can be an effective weapon. It is a strategy of the few to gain advantage over the many.

Of all national governments, the United States has enshrined transparency as a national value, reflecting a system deeply rooted in a tradition of openness—observed in principle if not always in practice. The American tradition of transparency in judicial proceedings is a legacy of English common law, which calls for every citizen accused of a crime to be judged by a jury of his or her peers and for the trial record to be public.

In the United States, this tradition of open debate extends to the deliberations of Congress, which over the years has held countless public hearings, enlisted the help of innumerable citizens groups and organizations, and invited comment from knowledgeable experts, officials, and citizens on proposed legislation. Still, over time, opacity naturally tends to assert itself in all systems of authority, as those who govern typically prefer to make their decisions without having to answer to or defer to public opinion.

Perhaps one of the greatest single contributions to the cause of transparency in American government occurred in 1966 with the passage of the Freedom of Information Act (FOIA). Under its provi-sions, American citizens can request copies of records maintained by all federal government agencies, departments, and the military. FOIA has become a popular tool for historians, journalists, educators, pri-vate companies, citizen interest groups, and ordinary people to gain access to the inner working of government. Under the Law of Unin-tended Consequences, private contractors bidding for government business have relied heavily on FOIA requests to determine what pre-vious contractors were paid on similar jobs, thus making FOIA an in-advertent tool of commerce.

In 2003, a number of events revealed the remarkable degree to which we, as a society, have accelerated the shift from a default posi-tion of opacity and secrecy to one of transparency. These changes were undoubtedly helped along by the 2002 summer of corporate scandal. The scandals were a profound wake-up call, alerting us—and in particular, investors—to the fact that for all the transparency we benefit from and now take for granted in the United States, there is much more ground to cover.

In some respects the degree to which we as a public felt deceived, lied to, and taken advantage of by these large public companies set the stage for a redefinition of what constitutes an acceptable level of transparency in a free society. The principle that you can run but you can't hide has begun in a fundamental way to change how all institu-tions deliberate on and ultimately decide what they must disclose.

Four examples of this fundamental cultural shift:

1. In the wake of the 2003 disaster with the space shuttle
   Discovery, NASA's behavior with regard to the release of
   information about its investigation was as different as night
   and day from the very same organization's reaction to the
   Challenger disaster of the decade before. When the *Challenger*
   exploded, NASA circled the wagons and conducted its
   investigation in secret. What little information it divulged
   came from independent investigations conducted by
   congressional committees operating in front of the television
   cameras. Following the *Discovery* tragedy, NASA went to
   unprecedented lengths to keep the public apprised of its

deliberations. While many people have freely criticized NASA for flaws in its flight safety program, the institution was effectively insulated from criticism of its response to the incident itself.

2. During the second war in Iraq, the second Bush administration arranged its press policy quite differently from that adopted by the first Bush administration during the first Gulf War in 1991. The policy of "embedding" over 500 journalists with the troops provided us with a unique vantage point and window on the war. Here, of course, transparency becomes a more relative term (as it always is to some degree), as embedded journalists provided us with only a selective and imperfect picture on events. Skeptics called this so-called transparency a distortion. How cynical you think the "embedding" policy was probably depended on your view of the war and the administration generally. What is unquestionably remarkable is the huge change that occurred in the last decade, even within a fanatically secretive administration, with regard to the minimum degree of transparency they felt was beneficial or required to gain the public support needed to wage the war.

3. The SARS (Severe Acute Respiratory Syndrome) outbreak in Asia, which first came to the public's attention in the spring of 2003, was initially hushed up by local Chinese officials, particularly in Beijing, when it first broke out in the fall of 2002. This response followed the default code of one of the most traditionally closed and secretive governments in the world. Once signs of the outbreak reached the World Health Organization—headed up, interestingly, by Dr. Gro Harlem Brundtland—they responded with admirable speed, openness, and a daily news update that far rivaled their handling of any similar situation. This transparency on their internal deliberations, as well as the information they collected to guide their decisions, caught other public officials, the news media, and even the rest of the medical establishment completely off-guard. Whether you agree or disagree with their specific decisions, their openness represents another

fundamental shift in cultural norms. It dramatically highlighted the degree to which the traditional Chinese secrecy was both totally out of step with the times as well as dangerous for the Chinese people and the world at large.

4. What set off the hundreds of disclosures among men and women across the nation who had lived with unbearable secrets for decades? Why was it now safe to disclose what was unimaginable to discuss when it happened? The sexual scandals that rocked the Catholic Church forced one of the most secretive cultures in the world to render its inner workings more transparent, as a means of regaining the trust lost by revelations that the Church hierarchy had placed a higher premium upon protecting its institutional image than the young people entrusted to its care, ironically tarnishing its image even further.

Corporate transparency has scored some significant victories in recent years, as well as suffered numerous setbacks. The greatest boost to transparency appears to have been, not surprisingly, the accounting and ethical scandals that arose at the turn of the twenty-first century. The Bush administration's primary response to the crisis of trust in public companies and the financial markets has been a push for greater transparency of financial reporting through the creation of the Sarbanes-Oxley Act, the main thrust of which is to tighten standards of transparency and disclosure for the nation's 12,000 publicly traded companies. While the administration response largely failed to address the larger systemic and ethical issues that were exploding in their laps, their narrow response was nevertheless a significant step in the right direction. Senior managers are required not just to disclose a wider set of information to the public, but also to gather it from their subordinates and place their reputations and jobs on the line in certifying its validity.

Among the specific requirements of Sarbanes-Oxley are: full financial disclosure of all off-balance sheet and related parties transactions; public certification of financial reports and internal controls by the CEO and CFO; reporting of most significant transactions involving company securities within two business days; and periodic reports to announce whether or not a Code of Ethics has been implemented as well as any change in or waiver of the company's Code of Ethics. These and many other disclosures must be certified by the CEO and the CFO, who will no longer be able to plead ignorance—as Enron president Jeff Skilling so egregiously did before Congress—of "what the accountants are up to."

Ignorance is no longer an excuse for fraud.

What role does the corporate social responsibility movement play in this drama? Amid the widespread public revulsion over the scandals, those of us in the socially responsible investment and socially responsible business community grew rightly concerned that Sarbanes-Oxley was focused on, at most, only half the problem. Greater transparency of financial reporting is of course critical to engendering trust, but greater transparency of social and environmental reporting is equally critical if companies are to truly persuade an increasingly skeptical public that they are committed to being good social actors. Other than litigation, the most powerful mechanism available to promote transparency among publicly held corporations on social and environmental issues, since the Securities and Exchange Commission has thus far failed to envision how they are relevant to shareholder concerns—has historically been the shareholder resolution.

In the United States, every investor in a corporation has the right to introduce a formal proposal addressing governance, business policy, operations, or disclosure as long as they can successfully navigate through the SEC's complex rules for doing so. The company is required to circulate these proposals to all of its shareholders and request a shareholder vote upon each resolution, generally through the annual proxy statement as well as in person at the corporation's annual meeting.

Unfortunately, both public companies and the SEC have placed increased restrictions on the proxy process. If a shareholder resolution didn't gather enough votes the first time around, it could be barred from being placed in front of shareholders again the next year. This hurdle was hard to overcome, and until recently virtually no resolutions obtained votes of more than 10–15 percent of all shareholders.

While a mechanism remained in place to allow shareholders to speak directly to the board of the company, the board could just as easily choose to ignore the resolution, and view the entire process as not just a nuisance, but a radical intrusion into their primary goal of letting management maximize profits and increase shareholder value.

Then, to the amazement of the corporate community, in 2003 everything changed.

At Gillette's 2003 annual meeting, 63 percent of voting shareholders backed a resolution filed by the Christian Brothers and other institutional investors calling on the company to improve its corporate governance by eliminating staggered board terms and electing all directors annually. That was just the beginning. A short list follows of some of the other shareholder resolutions introduced in that landmark post-scandal year by Wayne Silby's Calvert Fund, and the remarkable results achieved. Out of twenty resolutions filed by Calvert with top U.S. corporations for vote at their 2003 annual shareholder meetings, seven were withdrawn after the companies agreed to the substance of the resolutions or to enter into dialogue with shareholders regarding the same. This is itself significant, because simply the threat of the filing of a shareholder resolution—and the possibility that it might garner substantial shareholder support—had never been enough to force a company to revise its policies.

A few examples:

- Calvert filed a shareholder resolution asking Triquint Semiconductor to prepare an environmental, health, and safety report. The resolution received a 31.5 percent vote.
- Calvert joined Walden Asset Management in filing a shareholder resolution asking Dover to expand its diversity policies to include nondiscrimination based on sexual orientation. The resolution received a 42.8 percent vote.
- Calvert filed a shareholder resolution asking Danaher to diversify its board to include race and gender diversity. The resolution received a 28.6 percent vote.

- Calvert filed a shareholder resolution asking Gentex to diversify its board to include race and gender diversity. The resolution received a 38.8 percent vote.

The numbers here are unprecedented, showing record-high vote totals on a range of proposals involving corporate governance and social responsibility. Shareholder resolutions addressing board diversity, corporate governance, and the adoption of protocols covering clinical trials at pharmaceutical companies all received high levels of shareholder support. Barbara J. Krumsiek, the president and CEO of Calvert, drew a direct link to the widespread corporate misconduct uncovered in the preceding years:

> The strong results we achieved this year clearly indicate that shareholders want companies to adopt more responsible business practices in the aftermath of recent corporate scandals. Shareholders see a clear connection between stronger governance and improved corporate responsibility, on the one hand, and better financial performance and enhanced shareowner value on the other.

CERES and GRI

The use of the shareholder resolution as a tool for promoting social change dates back to the peace movement of the 1960s and the seventies campaign against apartheid in South Africa. In 1989, in the wake of the Exxon *Valdez* disaster, a group of socially responsible investors and environmentalists joined together to form the Coalition for Environmentally Responsible Economies (CERES), which initially concentrated on deploying the shareholder resolution process to persuade companies to adopt a set of environmental principles and produce public standardized annual environmental reports.

Among CERES' impressive roster of seventy noncorporate members are such wildly disparate entities as the AFL-CIO, the Calvert Group, Conservation International, Domini Social Investments, Environmental Defense, Friends of the Earth, Interfaith Center on

Corporate Responsibility, National Wildlife Federation, Walden Asset Management, and the World Wildlife Fund. Among the sixty corporate signatories to the CERES Principles—a ten-point code of corporate environmental conduct—are American Airlines, Bank of America, Ben & Jerry's Homemade, General Motors, Ford Motor Company, Nike, Sunoco, and Timberland.

Personally, although the CERES Principles represent an important step in codifying environmentally and socially sustainable practices, I believe that a more lasting legacy may have been gained on the disclosure and transparency front by an institution developed by CERES know as the Global Reporting Initiative. The GRI is an international, multi-stakeholder effort formally launched in 1997 to create a common framework for economic, environmental, and social reporting.

On my way to speak at the Harvard Business School on the subject of spirituality in business—which says something about the changing social relations of spirituality, Harvard, and business—I caught up with Bob Massie, the man who ran CERES for seven years before retiring for health reasons. It's fair to say that a huge part of the success of both CERES and GRI are attributable to Bob Massie personally, who graduated from Yale College and Yale Divinity School, after which he was ordained an Episcopal minister. After two years of ministering to his flock, he had something of a change of heart and applied to the Harvard Business School as a doctoral candidate.

During his first year in the MBA program, his expectations of having plunged into the "the belly of the beast where people were savage competitors and I was going to have to watch my back" were pleasantly belied by the people he met, as well as by the place itself, which, rather than being institutionally devoted to fostering cutthroat competition, "actively encouraged teamwork and cooperation." Massie brought a deep level of both passion and reflection to his work. In many respects he was the type of leader that CSR demands, a visionary with an unstoppable commitment to succeed executed with a style that is compassionate and self-deprecating, but firm and even aggressive when necessary.

Massie shepherded the GRI standards and protocols into existence out of a growing conviction that one of the most effective ways to induce corporations to change their behavior was not necessarily the use of pressure tactics such as boycotts, shareholder resolutions, law-suits, and going to the media with a hot story. Rather, he sought to induce them to disclose the negative and positive impacts of their operations, so that they might be encouraged to improve their own records.

What the corporate world really needed, Massie decided, was a mutually agreed-upon set of standards for environmental and social reporting. These standards would provide existing and prospective shareholders, creditors, and all those with a financial relationship with the company as well as the general public with a standardized, consistent, and independently verified window on the company's internal operations, their future risks, and the general health and viability of the enterprise.

The term "mutually agreed-upon" is a key concept here, and according to Massie the secret of GRI's success. The Global Reporting Initiative, he recalled, "started in a room with three people in it" in late 1996, and by the summer of 1997, this little group had raised enough seed money "to pay a few people to fly around and make contacts," with virtually all the other organizations trying to accomplish similar objectives.

Since companies in the United States are currently required to make only financial disclosures, GRI attempts to provide guidelines for disclosure and transparency on all the other aspects of a business's activities that may affect stakeholders. Given the increasing amount of requests for this nonfinancial information, GRI is also an attempt to standardize the disclosures that companies make as well as allowing for consistent benchmarking so that the performance of companies in the same industry can be objectively compared, as is the case with financial reporting.

Equally important, just as Massie had surmised, companies began finding that adopting and complying with GRI guidelines and its overall reporting process can be a fundamental driver of change in and of itself. General Motors recently compiled a detailed CSR report employing the GRI environmental and social reporting guidelines. According to Judith Mullins, director of GM's Public Policy Center in Detroit, GM was able to publicly identify and fix a significant number of environmental problems at its manufacturing and assembly plants that might have gone undetected before committing to the analysis and review that precedes public reporting. While few would argue that this made General Motors an environmentally responsible business, the company's commitment to making these disclosures followed by incremental changes has been accelerated by their participation in the GRI process.

By February 1998, the GRI had arranged for its first formal international meeting, at which Massie was able to gain a surprisingly high degree of cooperation from typically fractious and competing NGOs and businesses. "GRI was in the fullest sense of the term a coalition of the willing," he told me over a cup of tea and a plate of scones at his cozy house in Cambridge. Bob Massie was determined to create a process at least as transparent as the reports he hoped would one day flow from it. Massie and his fellow GRI members approached all of the groups that were trying to create competing disclosure standards and said quite straightforwardly to them, "We'd really like to work out a common standard and we'd like you to be on our steering committee and we'll provide the money for you to participate, and if you choose not to be involved we won't penalize you, we'll keep you fully informed, but on balance we'd really like you to get involved and help us to shape this thing, because this is an experiment and we really don't know if it's going to work out or not."

"No one I approached ever said no," Massie recalled. "Hundreds of people worked on this thing in a virtually seamless collaboration, with no line of authority being imposed from above, certainly not from me." The real recipe for success, observed Massie, was that "all that cooperation and shared vision and goodwill and teamwork" just happened to coincide with the rise of the Internet. "Because everyone was connected in real time and sharing everything simultaneously," he explained, "documents would advance through seven drafts between meetings. We'd break into working groups and get more work done. It was the most efficient piece of global cooperation I'd ever seen."

"This is not a secret plan for CERES world domination," Massie would assure numerous skeptics. "We'll review the program in two years, and if it succeeds, we're going to spin it off." In accordance with this promise, in 2003 a newly independent GRI directorate moved out of CERES' offices in Cambridge into a new headquarters in Amsterdam. At a Businesses for Social Responsibility conference in Miami in 2002, Judy Henderson, a member of the GRI global directorate, observed that the central precept underlying the GRI reporting framework is that "competitive advantage can be gained with transparency, as a question of managing risk and reputation, because discerning investors now recognize that a company managed according to interests broader than those of only shareholders is more likely to profit over the long term. Corporations with a stakeholder focus have been shown to enjoy greater sales and value growth than companies with a narrow shareholder focus."

"The GRI reporting is not an end in itself, but a tool to accomplish change," she emphasized. "It's inevitable that sustainability reporting will become as routine a process as financial reporting is today." That process is already occurring. In 2002, an estimated 2500 companies around the world produced some type of CSR report, of which more than 200 were produced in accordance with GRI standards. A majority of the fifty best global reporters identified in a recent survey conducted by the UK-based think tank Sustainability employed the GRI framework in writing their reports. In Australia, Japan, and the UK, government departments have adopted the GRI guidelines as a basis for possible legislation in this area. In South Africa, the King Committee on Corporate Governance has recommended using the GRI guidelines as a national standard for environmental and social reporting.

The advantage of the broader acceptance of any standard is that it levels the playing field. In the case of the GRI guidelines, the new voluntary rules promote transparency simply by making the requirements for disclosure clear, unambiguous, and equivalent for all players. The process, while daunting at first—especially for smaller companies—provides an exceptionally clear, step-by-step approach to completing a CSR report. Very tentatively, a few national governments have been getting into the act, with France taking the early lead in February 2003 with a set of New Economics Regulations requiring companies to disclose information on such social and environmental issues as stakeholder dialogue and human rights. The Paris Bourse has also passed a resolution calling upon all listed companies to produce environmental and social reports for the benefit of shareholders.

The fact that GRI compliance is strictly voluntary has led some critics to challenge its utility because no enforcement requirement currently exists to give GRI standards teeth, making the GRI just another form of greenwashing. While no CSR report that I've read complies with all of GRI's requirements, overall I regard this argument as false and misguided, since as more and more companies realize that adopting effective social and environmental policies is good for business, if not a necessary part of business, the pressure on them will grow to comply with a standard in place like the GRI.

After reviewing a collection of CSR reports that purport to follow GRI guidelines, it is clear that there is still much work to be done. I was particularly aware of the looseness of standards of disclosure for the environmental and social "footprint" imposed on the planet by business. The guidelines themselves are thorough enough, but even companies that choose to report on these issues remain free to be selective in terms of what they choose to disclose regarding their environmental and social impact and how broadly they look at their "footprint." Many reports, from those issued by Intel and Hewlett-Packard to Dupont, Procter & Gamble, and Unilever, proudly tout impressive-sounding reductions in toxicity levels of chemical discharges into the air and water. Yet no report we reviewed ventured close to even speculating about the absolute impact—much less the anticipated impact—that the use of those toxic chemicals might have on the people living in the communities in which they conduct their operations. By any definition, these impacts are a fundamental part of a company's "footprint."

Is it too much to ask how many additional cases of cancer or birth defects these discharges might be responsible for? This is an arena that, for obvious reasons, no reporting company is yet willing to touch. The risks of liability, and of handing ammunition to adversaries, are currently perceived by many companies to outweigh the benefits of fuller disclosure. But while it's all very well to tout reductions in water use and the elimination of excess packaging, or the use of packaging made from recycled paper, business has a vast range of often quite devastating human and environmental impacts. At some point, and somewhere—preferably on a Web site or CSR report— these need to be addressed in a frank and open fashion. Among other issues, these represent potentially huge financial liabilities.

At a recent CSR conference, a representative from the Ford Motor Company remarked that one glaring deficiency in the GRI, from the company's point of view, was that "there are no clear boundaries as to how to measure or define a company's footprint on the planet. Under the present system, companies get to define their own boundaries and measure themselves within the boundaries they set. There is no definition or consistency."

After critiquing all of these GRI reports, I was faced with yet another glaring inconsistency: Seventh Generation had never produced one of its own. We decided to dive in and do it ourselves. That process started an internal dialogue, which before long escalated into an internal conflict, which I was surprised and unprepared for.

We started with one of the toughest issues, leaving the small stuff for later. I figured that the biggest challenge would be critiquing our own products, which might end up requiring us to let our stakeholders know that many of the wonderful assumptions about our products were wrong.

We hear about these incorrect assumptions every day on the phone when customers call us. And while they aren't the result of anything untrue that we say, they are sometimes the result of what we don't say. Is our "natural" green apple dish liquid 100 percent natural? Well, in fact we don't say that anywhere on the label. Customers assume it is because we don't say that the preservative and green apple scent, which make up less than 1 percent of the formula, are synthetic. I and my intrepid colleagues on the Seventh Generation Values and Operating Principles Committee decided we needed to set our customers straight, and in the process of doing so, set ourselves straight as well.

This didn't mean that our dish liquid wasn't the best natural dish liquid around. Nor that it was not any better from a health and environmental perspective than Dove, Palmolive, Dawn, and all the rest of the traditional products on supermarket shelves. We also felt certain that it was superior to all the competitors who marketed their products as "natural" as well. But the problem was that our customers—or at least some of our customers—naturally assumed that it was a bit better than it actually was. The committee didn't propose taking out an ad, or putting disclaimers on our labels, but we did propose a "product self-critique" section on our Web site that would also be incorporated into our GRI report.

This idea of full disclosure elicited some grave caution and concern on the part of some members of our company's leadership team, who certainly raised some unanticipated good points: "Why is anyone entitled to know this stuff?" and "Our competitors will have a field day with this!" I realized that as deeply committed as I was to CSR reporting and disclosure, I hadn't brought everyone along with me by facilitating discussions, providing education and context for what we were about to do.

What most clearly emerged from this often excruciating process was that the discussions and debates regarding what constituted a meaningful and beneficial level of disclosure were in and of themselves worthwhile, and were indeed drivers of change. I can to some very small degree imagine what the leadership of NASA, the Catholic Church, and the Chinese health authorities have gone through in conducting similarly soul-searching dialogues over some of the true hot-button issues of our era.

The impact of the process led us to make better decisions more quickly than we otherwise might have, to look at our business in a new and fresh way, and in the end to help make us more authentic and transparent to our stakeholders.

One of the most interesting NGO initiatives in this regard is the "International Right to Know" (IRTK) campaign currently being conducted by the Friends of the Earth, which advocates for pushing the envelope of transparency to the fullest level of disclosure imaginable. Assembled by a consortium of NGOs including the AFL-CIO, Amnesty International, the Global Exchange, the Sierra Club, and Oxfam America, among others, the IRTK regards the current trend toward greater transparency on the part of business as the key to successful governance of international environmental and labor standards.

"Do you know under what conditions the clothes you wear were manufactured?" the campaign asks.

"Do you know how the gas you put in your car was extracted?"

"How the gold in the jewelry you wear was mined?"

"Where and how the television set you watch was assembled?"

Friends of the Earth is pushing for a level of disclosure and transparency modeled on the Toxic Release Inventory (TRI) currently in use in the United States, one of the few positive results of the deadly 1984 toxic cloud of methyl isocyanate that emerged from the explosion of a plant owned by Union Carbide (now a subsidiary of Dow Chemical) in Bhopal, India. In the wake of Bhopal, a chemical release at a sister plant in West Virginia underscored demands by industrial workers and U.S. communities to be provided with more accurate and timely information on the presence, storage, and use of hazardous materials. The result was the Emergency Planning and Community Right-to-Know Act (EPCRA), passed by Congress in 1986. The International Right to Know campaign hopes to apply similar standards in a wide-reaching program that will provide useful information on a range of global environmental and social issues.

The Pioneers

Ben Cohen's father, Irving J. Cohen, spent most of his life working for the New York State Department of Audit and Control assessing the veracity of financial statements put together by the school districts of upstate New York. The reason for the "J" was that in his high school there were two Irving Cohens, and Ben's father had the bright idea of adopting the name of his high school, Jefferson High, as his middle name.

When Ben and Jerry decided "to measure our success in the social as well as the financial realm," Ben knew from family history just what to do. What they needed to do was conduct a social and environmental audit, for precisely the same reason that a company needs to conduct a financial audit: so that you, the manager, and you, the customer or shareholder, can freely examine all your beauty marks and warts, with some assurance that the results are truthful and verifiable.

Ben and Jerry were pioneers in the movement to fragment the traditional financial bottom line into a "double" bottom line that includes environmental impact, which in the process of evolution would ultimately be supplanted by the "triple bottom line," which throws social reality into the picture. But once they started talking about having two bottom lines, they realized that they now needed to audit two bottom lines. Their first step was to call their senior managers into a room and tell them that from that day forward, they were going to be held accountable for two bottom lines: "To improve the quality of life in the communities in which we operate, and to make a reasonable profit."

"People stood up and applauded when they heard that," Jerry later recalled, but after a few months, the cheering stopped, and the arduousness of the task seeped in. "Hey Ben and Jerry," they later said—according to Jerry—"this sounded like a really good idea at the time, but now we've been forced to put our energy and our time and money into helping the community, and it takes time and money and energy away from increasing profits."

Ben & Jerry's solution to this problem was appropriately Solomonic: They told their managers to choose only actions that had a positive impact on both sides of the bottom line. Sounds simple, right? Easy to say, tough to implement. But since they knew from bitter experience that what gets measured is what counts, Ben and Jerry absolutely insisted upon counting and measuring quality of life issues as well, no matter how soft and intangible they would have seemed to most accountants.

They needed a feedback loop, they needed the rigor, they needed the hard-headed sense that they as a company were taking the environmental and social side as seriously as the financial side. As one of their impartial observers later wrote:

> Measurement is a key tool to convince boards of directors and core executives that the socially responsible company is a sound business strategy. As companies make more data from their efforts available, the story becomes more compelling. . . . To advocate transparency in business and for all of us to ascribe to that—that's the ultimate acid test.

But when they started looking around for environmental and social reports on which to model their fledgling efforts, they found only one. It was a report done by ARCO (the Atlantic Richfield Oil Company) that "had been printed in brown ink on brown paper, so you couldn't read it," Ben later recalled, with a wry smile. "We all felt this was indicative of the quandary that the reporting process had put the company in," because the company seemed to be signaling that they would prefer that it went unread. By all appearances, it had.

Ben & Jerry's first "social performance report" appeared in 1989 as part of its annual report to its shareholders. For third-party validation, they asked William Norris, the founder and chairman emeritus of the Control Data Corporation, to audit their audit. Ben and Jerry agreed beforehand not to in any way attempt to influence or censor the report, and to publish it in its entirety, edited merely for corrections of fact.

Ben & Jerry's audits have been studies in candor that I have rarely seen anywhere since.

On diversity circa 1991: "Vermont is 98.6 percent white, and Ben & Jerry's has done nothing to change that picture. At the end of 1991, only three of its 349 employees were black. . . . One high-ranking Ben & Jerry's manager told me that the company's tepid approach to recruiting blacks has been disappointing."

On administrative deficiencies circa 1992: "In many areas of the company, hiring of key personnel has been slow, even nonexistent. . . . Some feel that the relatively low management salaries, while they may be viewed as very equitable, have been an obstacle to hiring."

On community deficiencies circa 1993: "Locally the company is still meeting resistance to its plan to expand its Waterbury tour side to include more amusements for visitors and children. Objections include traffic, noise, and fear of its becoming part amusement park."

In 1992 and 1993, Ben & Jerry's Homemade hired Paul Hawken as its social auditor. Hawken published this statement in conjunction with his audit of their audit:

The only problem with Ben & Jerry's being so public about the intentions and flaws is that other companies aren't doing the same thing.

We have all these corrupt companies that no one says "boo" to, and then someone finds a nickel in a pint of Ben & Jerry's ice-cream and everyone goes ballistic. But if five hundred companies every year released their social audits at the same time, you wouldn't have this feeding frenzy by the media. . . .

Through the Social Venture Network, Ben got to know Anita Roddick, and soon they were collaborating and sharing ideas like the best of friends. As Anita and Gordon Roddick later wrote in their opening statement of their 1997 Values Report:

In 1995, we said that with our first social statement we had planted a flag. Nearly two years on, the flag is still flying and more businesses are committed to combined environmental and social reporting. . . . In our experience, these businesses will not just benefit from the approval of their stakeholders, they will be able to run their businesses better.

The Roddicks were admirably up-front—literally, in the sense that they placed the statement on the very first page of their report—about where they wanted to steer the company, what role the auditing process would play in setting that directional focus, and the fairly low priority they placed on accruing profits. Their mission statement—"Our Reason for Being"—made no mention of profits. Their first goal was to "dedicate our business to the pursuit of social and environmental change." Their second goal was "to creatively balance the financial and human needs of our stakeholders, employees, customers, franchisees, suppliers and shareholders."

Note that shareholders figured last on that list, but that was also the case at Johnson & Johnson. In a telephone conversation from her home in England, Anita recently recalled that in the mid-1990s, when she and Gordon first began to explore how to expand their company's long-standing commitment "to accountability and transparency in order to embrace its social performance," she found that "standards for social accounting did not exist."

The Body Shop and British Telecom jointly established an NGO called the Institute for Social and Ethical Accountability (ISEA) "to promote best practices and professional standards in social and ethical accounting and auditing." The group, which has since shortened its name to "Accountability," was chaired by Simon Zadek, the development director of the New Economics Foundation, chair of the Ethical Trading Initiative, and a visiting professor at the Copenhagen Business School.

At a recent conference in New York presented by the UK-based *Ethical Business* magazine, Zadek pointed out that a company's decision to put together a CSR report has everything to do with its level of interest in fundamentally changing its operating practices: "Do you want your reporting to just give you data, or do you want your report to be a driver of change? Deciding to pay attention to something new is going to push a lot of change inside a company. When you are building a new accounting system, you are in effect building *a new value system.*"

"It was a multiyear process," Anita told us, "and it really was a very long haul. It felt a little like playing a game to which we didn't yet know the rules. We had no real models, although I can dimly recall getting our hands on a copy of a tattered report produced by a Danish bank. The real point for us was to test out a stakeholder-based theory of management by engaging in meaningful dialogue with all sorts of stakeholders, not just employees and managers but also people in the community."

The 1997 Body Shop report ran several hundred pages, leaving me in awe of Anita and Gordon's effort. It contained enough new concepts and ideas to keep most companies going for a decade. While the Body Shop later fell on hard times, no one should ever forget the role they played in creating a model for all of the companies, including Seventh Generation, in trying to find their way down a road that often only Ben and Anita had traveled before.

The quest for corporate transparency remains very much in its infancy. While researching this book, I actually read a significant number of CSR reports, cover to cover. What characterizes the best of these reports are two traits: clarity and candor. Most of the best reports provide the first; very few provide the second.

I'd like to see a CSR report that candidly discusses the adverse health effects that an NGO might have *alleged* are associated with the company's products and practices. I'd like to see a McDonald's CSR report not print so many pretty pictures and instead confront head-on the health implications of a high-fat diet, the environmental and ethical implications of raising beef, and the justification for giving away all those stupid little plastic toys that quickly break and end up in the garbage—some of which, according to new reports, have been assembled in China using child labor. I'd like to see a Starbucks CSR report break out the total volume of coffee that it sells that is Fair Trade or shade-grown as a total percentage of its sales, and how much Starbucks is willing to commit to increasing those percentages in the coming years. I'd like to see Patagonia, Stonyfield Farm, and Aveda complete their first CSR reports.

———————

One day in 1997, a man named Marc Kasky opened his morning copy of the *New York Times* and read an article about a newly established Niketown in his native San Francisco. He was vaguely aware of organized protests over Nike's labor policies. The business model pioneered by founder Phil Knight outsourced all production to contract factories in Asia, which as a matter of policy the company did not own or control. When Kasky came across a number of negative reports on Nike's labor practices—one published by an NGO called the Vietnam Labor Watch, another by the Hong Kong Christian Industrial Committee, all alleging widespread abuse of workers in Nike contract factories in Indonesia and China—he had an idea.

"When a corporation holds itself out as a model for great behavior," he later recalled, "many consumers make their decisions based on wanting to support a company that's setting high standards. I believe there were a lot of people buying Nike products based on the reason that Nike was representing themselves in a very positive light. And here it turns out that it wasn't true. So I thought it was blatantly unfair to mislead people, hoping for their support."

Let's stop for a moment. I think there is something inherently subjective in Kasky's sentence: "And here it turns out that it wasn't true."

I see no reason to disbelieve the reports by Vietnam Labor Watch or the Hong Kong Christian Industrial Committee, but I also know that there is always another side. Kasky, somewhat of a professional agitator, got in touch with an attorney friend, Alan Caplan, who had helped stop RJ Reynolds from using the Joe Camel cartoon character to promote cigarettes to young kids back in the early nineties. In the spring of 1998, Caplan helped Kasky file suit against Nike alleging unfair business practices, employing an unusual and highly controversial California statute that permits an individual to sue companies on the grounds that they have gained an unfair advantage in the marketplace by misleading consumers.

According to a summary of the facts as established in the California First District Court of Appeals, Kasky's complaint alleged that Nike had in the course of its public relations campaign made a series of misrepresentations regarding its labor practices. None were advertisements. One was a letter to the editor of the *New York Times* signed by chairman Phil Knight; second, a posting on the Nike Web site; third, a letter to the CEO of the Y.W.C.A. of America; fourth, a press release; and fifth, a letter from Nike's director of sports marketing to university presidents and athletic directors. Among the misrepresentation of facts alleged by Kasky:

1. "that workers who make NIKE products are . . . not subjected to corporal punishment and/or sexual abuse;"
2. "that NIKE products are made in accordance with applicable governmental laws and regulations governing wages and hours;"
3. "that NIKE products are made in accordance with applicable laws and regulations governing health and safety conditions;"
4. "that NIKE pays average line-workers double-the-minimum wage in Southeast Asia;"
5. "that workers who produce NIKE products receive free meals and health care;" and
6. "that NIKE guarantees a 'living wage' for all workers who make NIKE products." In addition, the complaint alleges that NIKE made the false claim that the [Andrew] Young report proves that it "is doing a good job and 'operating morally.'"

Rather than address these allegations specifically in court, Nike claimed the protection of the First Amendment for these statements and asked for a dismissal. The trial court agreed with Nike, as did the appellate level. In a 4–3 decision, however, the California State Supreme Court found for the plaintiff, holding that the company had engaged in commercial speech with its public relations campaign and that they were thus liable under the state provisions regulating corporate enterprise. The California Supreme Court majority scoffed at Nike's claim that their free speech was being quashed.

"Our holding in no way prohibits any business enterprise from speaking out on issues of public importance or from vigorously defending its own labor practices," one justice wrote. "It means only that when a business . . . makes factual representations about its own products or its own operations, it must speak truthfully."

Part of what clouds the waters in a case like this is that the so-called doctrine of "commercial free speech" upon which Nike has based its First Amendment rights is a judicial creation that—according to the *New York Times*—"has flowered only recently as a result of a series of U.S. Supreme Court decisions beginning in the early seventies." It is a constitutional doctrine described as very much in flux, but is designed to protect speech that "does no more than propose a commercial transaction," in the words of one Supreme Court ruling.

Such speech is considered protected by the same First Amendment that protects all American citizens' rights, although not at the same level of "pure" or "political" speech. Nike appealed the ruling of the California Supreme Court to the United States Supreme Court, on the grounds that the communications in question were not "proposing a transaction" and were therefore not properly characterized as commercial free speech.

Both the U.S. solicitor general as well as the ACLU filed briefs in support of Nike, while Kasky had the Sierra Club and the California attorney general join his side. Kasky's brief asserted that Nike's purpose was simply "to induce consumers to buy its products." Nike's brief responded that the purpose of the communications was to engage in a free and open debate on a subject critical to determining the role of corporations in a free society.

Kasky noted:

Specifically at issue here is whether the speech that Nike was engaged in, in representing this Nike code of conduct, was private speech or commercial speech. Right now, the Constitution does protect a corporation when using private speech. Meaning a corporation can participate in a debate on a public policy issue without fear of being sued. But if it's not private speech—if it's commercial speech—then the states get to regulate business, and they get to regulate unfair business practices and false advertising. The Constitution does not protect a corporation for false advertising or unfair business practice. So the issue here is which one is it?

In the absence of a Supreme Court ruling—and indeed, the court sent the case back to California without comment in the late spring of 2003—I find the whole case a bit disconcerting. Nike's labor practices certainly were not flawless. In fact I believe they were negligent, naive, and utterly unfocused on what should have been both a core concern and competency. But I would also contend that they have made enormous strides toward improving conditions in their contract factories, and should be proud of those efforts. Differences of opinion as to the accuracy of these statements should, I believe, be the subject of debate and discussion, not litigation.

Nike was caught in the ever-widening net that the emerging definition of responsible business casts. I am firmly in favor of holding companies accountable for their behavior, their operations, and their social and environmental impacts on the planet and on society. But the question becomes: Do we want to leave it up to judge and juries to determine what is the "truth" in a debate, or do we want to or should we in fact be forced to assume the responsibility of making up our minds for ourselves?

Filing a "friend of the court brief" on behalf of Nike, the AFL-CIO—which has every reason to denigrate Nike's labor practices as antithetical to union organizing—castigates Nike's labor policies while nonetheless insisting that free discussions of the issue should be "an open speech debate under the First Amendment and not one subject to legal regulation under the commercial speech doctrine." Forty media organizations, including the *New York Times*, filed briefs in support of Nike.

The age of transparency is clearly upon us. My hope is that all businesses end up living in glass houses. Transparency calls upon business not simply to shed unobstructed light upon all business practice, but to do so in a humble manner, from a posture of openness and humility. Business can only do this if it has created a vision and culture that embrace this challenge at every level of responsibility. I do not underestimate the size or magnitude of the challenge. Embracing this challenge is one of the surest paths to—as David Batstone aptly titled his most recent book—*Saving the Corporate Soul.*

In the fall of 2003 the Nike case was settled out of court when Nike agreed to donate $1.5 million over a three-year period to the Washington-based Fair Labour Association to improve the quality of independent monitoring in countries where Nike produces its products. What looked like a storm was settled with a whimper, leaving no clear direction for where or how similar disputes may end up being resolved in the future.

chapter seven

Responsibility

In the first week of June 2002, as the corporate accounting scandals in the United States began to seriously hog the headlines, Microsoft CEO Steven A. Ballmer sent a 2,674-word e-mail memo to all 54,000 Microsoft employees, laying out an agenda for instilling the company's mission, values, and a culture of responsibility throughout its workforce. The memo made no mention of the scandals but, in the current climate, defining a company's ethics and living its values were clearly rising to the top of every CEO's to-do list.

At a gathering of Microsoft managers at an off-site retreat, Ballmer began, "simply put, our mission is to enable people and businesses throughout the world *to realize their full potential.*" Up until then, Microsoft's vision statement—which could have doubled as its slogan— had focused strictly on providing products and services: "Empowering people through great software—any time, any place, on any device." But Ballmer, who had been running the company for two-and-a-half years at that point, felt compelled to stress that even though Microsoft "uses software to help people get there"—"there" being the total nirvana of potential fulfillment—over time he expected the company's mission to evolve beyond "building great technology" to embrace "who we are as a company and as individuals, how we manage our business internally, and how we think about and work with partners and customers."

Needless to say, this was a new language for Microsoft, an organization that throughout its twenty-seven-year history had made it abundantly clear that it needed people mainly to buy its products and services. This hard-headed sentiment had governed the company throughout the twenty-five-year reign of Bill Gates and had been enthusiastically seconded by Gates's sidekick and best friend, "Bad Boy" Ballmer, the hard-charging Microsoft monopoly cheerleader, a man proud of his industry nickname, "Mr. Engulf and Devour."

Ballmer had become the fourth richest man in America through the ruthless conquest of market share at any cost, particularly to the company's competitors. But in his June 2002 memo, he tried to strike a conciliatory chord, and to adopt a tone and vocabulary that were mature and responsible. Microsoft was—out of the blue—beginning to speak the language of corporate social responsibility.

"The events of the last four years and the changes in our industry make this a good point to take stock of ourselves and our mission," Ballmer wrote, "and to understand how others perceive us, and to think about how we can do a better job explaining who we are and what matters to us. Many of us feel a disconnect in the way we see ourselves and our mission and motives, and the way we are portrayed, and only we can change that."

According to *Businessweek*, Ballmer had spent a fair amount of time since ascending to the CEO's post boning up on management literature like Collins and Porras's *Built to Last*, the central thesis of which is that visionary companies, in order to prevail, create a "cult-like culture" oriented around a clearly defined set of core values. In his memo to the troops, Ballmer spoke candidly of the challenges Microsoft faces in regaining the trust of its industry and customers, who despite their large numbers are not necessarily loyal, and often feel bound to the company more by coercion and contract than by fond goodwill.

"To meet the expectations people have of us as an industry leader," he wrote, "and to take advantage of the opportunities reflected in our mission, there are a number of things we must prioritize and value as a company." First and foremost, he insisted Microsoft needed "great people with great values." For those who might find the phrase a little warm and fuzzy, he sought to be more specific. Ideal Microsoft people are "creative, energetic and bright, absolutely passionate and committed to our mission . . . people who have their own strong personal values, as well as those necessary to be successful at Microsoft. These are the kind of people who, with their passion for helping others realize their potential, will push themselves to ask: What does the customer need? How do you build it? How do you make it successful? How do you support it?"

Placing the needs of customers first, a significant departure for Microsoft, may have been a critical first step in a major makeover. At a management retreat in March 2002, the company's sales chief, Orlando Ayala, had stood up to make a personal plea to his fellow Microserfs to think, for once, about putting customer's needs ahead of the company's. As *Businessweek* reported, "Ayala said customers often think Microsoft doesn't care about producing great products, and they believe Microsoft feels it can get away with shoddy work because it has a monopoly."

"Some of us should lose our jobs," Ayala proclaimed. "All of us are accountable!" For simply voicing out loud an imperative that at most companies hardly bears repeating, Ayala received a standing ovation from his peers. By the end of the retreat, Ballmer had decided to make "gaining customer trust" the focus of the next week-long quarterly "management sync" meeting, a Ballmer initiative at which executive staff and board members meet for in-depth discussions on synchronizing actions and values.

It's apparent from his memo that Ballmer is committed to turning Microsoft into a kinder, gentler, softer, more sober version of Bill Gates's 800-pound gorilla. No doubt this represents the right approach for repositioning his much-maligned company for the post-PC era. But if this mission was to have any hope of success, Ballmer conceded, "People [are going to] have to be very open, self-critical, almost relentlessly honest, and, at the same time, respectful." This is no easy change, as anyone who has ever tried to instill these values in their internal culture has experienced.

"At the exec retreat," Ballmer disclosed to his employees, "we agreed on the importance and value of people being open—with their ideas, thoughts, and in receiving input—and demonstrating respect for others. These values must shine through in all our interactions—in our work groups, across teams, with partners, within our industry, and most of all with customers. . . . Our industry wants us to be more actively engaged and open about who we are, and about our road map for the future. Our pending settlement with the DOJ [Department of Justice] adds new responsibilities that we must deliver on. We are committed to working with the DOJ and other government agencies to ensure that the settlement is a success and that our relationship is positive and constructive going forward."

This is an industry that, despite a laissez-faire ideology that sometimes even approaches anarchy, had over the decades gotten so bothered about Microsoft's putative monopoly that it took its troubles to the Justice Department, and cajoled it into enforcing U.S. antitrust law. The immensity of Microsoft's power in the marketplace was one market force that the "free market" proved unable to rein in.

So how did Ballmer's memo go over with the public and the press on the cusp of the summer of scandal? Much of the response was essentially, "I'll believe it when I see it." In the *New York Times*, Jeffrey Seglin expressed the reservations of many when he noted that after "tossing all the right 'values' words—integrity, honesty, respect, trust, excellence and accountability," the only concrete action Ballmer specified was a vague plan to ask "every employee to have a formal discussion of how they are doing on values with their managers" during their annual performance reviews.

As Seglin observed, the real challenge facing Microsoft would be to "balance the drive for innovation and big profits with the value of integrity [and] trust." More specifically, "How much does advancement and compensation depend upon bottom-line performance versus other values? And what happens to top performers who don't live by those values?" We might be skeptical of Microsoft's capacity to achieve the right balance, given its exceptional financial results, combined with a culture that has traditionally demonstrated little desire to balance anything other than some rough equity between its own profits and the pain it inflicted on competitors. Ballmer's memo could easily be interpreted as Microsoft's well-spun response to the tidal wave of popular revulsion over selfish corporate behavior and the cycle of "infectious greed" revealed during the summer of 2002. In this atmosphere, Microsoft could have put its money where its mouth was. It could, for example, have joined Coca-Cola, Berkshire Hathaway, and other leading public companies in announcing that from that day forward, stock options would be counted as expenses on its balance sheets. (Instead, nearly a year later, it announced that it would be revising its compensation system to favor grants of outright stock over options, a step widely regarded as being in at least the right direction.) It could have announced any number of specific measures to increase disclosure and transparency. It could have committed itself to correcting the culture of bullying, abusive behavior, and the take-no-prisoners attitude it had encouraged over the years, which had gotten it into trouble not just with the U.S. Justice Department but with the European Union, whose antitrust regulators are still weighing a decision on Microsoft's hardball business practices. The truth is that only executive insiders at the company may know the real intent of the memo. Time will reveal its sincerity, and Microsoft employees will—I suspect—reveal over time the depth or shallowness of Ballmer's commitment, because employee behavior typically reflects the true nature of the culture in which they are immersed.

For all its heartfelt tone and fresh outlook, the memo could just as easily be interpreted as a cynical response to a serious external threat, compared to which the one posed by the Justice Department might end up resembling a day at the beach. The "open source" software platform Linux, developed by the Finnish programmer Linus Torvalds, is a variant of Unix, a proprietary software platform developed by AT&T's Bell Laboratories in the late 1960s. In recent years, Linux has vastly outstripped Unix mainly because it offers the computing world the first viable means of loosening Microsoft's vicelike grip on its own industry.

The internal source code of Linux—its DNA—is freely distributed, and open to any programmer to create variations on it. What began as a radical student's strike at the bourgeois notion of intellectual property (Torvalds was still in college when he created it) has been embraced by such industry stalwarts as IBM and Oracle. Now Linux controls a quarter share of the world's $10 billion server operating systems market. But "the real virtue of Linux"—and the real threat to Microsoft, according to Doc Searls, editor of *Linux Journal*—"is not only that it's open and free, but that it's *transparent.* You can see through it. You can trust it because it has no secrets. The source of its integrity may not be obvious to everybody, but it's easy to find, to examine and even to improve."

One component of Microsoft's response to this threat posed by Linux is an initiative it calls "Trustworthy Computing," which Microsoft founder Bill Gates defines as "computing that is as available, reliable and secure as electricity, water services and telephony." This is an accurate description of any utility that provides a ubiquitous commodity in bulk to the masses, but the salient difference is that in this poker game, Microsoft has still chosen to keep its cards—its internal source code—close to its chest.

Microsoft has turned up the heat on Linux by adopting aggressive marketing methods that to some observers, at least, smack of the bad old days that the company was supposed to be putting behind it. It has been aggressively discounting Microsoft software to government and large private agencies, an effort that appears to have intensified since the government of China sent shudders through Microsoft headquarters by choosing Linux for its servers, reportedly because it did not want its computing needs and capabilities to be controlled by Microsoft.

A third component of Microsoft's response is that it has been giving away software to needy nonprofits around the world to the tune of nearly $1 billion annually. But as the *New York Times* headline describing the initiative indicates—"Microsoft Finds Some Doubters for the Motives of Its Largesse"—this recent development has left more than a few market watchers wondering if the new Microsoft isn't just the old one decked out in sheep's clothing.

Given that Bill Gates is frequently referred to as our era's John D. Rockefeller, it may be pertinent to recall that one of the many dubious methods that Standard Oil used to maintain its monopoly power was to lower its prices in a particular town to well below cost. Once it drove its rivals out of business, the company could turn around and charge what the market would bear. "Maybe it's just paranoia, or maybe it's historic perspective," noted a member of the Non-Profit Open Source Initiative, "but Microsoft could throw in all this software for the next two years and then just stop, and people will be hooked."

Critics like Lotus founder Mitchell Kapor have openly charged that Microsoft is simply trying to gain a monopoly in the software market for nonprofit organizations. As Kapor noted, based on bitter personal experience, "Microsoft's corporate culture is all about unfair competition." But Brad Smith, Microsoft senior vice president and general counsel, responded to these insinuations with ill-concealed irritation: "Maybe this is a case of no good deed going unpunished."

In June 2003, Ballmer added fuel to the fire by sending another long e-mail to his 54,000 employees in which he explicitly blasted IBM's endorsement of Linux as counterproductive because it "added credibility and an illusion of support and accountability" to open-source software. "The reality," he charged, is very different. With Linux, "there is no center of gravity, or control body, investing in the health and growth of non-commercial software, or innovating in critical areas like engineering, manageability, compatibility and security."

But isn't this lack of a "central control body" a major part of Linux's global appeal? Here is a classic case of a company (Microsoft) trying—with apparent sincerity—to turn over a new leaf and do the right thing, or at least say it is doing the right thing. The company commits itself to a strategy it calls "Trustworthy Computing" and goes out of its way to donate its products to nonprofits, and people instinctively wonder, what's the hitch? When it tries to construe its activities in altruistic terms—"helping people fulfill their potential"—this is seen as just another marketing ploy. People wink and smirk at what may be a sincere effort to reform the company's internal culture, yet there has been no credible context to support that claim.

As Ballmer attempts to invent a culture of responsibility at Microsoft, he may need to acknowledge that this particular challenge is going to require a lot more from senior management than shooting the shit at some off-site retreats, reading a few management books pushing "values," and then sitting down and dashing off a long soul-searching memo. What will it take to remake Microsoft into a truly responsible company? Installing a culture of responsibility can be compared to installing a software platform like Windows or Linux. It provides the entire organization, and every person in it, with a distinct set of operating instructions for controlling its behavior in the marketplace as well as inside the corporation. But instilling a culture of responsibility involves considerably more than downloading a source code or attending a few seminars and conferences about corporate social responsibility. It involves making hundreds if not thousands of decisions—many of which are unlikely to seem important at the time—at every level of the organization, which on a daily basis test a company's values against the often tyrannical short-term imperatives of the bottom line. It involves often painful and wrenching challenges to the habitual behavior of senior management, and the gradual building of responsibility and transparency into the culture and DNA of the company. It also involves creating transparent measurements and benchmarks so that others can objectively judge the company's progress against its objectives.

When Ben Cohen and Jerry Greenfield came up with the notion of a double bottom line—one that balanced environmental protection with "making the numbers"—it was a powerful motivating tool in the creation of a culture of responsibility for the entire capitalist system. The next iteration, John Elkington's triple bottom line, took that idea a step further and introduced social justice into the equation. If you start out with ideas like that, and carefully build outward and upward, magical things do occur. Those ideas can grow into a culture of responsibility that cannot be so easily deleted with a couple of keystrokes. As Mark Twain once put it, "If you tell the truth, you don't have to remember anything else."

Nike

One morning in the fall of 1972, the legendary University of Oregon running coach Bill Bowerman, then sixty-one and nearing retirement, was watching his wife make waffles when he had one of his brilliant ideas. He stayed home while his family went off to church, and stealthily heated up his wife's waffle iron. After a few minutes, when it was nice and hot, he put a piece of latex rubber in it. He let the rubber melt and spread across the iron like batter. After the iron was cool, he pulled a tacky rubber waffle out of it. The next morning, he took it to work.

In the tiny workshop he maintained on the university campus in Eugene, Bowerman cut the rubber waffle into two shoe-shaped pieces and glued them to the soles of a pair of running shoes he was making. The waffle-soled running shoes that hit the mass market the following year boasted hugely improved traction and shock absorption, and quickly became a best-seller for the small running shoe company Bowerman had founded a few years before with one of his former student runners, Phil Knight. After spending twenty-four years nurturing Olympians, All-Americans, record-holders, and NCAA champions, Bill Bowerman was about to become a multimillionaire many times over. Nearly every one of Bowerman's brilliant ideas—after the "aha" moment at the waffle iron—began hitting serious pay dirt.

Bill Bowerman was an unusual coach in that he regarded sports in general, and running in particular, more as a way of living than a way of winning. Sports and the healthy lifestyle that went with them, he believed, were not just for top athletes and members of high school and college teams, but for everyone without regard to age, sex, or level of natural ability. In the early sixties, he took a trip to New Zealand and observed a funny-looking half-run half-walk that the Kiwis did in their spare time to stay in shape, which they called "the jog." Bowerman returned to America convinced that he had just discovered a fountain of youth, and wrote a best-selling book with a Portland cardiologist on jogging, which helped to spearhead the national fitness boom that would very shortly make him and Phil Knight very rich.

Phil Knight had joined the University of Oregon track team in 1957, and under Bowerman's tutelage had blossomed into a pretty fair runner, if not a star. After graduating from college in 1959 with a B.A. in Business Administration, Knight spent a year in the U.S. Army Transportation Corps before enrolling in the MBA program at Stanford, with the goal of becoming a certified public accountant. He wrote a paper for one of his classes based on the premise that low-priced, high-tech athletic shoes imported from a low-cost Asian source like Japan might possibly unseat the dominant player in the U.S. running shoe market, the German company Adidas. After getting his MBA in 1962, Knight took a trip to Japan, where he put his idea to the test by setting up a meeting with the well-established

Onitsuka Tiger athletic shoe company. Knight pitched them on a joint venture to import low-cost running shoes from Japan to the United States. After respectfully listening to Knight's spiel, the gentlemen from Onitsuka humbly inquired which running shoe company in the states he represented.

"Blue Ribbon Sports," he gamely replied.

Upon his return, Knight approached Bowerman, and the two men ended up shaking hands on a 50–50 split as cofounders of Blue Ribbon Sports, which up until then had existed only in Knight's fertile imagination. Each man forked over $500 to pay for the first order of 300 pairs of Onitsuka Tiger shoes from Japan. After taking delivery in the fall of 1963, Knight stored them in the back of his folks' garage.

For the next few years, neither of the founders could afford to work for the company full-time. Knight was a CPA at Coopers & Lybrand and Price Waterhouse, while Bowerman continued his extraordinary run at the University of Oregon's famed Hayward Field. On weekends, Knight distributed Tiger shoes at local and regional track meets out of the back of his station wagon, while Bowerman kept tinkering away at his innovative footwear designs.

They built the business by word of mouth, by asking top runners to test out their prototypes, which Knight and Bowerman would often attempt to persuade Onitsuka Tiger to produce in limited editions. In 1968, Bowerman came out with his fastest, lightest running shoe ever—the Marathon, which sported a distinctive lightweight nylon upper—and quickly followed up with the Cortez, which became one of Tiger's best-sellers. Knight and Bowerman became convinced at this point that they could do better on their own.

By 1971, Blue Ribbon Sports had cut its ties to Onitsuka Tiger and had arranged with a Japanese trading company, Nisso Iwai, to subcontract its own shoe line. Jeff Johnson, the company's first full-time employee, came up with the name Nike, from the Greek goddess of victory. Since every new company requires a logo, Knight approached Carolyn Davidson, a young advertising and design student he had met while teaching accounting classes at Portland State University, and asked her to come up with something eye-catching and stylish that would look good on the side of a shoe. She whipped up the "swoosh," and for her trouble, Knight paid her a flat fee of $35.00.

By 1980, less than ten years later, Nike had achieved the extraordinary feat of capturing half of the U.S. running shoe market, which itself was growing by leaps and bounds, fueled by the health-and-fitness boom Bowerman's jogging had helped spawn. The company went public that year, with two million shares of stock outstanding, and within another five years of explosive growth, annual revenues were grazing the magic billion-dollar mark.

But in many ways, despite its size and its heft, Nike remained a culturally young company. It still regarded itself as an upstart, not one of those companies that took itself too seriously. Until the late 1980s, the company's environmental philosophy, not unlike most other companies in those days, including Interface Carpet, could be described as "comply, comply, comply," though with outsourced manufacturing of all of its products, there were few if any EPA regulations with which to comply.

In 1989, Phil Knight formed a long-range committee to study a variety of scenarios for Nike's future. One recommendation that emerged was that the company develop and adopt a comprehensive environmental policy before one was forced upon it. The small task force of employees that was formed to implement the suggestion quickly evolved into an environmental steering committee, which in turn quickly evolved into a full-fledged department. It called itself the Nike Environmental Action Team, or NEAT.

Formally launched in 1993, NEAT's maiden efforts focused mainly on the "green" issues of recycling and environmental education. Its most high-profile project to date has been Reuse-A-Shoe, which in its first year (1994) collected nearly two million old athletic shoes donated by consumers at sites established in partnership with Nike retailers around the country. These shoes are turned into something called Nike Grind, which despite its singular name is in fact three different materials: granulated rubber from the outer-soles, which is turned into playing surfaces for soccer, football, and baseball fields; granulated foam from the mid-soles, which is turned into synthetic basketball courts, tennis courts, and playground surfacing tiles; and granulated fabric from the uppers, which gets turned into the soft padding beneath hardwood basketball floors.

Sarah Severn, NEAT's originating director, recently discussed with

187

us the conception of the program. "We had been talking quite a lot about the fact that in the end of their life cycles all of our products were ending up in waste dumps and landfills. Since we found that disturbing, we created Reuse-A-Shoe, which remains to this day one of our best examples of the gradual shift that the company has been undergoing, away from open-looped to closed-loop systems."

If that language sounds familiar it should come as no surprise. In 1995, Sarah Severn invited Paul Hawken to talk to Nike's staff about issues of sustainability. As she later related to the authors of *Dancing with the Tiger*—a book tracing the Natural Step's advisory relationship with a number of organizations—Hawken's message struck a real chord at Nike.

In 1997, the Natural Step organized a workshop on sustainability at Nike's corporate conference center, and the year after that, the organization helped the company design a workable framework for fostering sustainable business practices. As part of this learning process, Severn invited Bill McDonough of McDonough Braungart Chemistry (MBDC) to speak to the company about refining its already well-honed design sensibility to take into account issues of sustainability as well as performance and style.

"Bill McDonough was instrumental in driving home to us the essential point that you can't just look at what comes out of the end of the pipe," Severn recalled, "but that sustainability issues need to be looked at from the point of view of design and innovation. That really clicked for us. Once we adopted that point of view, the sustainability issue began to fall into place."

In the fall of 2002, I had an opportunity to speak to Nike's Apparel Division about its environmental initiatives. I arrived at Nike during one of many difficult periods in their recent past. They had assembled a world-class team of activists and experts to plan and execute a long list of impressive environmental measures. What was most striking to me is that until I read through the materials they sent to me in preparation for my visit, I'd never heard of most of them.

Nike was still in the midst of a painful and protracted internal debate over how to react to what is referred to darkly at Nike as "the labor issue." Using mostly underregulated Third World labor to produce high-end expensive shoes for a largely First World market was part and parcel of Nike's originating business model, and was as firmly encoded in the company DNA as its devotion to environmental initiatives. To an outsider, the two impulses created a conflict, which the company, with varying degrees of success, was attempting to confront and if possible, reconcile.

The labor issue surfaced in a big way in the mid-nineties, but had actually been brewing for years. As you no doubt recall, the CSR movement evolved from a focus on exclusively environmental issues to the notion that social justice and workers' rights need to be included in the equation, hence the shift from a double to a triple bottom line. It took a long time for environmentalists to grasp that sustainability was not just about protecting the environment but also about protecting the lives of people and workers. At Nike, outsourcing its manufacturing to factories in the developing world rid the company of one problem, while it incurred another. It could recycle all the sneakers in the world, but if the workers who made them were routinely abused in the workplace, Nike could hardly hold itself up as a paragon of responsibility.

In its early years, Nike operated some domestic manufacturing facilities in places like Saco, Maine, and Exeter, New Hampshire—both in the one remaining (yet rapidly dwindling) shoe-producing region in the country. But Phil Knight's original business model states that the company should focus on design, promotion, and distribution—the high-value-added parts of the business—and leave the manufacturing to the lowest end of the wage and cost spectrum, mainly to contract factories in Asia. This strategy is certainly not unique to Nike. In fact, it forms the bedrock of globalization, and as such has become the subject of much spirited debate. To many observers, globalization smacks of neocolonialism, even slavery in capitalist disguise.

Nike's obsession with performance and quality meant that quality adherence has always been strictly controlled at its contract plants. But the conditions under which those high-quality products were churned out was never a primary corporate focus, and as a result, did not need to occupy the company's administrative time.

It took a few enterprising NGOs, helped out by the media, to call to Nike's attention—and simultaneously the world's attention—some of the flaws inherent in its business model. As tracked by the *Eugene*

Weekly, an alternative newspaper in the hometown of the University of Oregon, and—to Phil Knight's chagrin—the spiritual hometown of Nike, the "labor issue" first surfaced for Nike in 1988, when a newspaper published by an Indonesian trade union published a detailed investigative report exposing poor working conditions at a South Korea–based shoe company producing running shoes for Nike.

The following year, articles began to appear in other Indonesian newspapers reporting on wage protests at several local Nike contractors, each of which paid its workers an illegal "training wage" of 86 cents a day. These reports were closely followed by bitter strikes at two other Nike subcontractor factories in Indonesia, after which the Indonesian daily *Media Indonesia* ran a three-day report on abuses at Nike shoe factories headlined: "World Shoe Giants Rape Worker Rights."

It didn't take long for the Western media to pick up on these reports. In 1991, Thames TV in the UK, the *Economist*, and the Knight Ridder chain of newspapers all filed reports on poor working conditions at Nike contractors in Indonesia. The following year, after a lengthy report on Nike's Indonesian operations appeared in the *Oregonian*, in effect the company's local newspaper, Phil Knight fired off an angry rebuttal.

At the same, the company was sufficiently affected by these reports that it formulated its first "Code of Conduct and Memorandum of Understanding" for contractors, which unfortunately didn't stop highly critical investigative reports from appearing in the *New York Times*, the *International Herald Tribune*, the *Economist*, *Rolling Stone*, the *Boston Globe*, the *Los Angeles Times*, and the *Chicago Tribune*, in addition to on CBS-TV. In response, in 1994 Nike hired the large accounting firm Ernst and Young to conduct its first "social audits" of conditions at its Indonesian contract factories.

In 1997, in the wake of even more negative publicity, Nike hired former UN Ambassador Andrew Young to tour Asian factories, hoping that a clean bill of health from a well-known civil rights advocate would improve their public image, at home and abroad. But after reports came to light that Young had used Nike-supplied translators and guides throughout his tour, many labor advocates disregarded it as shallow and unhelpful—a classic case of "sweatwashing."

The fact that Nike wasn't doing anything substantially worse than thousands of other U.S. corporations, which in recent years have moved their production overseas, and often subcontracted it, was in many ways irrelevant to the debate. Nike became the global brand that exemplified the worst aspects of globalization. What has happened since—which the advocates of the original model certainly didn't envision!—was that the NGO community, frequently supported by organized labor in the First World, simply refused to let companies get away with this abdication of responsibility, and over time they have galvanized considerable public support for their position. The fact that a company like Nike hires other companies to make its sneakers simply does not—from their point of view—relieve it of responsibility for these workers' livelihoods any more than Starbucks or Chiquita is relieved of responsibility for the lives of its workers who grow coffee or bananas, simply because the workers are technically not employees but subcontractors.

Using cheap overseas labor to create products at low cost is arguably a necessary part of global competition. But after the spotlight of public disclosure illuminated the working conditions under which Nike's shoes were made, many responsible consumers couldn't feel good about running in footwear that might have been assembled by an underpaid child, working in a factory without adequate sanitary facilities or ventilation, exposed to dangerous or toxic chemicals. The question of why ten years after the problem first surfaced in 1988 Nike was still struggling to come up with a solution acceptable to the public is one that no one at Nike seems able to answer. As a result the "labor issue" became a profoundly important part of their brand image.

For fear of appearing to try to distract the public from their labor problems, Nike maintained near-total silence about having become, entirely upon its own initiative, the world's first shoe company to eliminate 100 percent of the polyvinyl chloride (PVC) used in its sneakers. This is an issue dear to my heart, as PVC is made with chlorine and has posed more dangers to the workers manufacturing it than just about any other product on the face of the earth. Nike has also taken the trouble to analyze the toxicity of every chemical used in every one of its plants all over the world, so it could develop a plan to eliminate all dangerous chemicals from its manufacturing process.

Under no particular pressure from anyone, it has introduced organic cotton into its apparel line, because reducing the use of toxic pesticides was clearly one of the most direct and viable methods of reducing the company's environmental footprint.

If the folks at Nike expected me to chastise them for using just 3 percent organic cotton in their products, and many of them were, they were in for a surprise. At the scale on which they are operating, there simply isn't enough organic cotton being grown in the world for them to do any different. Nike's mere entry into the organic cotton market could fundamentally change its economics and make organic cotton production more financially feasible. The company was working closely with organic cotton growers to fund an organic cotton association with the goal of greatly expanding the world's supply of this material. One of the least environmentally responsible raw materials on earth, conventionally grown cotton, would be replaced by a product that is one of the most environmentally responsible.

Nike's current goal is to move beyond 3 percent and for every Nike cotton-containing garment to contain a minimum of 5 percent organic cotton by 2010. As a step in that process, the company has introduced a collection of all-organic cotton clothing. From an environmental standpoint, I couldn't ask for much more, except for Nike to be less timid about telling this story to their customers, despite a well-justified fear that the initiative could be dismissed by cynics as mere window-dressing.

Nike's shift toward organic cotton can be compared to Starbucks' attempt to increase its consumption of organic, shade-grown, and Fair Trade coffee. Like Starbucks, Nike's heart certainly appears to be in the right place. Yet largely because of the scale on which both companies operate—combined with the fact that both companies are publicly held—these organizations are under considerable constraints and pressures that do not impact smaller, privately held companies like Seventh Generation. The basic question, which all socially responsible companies must constantly address, is how to strike a viable balance between, on the one hand, the potential damage done to their brand, their reputation, and their image by failing to implement changes fast enough and, on the other hand, the costs to the bottom line of just doing it.

Patagonia will always represent the high-water mark in this regard. The speed of Patagonia's switch from conventional to organic cotton was done with the conviction of an almost religious belief. From the outside, much of the caution, marketing research, and test marketing that often characterize consumer product companies were abandoned. To Yves Chouinard, the man guiding the company, this was the right thing to do, and being a privately owned company, he had no one to report to but himself. In spite of having to raise prices over 20 percent initially, the company did not balk at the possibility of lost sales.

Could Patagonia do the things it does if it were public, as Nike is? If it were financed by a venture capital group, or not led by a visionary leader who puts his money where his mouth is? The answer is clearly no. We often wonder why there aren't more Patagonias. It certainly isn't because Patagonia is perfect, or because they haven't made mistakes, or stumbled off in the wrong direction at times. It's that the personal vision of a committed founder and leader has driven the company to scale new heights in the relentless pursuit of sustainability. As a result sustainability is an integral part of the company's culture. I don't believe it would have taken ten years for Patagonia to address the same labor issues that Nike struggled with, a problem that Patagonia dealt with proactively enough that it never ended up in the news.

We also need to keep in mind that in an increasingly transparent marketplace the circle of responsibility is widening quickly and in unpredictable ways. Companies that fail to monitor this change and anticipate where it's headed are bound to be caught in a trap. Patagonia has almost always been ahead of the curve in this respect. Is Nike a bad company because of its historical inattention to the punishing labor conditions under which its products were manufactured? At the risk of being branded an apologist for globalization, I don't believe so. The fundamental flaw in Nike's perspective was its belief that these labor issues sat outside its circle of responsibility, a perception thousands of other companies share. What has happened to Nike could have happened to almost anyone. Therein lies a remarkable opportunity for positive change.

From the point of view of Marc Kasky and his allies in the activist community, Nike's goals of corporate social responsibility, particularly in the environmental arena, are nothing but a particularly pernicious form of *greenwashing*. The Oxford English dictionary has recently granted this neologism the honor of a definition:

> **green*wash:** (n) Disinformation disseminated by an organization so as to present an environmentally responsible public image. Derivatives *greenwashing* (n). Origin: from green on the pattern of whitewash.

According to the Berkeley-based NGO Corpwatch, Nike's true sins more accurately fall under the rubric "sweatwash."

> With child labor and sweatshop abuses at the fore of social issues, it is natural that companies notorious for use of sweatshop labor try to divert attention from their factories' practices. Examples include Nike's school curriculum about downcycling of sneakers, and Reebok's Human Rights Awards.

Fair enough?

Maybe yes, maybe no.

On May 12, 1998, Nike CEO Phil Knight stood up at a podium at the National Press Club in Washington and promised to institute sweeping changes. With considerable fanfare, he announced a six-pronged plan to improve labor conditions in the approximately 600 contract factories around the world that made Nike footwear and apparel, featuring these specific commitments:

1. To insure that all contract factories met the U.S. Occupational Safety and Health Administration (OSHA) standards for indoor air quality.
2. To raise the minimum age for all Nike factory workers to 18 years for full-time employees and 16 for part-time ones.
3. To include independent NGOs in its factory monitoring.
4. To expand Nike's worker education program.
5. To expand its micro-enterprise loan program to benefit 4000 families in Vietnam, Indonesia, Pakistan, and Thailand.

6. To fund university research and open forums on responsible business practices.

Knight candidly described a situation in which his company's cherished brand had become "synonymous with slave wages, forced overtime, and arbitrary abuse." He committed the company to adopt new labor policies for health and safety, child labor, independent monitoring, workers' education, and the protection of the rights of contract workers to organize in unions.

The national press was certainly impressed by the ardor and depth of his personal commitment. A May 1998 *New York Times* editorial praised Nike's stance as "setting a standard that other companies should match." The *Washington Post*'s E. J. Dionne Jr. referred to Nike's reforms as a "breakthrough for American and international human rights campaigners."

Still, what took them so long? How many conversations had taken place within the company since 1988, when the first news reports surfaced? Why did they wait ten years to take on the labor issue? Was Nike not taking the problem seriously, underestimating its significance, or simply not connecting these labor problems to the reputation and brand identity the company had worked so hard to build? Was it arrogance, ignorance, greed, or a lack of compassion for the plight of their workers? We may never know. But these have been and continue to be soul-searching questions for the CSR world as it has gradually widened its focus from green issues to issues of social justice. Anyone not paying attention to these matters now simply has no excuse.

Five months before Phil Knight's *mea culpa*, in January 1998, Nike had hired a new recruit, Maria Eitel, who had previously worked in Paris for the Corporate Affairs department of Microsoft Europe and who was instrumental in laying the conceptual groundwork for the speech. Eitel was brought in to spearhead Nike's CSR program, and to build on the efforts of a number of senior Nike executives, including NEAT chief Sarah Severn and Dusty Kidd, as Vice President of Compliance, in building a culture of responsibility. Her assignment was to pull the company's CSR efforts into a comprehensive package. Even her title—Vice President for Corporate Responsibility—"was a reflection," she recently told us, "of the fact that Nike was finally taking the idea of corporate responsibility and placing it at the very center of its business strategy." The creation of her position represented "a watershed moment" at Nike, she believed, because "it signaled the beginning of a substantive transformation at the company. At the highest levels, management had resigned itself to the fact that these issues were not going away."

In her first conversation with her boss, Eitel made it clear that doing the job right would require a substantial commitment of resources. "Phil's response was straightforward," she recalled. "Whatever it takes, we'll do it." With that in mind, the next thing she did was call up the San Francisco–based NGO Global Exchange, Nike's most vocal critic, and ask for a meeting. She went in "resolved to keep my mind open and my mouth shut and just listen to what they had to say." Having imagined that she might be meeting with one or two people, she found herself facing a panel of seven. Eitel was grateful that nobody raised their voices or made wild denunciations, but they were "very frank and straightforward about the issues they were concerned about. They explained why they were attacking us, and specifically what our shortcomings and failings were, from their perspective."

Eitel's response was to keep a low profile and to stress that she was new at the company and that she was hoping "to hear from them and learn from them and to not make any judgments until we had investigated what they were telling us." There was no point in being defensive. Since quite a few people at that point—mainly from outside the company, in the media, and NGOs—had conducted their own private investigations of Nike's contract factories, it behooved her to listen to the results they had compiled. The main lesson she took away from her meeting at the Global Exchange was that she "really didn't know much about what was going on in our contract factories," and that before she could do anything else, she needed to see for herself. After ten years of controversy, Eitel was starting her new job focused on an issue that just wouldn't go away.

The business relationship with contract manufacturers had traditionally been conducted at arm's length and that was how both parties had always preferred it. Now Nike needed to be looking into the factories through the same window that their critics used, as well as from the insider perspective that those working there experienced. It not only needed a viable means of monitoring what went on inside, it needed to know these things before someone reported in the media what Nike had failed to look at.

Conducting a comprehensive investigation of the charges "turned out to be difficult," Eitel told us, "because all the information we had to go on was so fragmentary and anecdotal. You know—'This worker in such and such a facility had this problem with their supervisor.' The most important thing we could do would be to create a reliable system of management oversight. Policing a specific facility has a certain utility—combined with independent monitoring and verification, of course. But at the end of the day, what you really want is a set of guidelines and business practices that are so clear and well articulated that *not* following them isn't an option."

Eitel employs an automotive analogy to describe this approach. "If reckless drivers see a policeman they'll slow down and drive safely, until the policeman is out of sight or radar range. We didn't want that to happen in our factories. We wanted a system in place that would have our people avoiding the risks to our reputation in the absence of specific oversight. We wanted a high-quality workplace. What we didn't want was a superficial or short-lived response to a specific initiative. Our goal was substantive transformation, and anything less than that would not be considered a success."

To handle this expanded oversight, Nike was obliged to create a comprehensive monitoring system, which in turn required the creation of a sizable CSR structure. With a virtual carte blanche from Knight, Nike quickly built up a centralized shop, which it has just as quickly tried to decentralize, in accordance with its own business model of pushing as much responsibility as possible out to the business units.

Over the last several years, Nike has invited more than 1100 people—ranging from NGO representatives to labor leaders to journalists to socially responsible investment groups—to tour its contract facilities in Vietnam, Indonesia, China, and elsewhere in Asia. This coincides with a broad effort to provide greater transparency and clarity for the outside world to see inside the company. "In many ways," Eitel said, "this has been the most challenging and profound transformation of all, because traditionally Nike had been quite an insular place."

The first phase of these efforts culminated on October 15th, 2001, with the release of Nike's first Corporate Responsibility Report. Phil Knight's introductory comments reflect both a sense of true personal commitment and personal bafflement at the breadth and elusiveness of these "soft" issues compared to the more tangible concerns he was familiar with as an accountant.

"In all of these areas of responsibility," he asked, "How are we doing? I know what makes for good performance when I see it on the running track. I know it when I read quarterly results from the finance department. I have to admit, though, I'm not sure how we measure good performance in corporate responsibility. I'm not convinced anyone does. Why not? Because there are no standards, no agreed-on definitions. . . . Until then, we have had to figure it out ourselves, with the help of our business partners, local and national governments, international organizations, and other interest and consumer groups."

On the contentious issue of monitoring its labor practices, Nike reported that in addition to external independent monitoring, it had devoted a staff of more than thirty employees "dedicated to ensuring that the workers at the nearly 750 contract factory sites throughout the world have good wages and a safe, fair and healthy work environment." Today, there are nearly 1000 subcontractor facilities in the network.

According to Severn, some eighty people are now working for Nike's Compliance Team, which is collectively responsible for monitoring and overseeing this vast network of factories around the world. Each of the three major business units—Footwear, Apparel, and Equipment—has a Director of Sustainability and a representative for labor compliance sitting inside its own staff.

The company stressed its productive relationship with the Fair Labor Association (FLA), a nonprofit established by a coalition of apparel and footwear companies, and pledged to have the FLA monitor 10 percent of its factory base in each of the first three years, and 30 percent each year after that. "We are building on what we have learned from managing issues in Cambodia, Indonesia and Mexico around unionization, worker abuse and age verification," the report stated. It also stressed its relationship with the Global Alliance for Workers and Communities, an NGO founded by Nike, the Gap, the World Bank, and two universities. Nike committed to spend $7.8 million over five years to underwrite a comprehensive research project to "determine the attitudes and aspirations of 4,000 workers in Nike contract factories in Indonesia." The Baltimore-based group conducts surveys of the workers in an attempt to identify worker concerns before they flare into controversy.

In a 2003 report entitled "Still Waiting for Nike To Do It," longtime Nike nemesis Global Exchange insisted that Nike has consistently failed to make good on the pledge made by Phil Knight at the National Press Club to abide by OSHA standards in all of its contract factories. One of the greatest unsolved problems, the report contended, is the lingering presence of toluene fumes, a chemical solvent used to glue sneakers together, known to cause central nervous system depression and liver and kidney damage. Toluene has been implicated in a serious case of nerve damage suffered by Nike co-founder Bill Bowerman, who inhaled it over years of tinkering with rubber and glue in his workshop. Though "the absolute amount of toluene has been reduced," Global Exchange admitted, Nike *appears* to be providing factory managers with advance notice of testing. If this is the case, "it gives [factory managers] considerable scope to change chemical use to minimize emissions on the day the test is conducted."

Medea Benjamin, Global Exchange's Corporate Accountability Director—and the woman who met with Maria Eitel in her first days on the job—summarized her report:

> There have probably been some improvements [in Nike labor standards], but we have yet to see any meaningful improvement in the areas of living wages or the right to organize.

I have great respect for Medea and the challenge Global Exchange has in congratulating the enemy. Recognition of positive achievements is critical and Nike has many to its credit. The question of whether they have changed quickly enough and created enough transparency about their accomplishments and their failings falls outside any clear guidelines. It's what makes CSR so challenging and messy.

Simon Zadek, in his excellent book *The Civil Corporation*, describes the same situation: "It is hard in many instances to distinguish success from failure. What to some appears to be 'progress' appears to others as 'failure.'" This is in part due to the recurring question of "boundaries." The reason for the different conclusions about how responsibly a business is behaving is because there is no shared agreement about how far that responsibility extends. A frustrated executive in *The Civil Corporation*, tries to understand how boundaries get defined:

> As a water utility we are a major landowner. We have been approached
> by representatives of the anti-hunting league and asked to stop renting
> out a parcel of land for use by sports-hunters. To be honest we don't
> have a corporate view on hunting, and do not particularly want to have
> one. Where does this all end? If there is a church but no mosque on
> our land, will we eventually have to have a view on God?

In the late fifties, Johnny Carson hosted a game show called "Who Do You Trust?" For all of us, the answer boils down to one of authenticity and credibility, which in turn boils down to a question of transparency. A related problem is perspective: If you believe that it's absolutely immoral to outsource manufacturing to low-wage countries to keep prices down, then Nike is by definition an immoral company. But if that is the case, so is the Gap, and so is just about every other apparel company in the United States.

Most of us, as consumers, have personally benefited from the low prices that one of the least savory aspects of globalization provides us. And if we are as brutally honest with ourselves as we expect companies like Nike to be, we must bear some responsibility for the success of the business model that fosters these labor practices. One of the most historically socially responsible companies around, Levi Strauss—a major supporter of the group Businesses for Social Responsibility—not long ago had to move much of its manufacturing capacity overseas, or see itself go under in competition with rivals like the Gap.

If you are a realist, the question becomes not how to defeat globalization, but how to improve it. Surely, a company that puts dozens of people to work on the problem of improving the lives of its overseas workforce is in better shape to assume the challenge and responsibilities of this business practice than a company that outsources all of its manufacturing to developing countries and ignores the problem altogether.

A culture of responsibility involves making serious commitments to improve basic practices and processes, and if the company fails to live up to these commitments, it will suffer far greater criticism than a company that never made them in the first place. In Nike's case, this generated a virtuous cycle in which the company became more vulnerable and transparent in response to attacks, rather than more opaque and defensive.

Nike's culture of responsibility is reflected in the enormous amount of time, effort, and money it has poured into trying to "do the right thing," even in the face of considerable cynicism. Since I haven't personally visited a Nike contract factory in Indonesia or Vietnam or China—although the company's Web site offers a virtual tour of one—I can only speak from my experience, which validates the sincerity and authenticity of the commitment to change at Nike.

At the same time, one has to respect the hard-working, underpaid people at the NGOs who created the pressure that forced the company to expand its umbrella of responsibility far beyond its original focus, just as one has to empathize with the hard-working, underpaid people whose rights they have defended so vigorously.

It's safe to say that the experience of being called upon to change has been a growth process for Nike. "On one subject," Maria Eitel told us, "I am a total maniac: the idea that in this area, there truly is no finish line. There is no perfect factory, just as there is no perfect community. There will always be issues that have to be addressed, problems to fix. The point is to create a system and a framework within which these issues can be addressed, and expressed. We continually have to improve our practices."

On that point, at least, there can be no dispute.

Hewlett-Packard

On March 8, 1960, three years after his twenty-three-year-old company had sold its first share of stock to the public, David Packard delivered an address to the executives in charge of Hewlett-Packard's management development program. Rather than emphasize the usual things—growth, profit, or the benefits of advancing technology— Packard began by ruminating on the reasons for a company's existence. Not just his company's, but any company's.

> I want to discuss why a company exists in the first place. In other words, why are we here? I think many people assume, wrongly, that a company exists just to make money. While this is an important result of a company's existence, we have to go deep and find the real reasons for our being.

Indulging in what authors James Collins and Jerry Porras, in *Built to Last*, aptly called "corporate existentialism"—Packard answered his own question:

> As we investigate this, we inevitably come to the conclusion that a group of people get together and exist as an institution that we call a company so they are able to accomplish collectively what they would not be able to accomplish separately. *They make a contribution to society, a phrase which sounds trite but is fundamental.*

The goal Packard and his partner William Hewlett strove to achieve at HP was simple: "to make a contribution to society." CEO John Young (1976–1992) freely admitted to Collins and Porras that "maximizing shareholder wealth has always been way down the list" of objectives at HP. "Profit is a cornerstone of what we do . . . but it has never been the point in and of itself. The point is to win . . . by doing something you can be proud of."

Nearly two decades after Hewlett and Packard founded their oscilloscope company in a Palo Alto garage—the true birthplace of Silicon Valley—the HP Way was formally codified. But its principles had already guided the company through several tech booms and busts, and would—unless the company lost its way—continue to guide it in the future.

HP, for example, consistently eschewed the "hire-and-fire" mentality common to many tech companies. Even in its early years, when it was still a struggling start-up, HP would turn down lucrative government contracts—its bread and butter in those days—if the contract called for recruitment and retention policies that entailed a high rate of employee "churn." Early on, HP offered its employees something practically unheard of in Silicon Valley, and remarkably rare to this day: job security. And as early as the mid-1940s, HP introduced the rudiments of a profit-sharing program by awarding what it called a "production bonus," which paid the same percentage to every employee from the janitors on up. When the company went public in 1957, all employees who had worked at HP for more than six months were allowed to participate in a stock-purchase plan.

In 1974, with the U.S. economy in the midst of one of its periodic slumps, HP avoided layoffs by shifting to a four-day workweek, obliging all employees to shoulder the burden of the downturn equally by taking a one-fifth pay cut. In both up and down times, managers were taught to trust an individual's own motivation to work and to treat co-workers as family members. Employees were encouraged to call each other by the first name, regardless of rank, and it became *de rigueur* to call the two founders Dave and Bill.

After Dave and Bill retired, some old-timers believed the HP Way died a dozen deaths. Invocations of the HP Way are frequent at the company: One disgruntled employee allegedly insisted that a decision to no longer provide free doughnuts with morning coffee was not consistent with its precepts. Despite this appeal to principle, free doughnuts did not survive the latest tech slump, or the contentious merger of HP and Compaq.

During the proxy fight preceding the merger, both Walter Hewlett and David W. Packard, scions of the founding families, vigorously opposed the merger, in part because it would inevitably lead to massive layoffs—more than 15,000. Carly S. Fiorina, the new CEO, was constantly chastised for abandoning the HP Way, even while she stressed that David Packard had considered profit an important goal, right up there with making a contribution to society. The layoffs were required, she argued, to return the company to a financially sustainable position. And she insisted that the only change she would make to the HP Way was to add "speed and agility" as a core virtue.

Jerry Porras, who regards himself as something of an expert in the

HP Way, has publicly voiced doubts that the credo has survived the merger with Compaq and Carly Fiorina's ascendancy. Fiorina, for her part, has responded to these criticisms by creating a new set of guiding principles called "The Lessons of the Garage," a nostalgic reference to the legendary garage in which Packard and Hewlett founded the company.

RULES OF THE GARAGE

Believe you can change the world.

Work quickly, keep the tools unlocked, work whenever.

Know when to work alone and when to work together.

Share tools, ideas. Trust your colleagues.

No politics. No bureaucracy. (These are ridiculous in a garage.)

The customer defines a job well done.

Radical ideas are not bad ideas.

Invent different ways of working.

Make a contribution every day. If it doesn't contribute, it doesn't leave the garage.

Believe that together we can do anything.

One part of the HP Way that has survived both the tech slump and the often bitter merger battle is the emphasis on the company making a positive contribution to society: "Make a contribution every day. If it doesn't contribute, it doesn't leave the garage." Before the merger was formally approved, at a conference sponsored by the UK-based magazine *Ethical Corporation*, Debra Dunn, Senior VP for Strategy and Corporate Affairs, presented a lucid overview of current CSR efforts at HP:

> Our cause for some time has been bridging the digital divide, which we have approached through what we call the e-inclusion initiative. We believe that technology has huge potential as a driver for poverty alleviation around the planet, but we view these community engagement projects as market development projects, seen for the long-term.

"A key issue here," Dunn went on, "is time horizon. A long-term time horizon is embedded in the DNA of our company. . . . What the

HP Way tells us, in no uncertain terms, is that if you're exclusively focused on meeting next quarter's or even next year's financial goals, making a meaningful contribution to society may well not be possible, but that would represent a *huge* missed opportunity."

When HP's managers first began talking about setting up a CSR structure, Dunn recalled, they found that the employees "had the desire, the passion, and the commitment to contribute to society, but few or no outlets or appropriate vehicles in which to express these desires." The job of the CSR department became providing the outlets. The theme of closing the digital divide provided a tight focus for these altruistic feelings.

> We realized that what we had to contribute at HP, apart from money, was skill and competence in certain clearly defined areas. So we sat down and provided people with access to opportunity to invest their time, energy, and emotion into something that we consider ultimately profitable—developing new technologies appropriate to developing markets. We didn't want just to write a check, or hand out charity. We considered this a form of building markets over the long haul.

The overt recognition that HP was going to build new markets for its products as part of its CSR efforts seemed like a new twist for the company. When I first read about this in their CSR report, I thought to myself, "Hey, wait a minute, isn't this really a new sales and marketing program disguised as a community outreach?"

The company insists that they want to test the general idea that technology can have value in health care, environmental protection, and conservation. And the company considered it equally important that these test projects in developing countries not be viewed as philanthropy, but as "test-beds" and incubators of solutions that can one day be scaled up and applied elsewhere under similar circumstances.

We spoke to Walt Rosenberg, Vice President of Corporate Social and Environmental Responsibility for HP—a former Compaq employee. "At present, we figure that our products and services reach about 10 percent of the world's population," he explained. "When you start looking into serving that other 90 percent, you start looking at business models very differently."

The HP approach to bridging the "digital divide" now has a title —"e-Inclusion"—which currently embraces a number of promising projects in both the Third World (embracing tribal villages in Asia and Africa) and in the United States. These projects work on the ground with HP acting as orchestra conductor, bringing together citizens, governments, local NGOs, multilaterals, and other corporations to solve problems on a local level.

In India, every government service is made accessible only through a government-issued photo ID card. In order to get one of these ID cards, people who live in the countryside typically have had to make a long, expensive, arduous trip to a government office in a large city. By present methods, this process typically takes half a day. This time taken away from work or family places a significant stress on those living in the countryside. Working in partnership with an Indian nonprofit, HP created a solar-powered backpack that includes an entire portable digital photography system. Individual entrepreneurs can buy or lease one of these products and head for the countryside and find prospects willing to shell out a few rupees to have the technology brought to them, as opposed to them having to travel to the technology.

"After developing that product," Rosenberg recalled, "we started thinking more clearly about how to serve markets where there is little reliable or even no electricity, and no local power systems. That got us into working on solar power, and other local power plants, which can enable people who live in rural areas to gain access to our technology."

I wondered, "Do you look at this strategically, as in where do we have a business opportunity for HP, or do you first try to figure out where the greatest social problems lie?"

"We tend to go into communities where we already have an established presence," he replied, "because we don't have a lot of confidence in the model that we can just parachute our people into some place and expect them to hit the ground running. We favor places where we have a presence, where we have people from the community already working with us, people who know us, and if possible, a pre-installed R&D capability. We find that that can be leveraged to create a productive program, and that way we get a head start."

Here are a few examples of HP's e-Inclusion projects:

Dikhatole Digital Village, South Africa

Dikhatole, the name of a community of 8000 tribal people not far from Johannesburg, South Africa, literally means "lost" in the tribal language spoken there. The town lacks running water, electricity, and the most basic housing, and with an unemployment rate constantly hovering in excess of 30 percent, most of the people who live in Dikhatole spend their days wondering if they might ever find work, and knowing that they have no job skills. In partnership with a consortium of local NGOs and businesses led by HP-South Africa, the Dikhatole Digital Village—the largest facility of its kind in the country, equipped with more than 90 Internet-enabled workstations donated by HP, with software donated by Microsoft—has become a training center for the community. The village is being managed by a local affiliate of the international nonprofit Organisation for Rehabilitation and Training (ORT), and in the first phase more than 1000 unemployed youth are being tutored in computer literacy, resumé writing and preparation, communications and presentation, and entrepreneurship. Five hundred and forty local women are also being trained in basic Internet use for networking and support, as well as in starting and running small businesses.

Kuppam, India

In Kuppam, a community of 320,000 people scattered across four rural villages in the Indian state of Andhra Pradesh, HP has begun a collaborative project designed to automate various government services, including the maintenance of land records, birth and death registration, and bill payments. The collaborative is planning to provide digital connectivity to local schools, colleges, and hospitals, to provide vocational training through direct and distance learning, and to help improve health and agriculture services by providing technical support.

Tribal Digital Village, Riverside County, California

Nearly a third of the more than 7600 Native Americans who live on reservations in isolated and scattered rural communities stretching from the California–Mexico border into Riverside County, California, live below the poverty line, and around half are unemployed. Exacerbating the poverty, lack of work skills, and lack of jobs in the area is the fact that these people have no means to regularly communicate with each other, or with the rest of the world.

HP is currently installing a high-speed Internet backbone to connect eighteen American Indian reservations in San Diego and southern Riverside Counties as a means of building communities of interest among tribal members in ways that deliberately resemble long-standing family and community networks. "The goal," as HP puts it, "is to create a distributed digital community that mirrors and amplifies the community and kinship networks that have historically sustained these tribal communities."

Each tribe is being given a Hewlett-Packard equipment grant to provide basic Internet access in their community, while a team of local Native Americans—trained to use topographic software to identify potential sites for the solar-powered high-speed wireless network nodes—has been hiking out to specific sites and marking them using a GPS (Global Positioning System) device. The team has already mastered this relatively complex surveying exercise, and has used the specialized skills it acquired to place six sites in the northern part of the county. It has also been working with local Native American high school students to give them hands-on training and to transfer the skills that they developed, to sustain the knowledge base for the next generation.

Costa Rica

In Costa Rica, HP has been working with an NGO led by Costa Rica's former president, Jose Maria Figueres Olsen, to develop low-cost "telecenters" designed to provide isolated villages with connections to the outside world. These telecenters, called LINCOS (Little

Intelligent Communities), are actually housed in recycled shipping containers and come fully equipped with solar-powered computers and high-speed Internet connections. Their target applications include telemedicine, education, agriculture, micro-banking, access to world markets, environmental monitoring, and communications. The LINCOS program is expected to spread beyond its pilot sites in Central America and the Caribbean to Asia, Africa, and Central Europe, with a similar project currently being pursued with Muhammad Yunus's Grameen Bank to develop telecenters in Bangladesh.

If defined merely as traditional corporate philanthropy, it might be easy to dismiss all of these projects as mere drops in the bucket, certainly compared to the widening chasm—the digital divide—that they are designed to address. But the fact that HP is pursuing these projects with the stated intention of making them "test-beds" for future business development makes them more significant, in my opinion, not just because they have a greater chance of being replicated elsewhere, but because they represent tangible examples of the current shift away from corporate *philanthropy* to corporate *responsibility*.

But it's certainly a reasonable question to ask, What's the difference between Microsoft donating software to needy nonprofits around the world and HP developing "test-beds" in the Third World? Aren't both attempts to develop new markets under the guise of altruistic behavior?

Yes, but the critical differences are both circumstantial and historical. Microsoft is a near monopoly, with a history of monopolistic practices. By donating its Windows software to nonprofit organizations, it is effectively preventing them from turning to the only viable competition—Mac and Linux—and thus extending its already massive market share. Once they accept this largesse, these nonprofits must continue to buy Windows-compatible hardware and software, or incur the huge expense of starting over.

Whether this was the plan all along, the effect of its actions cannot have escaped the Microsoft management—a fact that calls the program's intentions into question. HP, on the other hand, is not a monopoly and its history is very different. Its programs extend technology generally to people and communities that otherwise would not have access to it for many years. As business initiatives, these efforts benefit HP by expanding the market for technology generally, not by tying new groups of users specifically to HP products.

By attempting to bridge "the digital divide," HP appears to be trying to improve the business climate for the tech sector as a whole, not just expand its own market share. Its claim to promote a win-win situation—with actions that are both philanthropic *and* good for its sales—merits less skepticism. Does this compensate for thousands of layoffs in the wake of its merger with Compaq? Does it compensate for the adverse health effects endemic to the high-tech world of chip manufacturing? How do you weigh and approve or disapprove of the balance HP has chosen to strike? Is HP a responsible company? Is it responsible enough?

The fact that we have no definitive answers is a sign of a cultural shift still in flux. The business community is still trying to figure out what world they are really operating in. There is still more art and intuition than science to corporate social responsibility. While this provides room for some companies to avoid making a real shift in their cultures, values, and behavior under the cover of what appear to be "good deeds," we need to reward signs of genuine innovation from those businesses that are truly committed to inventing new ways in which businesses can help address the world's problems.

chapter eight

Ownership and
Social Responsibility

In April 2000, the news that Ben & Jerry's Homemade had agreed to be acquired by Unilever for $326 million sent shudders and shivers through the socially responsible business community. To many of us who had been present at the creation of the CSR movement, it seemed like the end of an era. Ben & Jerry's, our icon and role model, our best-known example of "caring capitalism," had been gobbled up by the enemy.

Most of us knew almost nothing about Unilever except that it was huge. We later learned that Unilever is a nearly $50 billion company that makes and markets foods, home, and personal care products in 88 countries around the world. It was the world's first multinational food company, formed by a merger in 1930 between British soap maker Lever Brothers and the Dutch margarine company Uni. Ben & Jerry's was slated to join a bulging portfolio of brands that included Breyer's and Good Humor ice cream, Lipton tea, Dove soap, Hellman's mayonnaise, Knorr soups, Bird's Eye frozen foods, "I Can't Believe It's Not Butter" spread, Ragu tomato sauces, Lawry's seasonings, Bertolli olive oil, Close-Up and Mentadent toothpaste, Vaseline, Ponds cold cream, Lux, and Wisk—all of which Unilever sells just about everywhere in the world. Did Unilever "get" Ben & Jerry's, we wondered, or did it just get a best-selling brand that would provide entrée into the super-premium ice cream market?

By the time of the takeover, Ben & Jerry's and the Body Shop had come to mean something specific and special to the socially responsible business community. Both companies' commercial success represented sweet vindication of much that we had stood and collectively fought for over the years—doing well by doing good was *not* just a pipe dream. Maybe you really could build something of lasting value based on your values, and that those values could also translate into the financial language of business—sales and profits.

What had Ben & Jerry's become? To many of its loyal customers, the company had remained just what its name suggests, the tangible extension of its founders' personalities: Ben and Jerry, two big-hearted Jewish guys from Merrick, Long Island, who had made it big by not selling out. "Selling out" is of course a normative term, and possibly an outdated one. Selling out meant that you were betraying yourself, your cause, and your values, that you were willing to compromise who you were at heart, in exchange for the two commodities the power structure could invariably provide: money and security. Not selling out meant retaining your integrity and your independence at just about any cost, especially if it involved turning down money and security.

But April 2000 also marked the sobering end of a different era: the Roaring Nineties. This was a period in which an outfit like Ben & Jerry's could rocket to the top of the capitalist charts by proudly letting its freak flag fly, as David Crosby once sang; when there was no apparent contradiction between Ben & Jerry's progressive politics and its runaway financial success. But the Roaring Nineties, as we know now, also turned out to be a period of unparalleled greed, marked by such systematic abuse of the popular trust by some of the nation's best-known companies that it may take years for the markets to recover.

By selling out at the peak of the bubble, at more than a 150 percent premium over the trading price of its stock before the battle began ($17 versus Unilever's final offer of $43.60 a share), Ben & Jerry's (more specifically, CEO Perry Odak) had made a sweet deal for itself and the company's shareholders. By the time the deal was finally done, Odak was reported to have earned $30 million after less than three years on the job, while Ben Cohen was understood to have taken away nearly $40 million. Jerry Greenfield, who had sold much of his stock and taken a much less active role in running the company in recent years, pocketed just under $10 million.

As socially responsible entrepreneurs ourselves, much as the deal pained us we couldn't help feeling validated by the high purchase price, which could be ascribed to the value added to the brand by the company's highly publicized social and environmental efforts. One of the central tenets of the socially responsible business movement right from the beginning has been that authenticity forms the bedrock of our legitimacy. Ben and Jerry's had consistently conducted those time-consuming and expensive social audits, donated 7.5 percent of its profits to charity, and openly and often courageously advocated sometimes controversial social causes at the risk of alienating customers, shareholders, and stakeholders.

After the acquisition, it was hard to imagine that a subsidiary of Unilever—even if nominally independent—could do all these things with the gusto and conviction that Ben and Jerry had brought to the party. It was far easier to imagine the company becoming a dull simulacrum of its former self, an ersatz flavor-of-the-month "CSR company" hollowed at the core. We could see its altruistic behavior having all the cold calculation of a "cause-related" marketing campaign for Procter & Gamble's Dawn, portraying its petroleum-based dish detergent effectively cleaning the feathers of birds damaged and poisoned by oil spills.

When we had lunch with Ben Cohen in early 2003, he told us a revealing story about Peace Pops™. He believes the United States should take advantage of the peace dividend that should have come at the end of the Cold War to improve society. Despite the threat of terrorism, Ben doesn't believe in beefing up our own already bloated capacity to fight conventional wars. He believes our taxpayers' money would be better spent on schools, housing, and other urgent social needs. As a shorthand for that message—which he promotes through two nonprofit organizations, Business Leaders for Sensible Priorities and the True Majority—Ben decided to call the new line of popsicles

Peace Pops. But not everyone even within Ben & Jerry's was entirely in tune with this idea.

"We had this big controversy over Peace Pops," Ben told us. "The internal argument in opposition was that the company, any company, had no business adopting political positions, that in some sense this was morally wrong, and an abuse of our corporate charter." After Perry Odak became CEO, he changed the name to reflect Ben & Jerry's new, more corporate image. But recently, Ben was amused to learn that "the Unilever guy got in and changed it back—a decision he made from a marketing perspective, I assume."

That is an excellent example of what happens when a socially responsible business is bought out by one of the big conglomerates—which, by the way, is a powerful and disturbing trend. When Ben & Jerry's sells Peace Pops as an extension of Ben Cohen's own political and social convictions, that's a different thing from Unilever selling Peace Pops because they are part of the Ben & Jerry's brand identity. Or is it? The first instance seems authentic and human, while the second seems synthetic and somehow deceptive. How can Ben & Jerry's "stand" for a political position that its management adopts because it believes that's what its customers want to see? Still, to be fair, it's hard to imagine that Unilever management does not feel positive about peace.

Did the Ben & Jerry's sale to Unilever constitute a happy ending? For Ben, it pains him to have sold the company he spent his life building. But in fact the company had not been really his for some time. Like all public companies, it belonged to its shareholders, who unlike the loyal customers tend to be more than happy to sell their stock to the highest bidder.

Other answers to that question, more than three years after the closing, are still ambiguous. To Judy Wicks, owner of the White Dog Café, for whom scale is *the* issue and globalization and large conglomerates the enemy, the answer is simple: "This is absolutely not a good thing," she told *Mother Jones*. Takeovers of small, socially responsible businesses by multinationals are "a threat to democracy," in her view, because they exacerbate an already pernicious trend of "wealth and power being concentrated in a few hands." Whether a multinational company the size of Unilever can ever be regarded as socially responsible is a question that is bedeviling the community of small, socially responsible businesses, as more and more of them contemplate selling out, with varying degrees of eagerness and remorse.

In many respects, the jury is still out on what Ben & Jerry's has become since the takeover. Unilever has put enormous effort and expense into positioning itself among the most socially responsible of the giant companies. In its 2002 CSR report, entitled "Listening, Learning, Making Progress," Unilever cochairmen Antony Burgmans and Niall Fitzgerald frankly acknowledge that the debate over globalization is a serious one, and that as a globe-straddling conglomerate Unilever is smack in the middle of it.

> Poverty and inequality between nations remain acute. We believe part of the answer is to realize and spread the benefits of globalization more widely. We recognize that the change implied by globalization can be threatening and the benefits remote. But the active participation of business—responsibly and sustainably conducted—is essential in creating and spreading wealth. Business has a major part to play, in partnership with others in society.

Is Unilever sincere? Does its corporate mandate to focus on "profitable growth," in which sustainability plays an assigned role clearly subsidiary to profit, inevitably erode its professed desire to be a positive force in society? Always with such assessments, the problem tends to get wrapped in issues of ideology. The answer ultimately depends on your opinion of global capitalism. For an example of what this looks like from the radical perspective, let's take a look at the way the Ben & Jerry's takeover is presented on a Web site called Oligarchy Watch, put up by an organization that avowedly keeps a jaundiced eye on the mischief being committed by the world's corporate juggernauts.

Oligarchy Watch

Tuesday, April 15, 2003

The real Ben and Jerry's story
Two big trends we've noted in the new oligopolies:

215

1. They buy up successful new startups with innovative ideas.

2. They offer a "pseudo-choice," that is, a way to buy their product while thinking you are protesting against multinationals or being more sophisticated than other shoppers.

Ben and Jerry's ice cream is a case in point. The socially-conscious, enlightened-management Vermont-based company started having growth-related problems in the late nineties. The company had been too successful and the "hippie" founders had tired of running an increasingly complex company. . . .

The idea is that the organic, eco-active image of the brand will translate into a European market where organics are growing rapidly. To that end, Unilever has maintained the funky, privately-held image, barely mentioning the parent company on the company's home page. It's also continued contributions to socially conscious causes. But internally, decisions are being made as in any other division of a big company by people who think like Unilever. For example, layoffs are in the air as Unilever tries to reduce overall staffing. And payments to Vermont dairy farmers are less generous than they used to be. Gone too is the idea of making executive compensation have some tie to assembly-line worker pay.

But the illusion of independence works. The average shopper still thinks that passing by the Breyer's and picking up a pint of Cherry Garcia is an act of social defiance.

Seen from this point of view, Unilever is part of an "oligarchy" and is intent on crushing everything quirky, original, authentic, and subversive out of Ben & Jerry's. By buying a funky, politically progressive brand, it gets to masquerade as cool and progressive for the unsuspecting consumer. Seen from the perspective of the food industry, however, the merger looks like a no-brainer. As any number of industry analysts have pointed out, it can cost up to $100 million to create a brand from scratch with a fraction of Ben & Jerry's recognition. It makes far more economic sense for Unilever to let people like Ben and Jerry innovate and then cherry-pick the most successful brands than it does to build one from scratch.

Layoffs are more than in the air, they are in full swing. Over 20 percent of the staff has been let go since the acquisition. That includes their entire sales force. Today, Ben & Jerry's Peace Pops™ and Cherry Garcia™ ice cream are sold by the Good humor sales force.

What may matter more than staffing issues is the way the parent company defines CSR. In this case, the concept is starkly different from the way it was once defined by Ben and Jerry themselves. At a BSR conference in Miami in November 2002, Charles B. Strauss, president and CEO of Unilever in the United States, gave a presentation of CSR efforts at Unilever. Strauss started out with an unusually broad definition of CSR, working from the premise that everything at Unilever is inevitably scrutinized from the perspective of the brands and the relationship to the consumer.

> Each of these brands . . . [is] built on a deep understanding of people's everyday needs. In Unilever, we define a brand as an intimate relationship with its consumer . . . a bond . . . an expectation . . . a promise. And we take that responsibility seriously.

This is where "corporate social responsibility" begins for Strauss and Unilever. Safeguarding the health and welfare of the employees under its capacious umbrella comes in a clear second.

> We are also responsible for the nearly 254,000 people who work in our company worldwide. With our brands, their talents and commitment are our most important assets. Without them, and our relationships with many partners across the value chain, Unilever today would not be a $50 billion sale enterprise.

The interests of the shareholders come third. These people "have invested their faith and their capital in the ingenuity and hard work of our people. . . . Our investors deserve a return that's fair, competitive and sustainable." But when Strauss cited some case studies of CSR at work at Unilever, he began with—Suave. Suave shampoos and conditioners, he said, are a value as opposed to a premium brand, yet the brand enjoys "the highest consumer loyalty of all personal care products [in the United States] because it's so in tune with the needs of its customers. . . . Suave has been built by delivering value and quality consistently to its consumers. Sales this year will exceed $700 million." To put forward a shampoo made from nonrenewable petro-leum-based surfactants with synthetic dyes and fragrances as an example of corporate social responsibility is almost laughable. It changes the definition of the term, and not for the better, and certainly does little to save the world.

There's nothing wrong with companies selling products at good prices to consumers of modest means, just don't call it CSR. Unilever does, on the other hand, invest substantial sums in employee development, which has a strong component of self-interest, but also arguably benefits the societies and communities in which the company operates—a critical stakeholder. In a country like Brazil, where half of the children fail to complete secondary school and nearly one in five citizens is illiterate, Unilever's Educare program—launched in 1996 with a pilot program at Unilever's personal care products plant just outside São Paulo—has been a rare bright spot on an otherwise bleak educational scene.

But what about nonemployees? The great challenge here, Strauss acknowledges, is sustainability.

> The first order of business of a company like Unilever is to improve the environmental impact of its own operations—from the design of our products to the efficiency and cleanliness of our production.

To its credit, Unilever has become intimately engaged with three areas of sustainability that are directly related to its business: (1) sustainable agriculture, (2) sustainable fisheries, and (3) clean water. The fact that they choose to virtually ignore everything that falls outside of those three areas, including a simple acknowledgment that they have chosen to do so, leaves much to be desired.

And yet,

- On the agricultural front, Unilever is sponsoring projects in nine countries designed to create a system of "best practices" to grow five key crops—palm oil, tomatoes, peas, spinach, and tea—more sustainably.
- As one of the world's largest buyers of fish, Unilever partnered in 1996 with the Worldwide Fund for Nature to

create an organization known as the Marine Stewardship Council (MSC). Modeled on the Forest Stewardship Council, which has created a certification system for sustainable timber, the MSC has established a certification process for sustainable fisheries, and has made a commitment to "sourcing all of our supplies from sustainable fisheries by 2005."

- As an example of its focus on clean water, Unilever has adopted a village on the banks of the heavily polluted Brantas River in Indonesia as a pilot program of its SWIM (Sustained Water and Integrated Catchment Management) initiative— the catchment area, where fish are caught, which might also serve as a source of drinking water. Having improved water treatment practices in the village, Unilever is now working with more than a hundred companies with operations along the Brantas to clean the entire river.

In the end, Unilever defines "corporate social responsibility" as "looking at the consumer not simply as a buyer of competing products and brands but also as a global citizen who has social and environmental needs and concerns." To what extent does the company deliver on this admittedly vague promise? While demonstration projects and model plants are important and commendable, Unilever seems a long way from honestly beginning to quantify the impact that it has on the planet and its people. For example, how many pounds of pesticides does it take to produce the ingredients in each box of Bird's Eye frozen vegetables? How much water was polluted and soil eroded? What were the health implications for the farmers who handled those pesticides? Answering these and countless other questions would be a critical step in Unilever's beginning to take real responsibility for its own environmental and social footprint. Recognizing that they need to be asking these questions of themselves would be a step in the right direction.

As Simon Zadek notes in *The Civil Corporation*, "Defining boundaries of responsibility is the single biggest dilemma for companies wishing, or having been pressured to take fuller account of their responsibilities." Yet if Unilever believes that it can set these boundaries itself rather than through a process of discussion with its stakeholders, it will have misunderstood one of the most basic tenets of CSR.

Financial Structure Is Ownership Structure

Ben & Jerry's was launched in 1978 with $4000 in savings from Jerry, $2000 from Ben, and $2000 borrowed from Ben's father. Since they needed about $20,000 to get started, they went to a local bank looking for a loan, and in order to complete their application, they needed to draw up a business plan. Conceiving it required some chutzpah. Since it wasn't easy to project annual revenues for an ice cream parlor in Burlington, Vermont—the town stays pretty cold for about half the year—Ben and Jerry projected first-year sales of just under $100,000. Of that total take, they estimated that around $8000–or 8 percent—would flow to the bottom line.

A local banker agreed to a loan of $18,000, provided the Small Business Administration (SBA) would back it up. When the SBA turned down their application, the banker reduced his commitment to $4000. "When we were looking to start up," the two founders later wrote, "we had two choices: take the bank loan, or look for someone to sell a share of the company to." They decided to take the bank loan and keep the equity for themselves. They did that for one simple reason. They wanted to keep control of the business.

By 1983, after just four years in business, the place was pulling in between $3 and $4 million in annual sales, and the partners' self-definition slowly began to change. "When we started making ice cream in 1978," they later admitted, "we had simple goals. We wanted to have fun, earn a living, and we wanted to give something back to the community, only we didn't know what that last item meant."

Spurred in part by kindred-soul Anita Roddick, whom they encountered at various Social Venture Network conclaves, Ben and Jerry resolved to become values-led rather than profit-driven. Their first decision involved whether they should take a big chunk of their profits for themselves or reinvest it in a new physical plant? Since the working conditions in their antiquated factory could be charitably described as "pre-ergonomic," they didn't feel good about their employees working there. But in order to justify the expense of building a new plant, they needed to grow their business dramatically.

"We believed that the best way to make Ben & Jerry's a force for progressive social change," they wrote many years later, "was to grow bigger so we could make more profits and give more money away." Their firm commitment to give away 10 percent of their profit every year to social causes, ironically enough, provided them with an irreproachable rationale for growing the business. As they later put it: "Ten percent of the profits of a $100 million company could do a lot more good than 10 percent of the $3 or $4 million we were currently doing."

But how to become a $100 million company and not compromise their values? Having made the decision to "bring the business to the next level," they now faced an even more urgent question: How best to finance the required expansion? A few years before they had faced a similar choice between taking a bank loan or taking on an equity partner. Now their choice was between "selling out to a big corporation or take in investment money from venture capitalists."

They didn't want to do either. "In the first scenario," they later wrote (before the sale to Unilever), "the company can't be values-led unless the corporation that buys it shares its values." They noted, ironically in light of subsequent events, that "the trend of small companies being swallowed up by big companies exacerbates the trend toward concentration of wealth in the hands of the few. . . . If, on the other hand, a values-led business takes in venture capital, the venture capitalists are unlikely to allow the company to maintain its social values, because most of them hold the mistaken belief that social values will make a company less profitable." A rare exception to this rule was a venture fund like Calvert Social Ventures, founded by Wayne Silby's Calvert Group specifically to solve this problem. But at the time, Calvert Social Ventures (which later invested in Seventh Generation) was barely a glimmer in Wayne Silby's eye.

So Ben, being Ben, had a brainstorm. Why not "turn to the community" for financial support, in the form of a very unusual public stock offering restricted to citizens of Vermont? Every stockbroker they spoke to, not surprisingly, thought they were nuts. "Talk about swimming upstream and fighting against conventional thinking,"

Jerry later said. "All the so-called professional experts highly recommended against it."

Ben & Jerry's first public offering of stock, priced at $126 for twelve shares at $10.50 a piece, sold out in a few days. It was handled not by conventional brokers and underwriters but by selling stock directly to the public. They took out ads in local newspapers near the grocery coupons, where the regular folks could see them. They crafted a headline that proved irresistible: "Get a Scoop of the Action." The public offering not only raised the $750,000 they were seeking but had proved a point: It was possible to do things a little differently, and yet still win by all the conventional yardsticks.

Having pulled off this community-based, counter-cultural stock offering, Ben and Jerry were happy campers—for a while. Here's Ben and Jerry writing—somewhat naively, in retrospect—in *Double-Dip* (1997):

> You sell to the people who support your company, people who have been buying your products for years, people who believe in your values-led company and therefore aren't in it for the short-term. They're people who want to combine their values with their wallets. They want to feel good about the company they own a part of, and not have to close their eyes to feel okay about an impersonal numbers transaction.

It all worked like a charm, up to a point. What they didn't realize then—but know now—is that however closely your values might be aligned with your original shareholders, many of them over time end up selling their shares to other people who don't necessarily buy into the same values. With a privately held company, ownership can be restricted by the board of directors to just those people who you believe share your values. Through a shareholders agreement, a predetermination can be made as to how, when, and even to whom selling shareholders must sell. While a majority of the shareholders can usually elect new directors, the options for controlling your own fate are endlessly wider if you are privately held. By 1998, it had dawned on Ben and Jerry that they had lost control of the company, just as they began receiving nibbles from larger buyers. They were in a weak spot because "the stock had done nothing for the past ten years," Jeff Kanter, an analyst for Prudential Securities, later told the *Associated Press*. In response to the muted reception the company was receiving on Wall Street, Ben and Jerry had recruited a new CEO, Perry Odak, whose mandate for change was appealingly straightforward: Get that stock price up, and fast. Getting the stock price up was an urgent matter because the company's low valuation was what made it an attractive takeover target. Ironically enough, one of the most reliable methods of boosting a stock price is to *become* a takeover target, and that is precisely what Perry Odak set out to do.

The first bidder was Dreyer's Grand Ice Cream—the domestic ice cream giant that produces the Starbucks brand. Ben & Jerry's successfully fended off that first takeover bid, but now, as they say on the street, the company was "in play." By the fall of 1998, Ben and Jerry had cautiously agreed to meet with Unilever "to see if they could work out a partnership," Jerry later recalled, "that would permit the company to remain independent." In other words, they were hoping Unilever might act as a friendly investor, or "white knight," that would save them from being gobbled up by an even less desirable party. Shortly after the meeting, four more unsolicited and much higher bids quickly came in.

The bids came from Dreyer's, from Italian ice cream maker Roncadin, from Nestlé, and from Britain's Diageo PLC, owner of rival Häagen-Dazs. Meanwhile, a stock that had languished in the teens for years had nearly doubled in a few months, from $17 to $30. All of a sudden, all that tall talk about keeping a values-led, shareholder-controlled business independent fell by the wayside. Not that Ben and Jerry weren't desperately hoping to land a suitor in alignment with their values. But like it or not, Adam Smith's invisible hand was driving the train, and the two founders were merely passengers.

By early 1999, a number of Ben & Jerry's franchise owners who didn't have a warm feeling about working with Unilever, Nestlé, Roncadin, or Diageo tried to put the brakes on by launching a spontaneous campaign to save Ben & Jerry's from the conglomerates. The "Save Ben & Jerry's Coalition" organized a protest, held fittingly enough at a Ben & Jerry's scoop shop on San Francisco's Haight Street, complete with celebrity hippie Wavy Gravy—for whom Ben & Jerry's had named one of its best-selling flavors—who yelled out to the crowd: "Calling all cows, calling all cows, corporate land sharks are circling the scoop shops! They want to scoop up Ben & Jerry's. We need to save it from this megamerger!"

It was an unforgettable culture clash of sixties values with nineties numbers. Medea Benjamin of the Global Exchange spoke for many in the socially responsible business community when she protested:

> This proposed corporate takeover shows how insane the drive for profits at any cost has become. The directors of the company could actually be sued if they decide to put the interests of their employees, family farmers and local communities above the interests of Wall Street. It would be a disaster if Ben & Jerry's were to sell out, especially to a multinational like Nestlé that is renowned for its social irresponsibility. We have so few companies that truly have a social conscience—we can't afford to lose this one!

"I wanted the company to remain independent. . . . I tried real hard to keep it independent," an anguished Ben Cohen later told a reporter. One of the last-ditch efforts to save the "values-led" business from the relentless current of market forces was cobbled together by Meadowbrook Lane Capital, a Massachusetts-based socially responsible private equity firm headed up by SVN member Joseph Sibilia. Meadowbrook's original deal (in which it enlisted Terry Mollner, formerly of the Calvert Group, to form a group called Hot Fudge Partners) at one point envisioned bringing in Unilever as a white knight, which suggests that Unilever was, of all the conglomerates, the one whose values were perceived to be most in alignment with management.

Meadowbrook's Hot Fudge Partners offered $268 million for the company's 8.36 million outstanding shares, or about $38 a share. Ben strongly supported the Meadowbrook bid and told a radio interviewer at the time: "My personal belief is that the long-term value of the stockholders is best maintained by keeping the company independent." Yet he also acknowledged—as Medea Benjamin had pointed out—that under federal law, "it is the directors' responsibility to make decisions that maximize shareholder return in the short term." After word leaked out of these confidential deliberations, and an article describing them appeared in the *New York Times*, three shareholder groups sued Ben & Jerry's under the provisions of that law for allegedly failing to get the best possible deal for its shareholders. The Meadowbrook deal collapsed.

Marjorie Kelly, the editor and founder of *Business Ethics Magazine*, recently shed some light on a little-known Vermont law that might have made a big difference. Colloquially called "Ben & Jerry's Law"—and strikingly similar to stakeholder laws in place in thirty-two states, including Illinois, Massachusetts, Minnesota, New Jersey, and New York—the Vermont law asserts that corporate boards need not sell to the highest bidder, but may take other countervailing factors into account. Such "stakeholder laws" permit management to consider factors other than price—including well-being of employees and the community—in deciding who should own a company.

As Joe Sibilia of Meadowbrook Capital recently recalled to Marjorie Kelly of *Business Ethics*, when the possible application of Vermont's obscure stakeholder law was first brought to his and his partners' attention, "We paused and went into the other room. And we said to ourselves, if we use this law we'll lose and have to appeal. It could go to the Supreme Court." The group decided that this was one battle it could not afford to fight. Just the same, "Stakeholder laws represent a potential Copernican revolution in corporate purpose," Kelly wrote. One might call this an understatement. If stakeholder laws ever do became the uncontested law of the land, legacy issues like those faced by Ben Cohen and Jerry Greenfield may end up being resolved very differently. It may in fact be the best bidder that prevails, as opposed to the one with the deepest pockets.

On April 11, 2000, Ben & Jerry's board met with representatives of the two final bidders, Dreyer's and Unilever, and, as expected, Unilever won the auction with a bid of $43.60 per share, a 25 percent premium over the then current trading price and up 156 percent from the $17 it was trading at only 24 months before. Unilever further sweetened the pot by agreeing to a series of commitments extracted from them in a last-ditch effort to keep Ben & Jerry's true to itself. Under the agreement, Unilever promised to:

- Maintain the company as an independent entity, with a board of directors independent of Unilever.

- Keep the company in Vermont.
- Maintain the company's policy of donating 7.5 percent of its profits to charitable causes.
- Make a substantial donation to Ben & Jerry's Foundation in support of the company's social agenda, and to maintain an annual gift of at least $1 million a year.
- Buy rBGH (recombinant bovine growth hormone) -free milk from local farmers.
- Increase the number of suppliers who use Fair Trade products (these are products that pay premiums to the small farmers who grow them).
- Explore the opportunity for an organic line of ice cream.
- Work with a reputable consultant to do a "social audit" of Unilever's business practices.

With those commitments firmly in hand (or so they thought), Ben and Jerry told themselves that they had salvaged the best possible deal to maintain the socially responsible principles of the company in its new incarnation. "While we and others certainly would have pursued our mission as an independent enterprise," they proclaimed in a statement issued on the day of closing, "we hope that, as part of Unilever, Ben & Jerry's will continue to expand its role in society."

The founders concluded on a hopeful note.

> Neither of us could have anticipated, twenty years ago, that a major multinational would some day sign on, enthusiastically, to pursue and expand the social mission that continues to be an essential part of Ben & Jerry's.

Richard Goldstein, president of Unilever Foods North America, seconded that emotion by insisting that the company's distinctive social policies were integral to its brand identity. "Much of the success of the Ben & Jerry's brand is based on its connections to basic human values," Goldstein elaborated, "and it is our expectation that Ben & Jerry's continues to engage in these critical, global economic, and social missions. We feel that Ben & Jerry's has a significant opportunity outside of the United States, and that Unilever is in an ideal position to bring the Ben & Jerry's brand, values, and socially conscious message to consumers worldwide."

Does it matter if a company pursues a social agenda for marketing reasons rather than out of heartfelt commitment? Possibly all that focus on "brand identity" should have been the tip-off of trouble. By January 2001, only eight months after the deal had closed, the warm and mellow feelings that had surrounded the closing were growing frayed. One major point of contention between the founders and the new owners was Unilever's refusal to appoint a CEO favored by Ben & Jerry's advisory board. They picked instead a twenty-four-year Unilever veteran who gave no indication of expertise in selling values, but knew one heck of a lot about selling ice cream. In response, Ben and Jerry issued a doleful statement.

> We strongly supported a different candidate, a longtime member of Ben & Jerry's Board of Directors, whose commitment to our social policies was clear and established. As owner, Unilever of course has the legal right to manage Ben & Jerry's in the way it sees fit. We have not decided whether or not to remain with the company. . . .

To the press, Ben openly expressed concern that the ostensibly iron-clad commitments made by Unilever to maintain the company's social policies were not as legally binding as he had been led to believe. He wasn't explicit about which commitments he was referring to, but one of the key ones—to not lay anyone off for two years—was upheld by Unilever only to the letter of the agreement, at which point Unilever began wielding the ax with abandon. In October 2002, it issued pink slips to a quarter of the headquarters staff at Waterbury, letting go fifty-two people. This came on top of an earlier decision to close two factories elsewhere in Vermont, at a cost of 124 blue-collar jobs. At the end of three years a total of 20 percent of all employees had been let go. Ben let it be known that he was very, very upset by these actions.

In light of the layoffs, he was inclined to believe that "the values of Ben & Jerry's at its height are not the values of Unilever," as he bitterly informed a reporter for *Mother Jones*. He further went out on a limb by stating, "most of what had been the soul of Ben & Jerry's is not gonna be around anymore."

In all fairness to Unilever, the difference between April 2000 and April 2002 was pretty profound. In those two years, the economy had slowed, and nearly everyone was hurting. Nevertheless, the new Ben & Jerry's responded to Ben's charges by pointing out that the company had just made its biggest environmental push ever, with a campaign starring the Dave Matthews Band to fight global warming, and that an independent social audit conducted by Institutional Shareholder Services had recently concluded that "fears that Ben & Jerry's would abandon its commitment to caring capitalism have so far proven unfounded."

Most industry observers agreed that the best way to appease Cohen and Greenfield and improve the image of the brand would be for Unilever to use its marketing muscle to do what Ben and Jerry had never been able to pull off: to bring out a line of organic ice cream. On this point at least, Ben Cohen wholeheartedly agreed: "I have always thought that Ben & Jerry's is the perfect brand to introduce organic to a wider consumer audience."

In June 2003, they did it. Ben & Jerry's Homemade announced plans to test-market organic ice cream in two major U.S. cities, San Francisco and Boston, while somewhat tentatively living up to their commitment to purchase raw materials locally, by promising to buy as much organic milk as Vermont farmers could provide. This news was met with cautious optimism by Vermont's depressed dairy community, who could expect to be paid about $20 per hundredweight for organic milk, a significant premium over the roughly $12.50 per hundredweight paid at the time for the conventionally produced variety.

This was certainly a win for the environment, for the Vermont dairy industry, and very possibly for Ben & Jerry's. In fact there was just about no major stakeholder group, including the consumers who would be given the privilege of snacking on pesticide- and hormone-free ice cream, that would not benefit from the change. Which certainly raised the question: What took them so long?

When I ran into Gary Hirshberg, founder of Stonyfield Farm and one of the country's pioneers of the organic food movement, shortly after the Ben & Jerry's organic announcement was made, I asked him what he thought. "If Ben & Jerry's had gone organic ten years earlier," he answered, without hesitation, "the company might have been able to maintain its independence, and Ben might still be in control. It's ironic that it's happening under Unilever and it never could happen under Ben. By not being organic already," he elaborated, "Ben's social mission and his product line were not intersecting. They were separable. By being organic, your mission and your product are no longer distinguishable or separable."

He continued: "That made it okay for Unilever to come in and say, 'Ice cream? We know ice cream. All this social mission stuff, great, we know how to do *that*.' But had Ben & Jerry's been organic already and had Ben known how to make his company and his product organic, if he had had the infrastructure to prove it, the takeover story could have turned out very differently."

So why didn't Ben and Jerry create that infrastructure themselves? They have said that they were focused on too many other things—including a campaign to produce their ice cream cartons out of chlorine-free paper—that they simply couldn't take on the challenge. On the issue of the layoffs, Gary's take was also not quite what you'd expect from a socially responsible entrepreneur.

Ben & Jerry's people say Unilever must not be socially responsible because of the layoffs. But you could also say that Ben & Jerry's wasn't being responsible because there was fat in the overhead. If his overhead hadn't gotten to the point where it had, maybe his financial results would have been different, and maybe the stock price would have reflected that. That's a lot of maybes. But I'm not sure anyone anywhere in business can say that we guarantee permanent employment to anyone.

A few days after Unilever had made its announcement, Gary had run into Ben Cohen, and said, "You know, it's really kind of amazing that Unilever is launching an organic ice cream line."

To which Ben somewhat caustically replied, "Well you know, they're not doing it because they believe in organic. They're doing it to make a buck."

Gary responded, "Yeah? What's wrong with that?"

His point was that this was the essence of the socially responsible enterprise: to make money by doing the right thing. "After all," he later told me, "they were taking toxins out of the food chain that he wasn't taking out. At the end of the day isn't that what really matters?"

Maybe not. The organic result is great, but the why and how matters as well. If a company's commitment is exclusively to aspects of social and environmental responsibility that can be marketed to the public, one has to wonder whether the moral and ethical commitment will carry through to aspects of business that are harder to see and evaluate. That's what transparency is all about, and as we know it's an imperfect art at best.

The Selling of the Socially Responsible Business: A National Trend

If you buy a carton of Odwalla premium, fresh-squeezed, organic orange juice, you are patronizing a supposedly "alternative" brand now owned by Minute Maid, a subsidiary of Coca-Cola. If you buy a bottle of Mad River Traders natural juice, you are also buying from Coca-Cola. Boca Burger natural and soy burger and Balance Bar energy bars are both owned by Kraft, a subsidiary of Philip Morris, now known as Altria, which also sells Marlboro cigarettes and Virginia Slims.

Cascadian Farm, an organic food company, is now owned by General Mills, which also sells Hamburger Helper. Muir Glen organic tomato sauce is now also a part of General Mills, while Earth's Best organic baby foods has been acquired by Hain Celestial, which is 20 percent owned by H. J. Heinz. The list goes on, and it is likely to keep growing until just about every small, organic, natural, socially responsible company in the world is either owned or partly owned by a major player. (For a fuller accounting of this trend, see the appendix Who Owns Who.)

Why is this happening and what does it mean for the future of leading-edge socially responsible business? There are many reasons: founders who are burned out and want to retire and are willing to sell to the highest bidder; companies with a minority venture capital shareholder who aggressively pushes a transaction that generates the financial return they need to meet their own financial objectives; companies that end up in financial trouble and can't find any other way out. There's no question that a lack of alternatives is a real problem, particularly when they are limited to being engulfed in the sale to a multinational or the other most common option, "a venture capital roll-up," when a venture company sets out to acquire a cluster of related companies, under the theory that one plus one equals three. All of this is also driven by the scale issue—the largely unchallenged notion that bigger is always better. In the larger companies' defense, this rationale has been expressed by many socially responsible businesses themselves over the years.

The market for organic foods has grown by a robust 20 percent a year since 1990, according to the Organic Trade Association, and hit a whopping $11 billion in 2002. If this trend continues, the 2 percent of the nation's grocery bill that now goes to organic food will get considerably bigger in a few years. With organic now growing at a rate five times as fast the conventional food market, and with nearly 40 percent of organic food now sold through mainstream grocery outlets like Safeway, Krogers, and even Wal-Mart, the big food companies are extremely interested in the organic market. It takes tens of millions of dollars to build brand recognition in today's crowded marketplace, and the big boys would rather buy a brand perceived as "authentic" by the natural-food crowd than spend the time and money trying to build one from scratch.

To some observers, this trend means the death of the CSR movement as we know it. While I wouldn't go that far, it is certainly a sign of maturation that is not restricted to the food business: Socially responsible companies are being bought up by giants in practically every category where they exist.

Ben Cohen's less-than-satisfying experience with Unilever has prompted him to offer some timely advice for socially responsible entrepreneurs who might be tempted to sell out to large corporations: "Don't do it!" he told *Mother Jones.* "Stay independent. I certainly tried to keep Ben & Jerry's independent. I lost that battle. But that doesn't mean that other people can't win it."

But then, what is the long-term solution? To many companies, it is to remain private, or as many public companies (including Seventh Generation) have done of late, take themselves private by purchasing all of your stock back from the public before someone else does.

When we asked Anita Roddick what she might have done differently to avoid being relegated to the nonoperational, advisory role in which she now serves at the Body Shop, she replied with her characteristic forcefulness: "I'd tell anyone *don't take the company public.* Stay private at any cost. Going public is, in my experience, a total bloody disaster!"

In May 2003, *Fortune* ran an article entitled "The Burden of Being Public," which began, "Angry shareholders. Aggressive regulators. Onerous record-keeping requirements. As thousands of small firms face the new realities of life as a public company, many are saying: 'Who needs it?'"

The article described in some detail the slow expiration of the publicly held corporation as the absolute pinnacle of capitalist success. *Fortune* charted a number of cases in which public companies decided to take themselves private, all for pretty much the same reasons Seventh Generation did, although by no means all had a social focus. In the case of the pharmaceuticals-testing company Quintiles, company founder Dennis Gillings was described as having become "fed up with analysts' focus on quarterly earnings and their failure to grasp that his long-term growth strategy required the company to make expensive investments today." He took Quintiles private with a $1.7 billion leveraged buyout, in company with an increasing number of other once publicly held firms.

Fortune pointed out that one unintended consequence of the 2002 Sarbanes-Oxley Act, designed to safeguard shareholders against corporate malfeasance, has been that it is much more expensive to become a public company today. For a small public company to comply with the basic provisions of Sarbanes-Oxley can cost up to $1 million in additional accounting and legal fees. The recent crackdown on conflicts of interest in stock market analysis has had another unintended consequence: Brokerage firms have cut way back on their coverage of small-cap firms, which tends to make their stocks illiquid, which further reduces the advantage of being public.

Like Ben & Jerry's, Seventh Generation had gone public in the early nineties to avoid taking money from venture capitalists, most of whom we didn't believe would share our values and possibly wouldn't be patient enough for us to accomplish our long-term objectives. In general, most venture investors want to "cash out," meaning that they want to realize a return on their investment, within a three- to five-year time horizon. When you've been working, as I have, on something like Seventh Generation for fifteen years and are just beginning to hit your stride, that feels like an awfully short period. Perhaps worst of all, many venture investments are structured so that if the entrepreneur fails to hit the numbers in the financial projections, the venture investor can assume a larger ownership position—if not assume outright control—and even fire the founder and bring in their own "professional" management team.

But just like the disgruntled executives and company founders cited by *Fortune*, we found over time that our long-term focus on building the business did not always square with the short-term goals of stock market analysts, most of whom we couldn't get to pay attention to our tiny company anyway. If you're a Johnson & Johnson or HP, you are in a better position to make a case for the long-term perspective of investing in CSR, although as Bill Ford found out at Ford, they aren't very forgiving once you start losing money. As a micro-cap company, we found it surprisingly difficult to sell our long-term focus to our public shareholders, who tend to follow the advice of stock market analysts and brokers, who frequently focus on two factors, and only two factors: last quarter's sales and earnings.

With the help of our chairman Peter Graham, a longtime friend, prominent New York investment banker, and investor in the company since 1993, we took the company private in 1999. We've never looked back. Other companies that have cited—to us—the benefits of private ownership as a path to social responsibility are Patagonia, Eileen Fisher, and Working Assets.

Let's Make Another Deal

As I mentioned earlier, in 2001 the French multinational food conglomerate Danone agreed to acquire 40 percent of Gary Hirshberg's Stonyfield Farm for $125 million. This was certainly selling out, but the sale included certain iron-clad commitments on Danone's part, which it would need to honor before taking full control of Stonyfield Farm sometime in 2004. Gary has set the deal up, or so he says, to keep the company independent in spirit, if not in fact. He has made it his mission to "infect" Danone with his own life's work and message: selling the value of organic agriculture, for both human health and the environment.

Gary is a "former windmill-building hippie," as he puts it, and a longtime member of the Social Venture Network. He started out as an environmental activist, whose primary qualification for running a major food company included a stint as executive director of the Cape Cod–based New Alchemy Institute, which was devoted to spreading the gospel of sustainability as it related to renewable energy and agriculture. In the course of running his nonprofit, Gary made contact with Samuel Kayman, who ran a school for organic farming in Wilton, New Hampshire. Kayman's organic yogurt was very popular, but his fledging business was turning sour.

In 1982, Kayman persuaded the twenty-nine-year-old Hirshberg to step in and run the business in a more businesslike manner, which included getting up at five in the morning to milk the cows in subzero temperatures, mastering the complex and often frustrating craft of raising dairy cattle, and producing milk according to strict organic (chemically-free and all-natural) principles.

As the company grew, Gary inevitably needed financial help to expand, so he rounded up a few hundred investors, primarily friends and family members, to fund his growth, which to their delight verged on the explosive. Those investors, he hoped, had signed on to his values and his firm conviction that converting to organic agriculture would make the world a better place.

Until the late nineties, the 297 private investors couldn't have been happier to let Gary use the company as a platform to push a variety of environmental and social causes—it was good marketing, and most of them believed in these same causes. By 2000, after a decade and a half of runaway growth, Stonyfield Farm was selling more than $70 million worth of organic yogurt and other dairy products a year.

Gary's business was lending tremendous support to organic farming and farmers throughout New England, as he made a point of purchasing his raw materials locally. When I spoke to him in California, he knew the exact number of farms Stonyfield had encouraged to convert to organic in New England—120. That meant a lot less pesticides going into the ground, fewer cows munching on genetically modified corn, and in general a lot less reliance on agrichemicals—almost all of them petroleum based, and nearly all of them in some way toxic. Gary also told me that he regarded conversion to organic as the salvation of the small family farm, an accomplishment of no small significance as the New England landscape was under siege by developers devouring small farms right and left.

"There were forty-five dairy auctions in Vermont this spring," he told me. "The conventional dairy farmers are just going under in record amounts, while the organic farmers are thriving." An early proponent of sustainability, Gary started using his plastic yogurt containers as "mini-billboards" to get out messages that ranged from fighting oil drilling in Alaska to the long-term implications of global climate change. Stonyfield donates 10 percent of its profits to environmental causes and has invested significant sums in making its production processes sustainable. Its plant near Manchester, New Hampshire, features recycled wood floors, ultra-energy-efficient lighting, and recycled plastic stalls in the bathrooms. He also focuses on issues like making his plastic containers recyclable and as light as possible, and recently he eliminated the reclosable tops—although he'll send you some from his Web site if you ask.

Everything ran smooth as silk until the late 1990s, when a few investors (one of the largest of which happened to be a "socially responsible" venture capitalist) decided they wanted to sell their shares, at a price that was more than Gary and the company could afford. Ironically, this desire to cash in was undoubtedly the result of the company's success, and the extremely high valuations it could receive in the marketplace.

Gary pondered his options and took a look at a number of comparable cases. Never far from his mind was his friend Ben Cohen's growing disenchantment with the way that things had turned out with Unilever (although Gary was not so skeptical of Unilever's motives).

He watched as a larger competitor, Horizon Organic, went public only to see its stock sink and later be sold to Dean Foods, which had earlier purchased White Wave, the largest brand of soy milk, called "Silk." He did not want to buy out his restless investors with an initial public offering. So he became determined to do a deal that would be right for him, right for his company, and right for the environment, which would mean leaving him in charge to run the company pretty much as he saw fit—just as long as he made his numbers.

When I spoke to him, Gary was positively ebullient over his deal with Danone, not only because his family reportedly made about $35 million from it. Gary told me he considered Ben Cohen's deal a cautionary one, and he had deliberately set out to craft something different.

"The deal with Danone is turning out to be an unbelievable deal. It's the solution to the money-raising problem you and I have been working on for two decades. I've got total influence, total control, and total freedom from having to worry about money!"

Gary eagerly filled me in on the details. "That freedom is all dependent, of course, on my ability to generate results as a business. But here's the deal with that: I have to have *two consecutive years* of coming in below budgeted revenues by more than 20 percent for there to be any negative repercussions with regard to our independence. If I stumble in the first year, my adjusted second-year goal is a reduction from my first-year results. It's not like I have to come back to the originally budgeted second-year goal if I stumble. So in order to fail that badly, I would have to go on heroin and become a complete junkie and do something really irrational, and I would have to do it for more than a year."

We agreed that it certainly seemed from the outside like a good deal. Gary passionately insisted that his personal values had become so deeply "genetically encoded" in the product that no matter who controlled Stonyfield Farm in the future—and presumably once Danone takes full control it could sell it to General Foods—those values will survive intact as a core code embedded deep inside the brand. But what really made Gary excited about the deal with Danone was not so much the preservation of that code at Stonyfield but the opportunity it presented to instill it in the much larger parent company. He wanted to leverage economies of scale to spread the gospel of organic farming and organic food to a broader, global market.

Marjorie Kelly of *Business Ethics* was not convinced. She agreed that Gary's organic proposition was probably safe, but wasn't nearly so sure about "issues peripheral to consumers—like layoffs or employee benefits—where a company can cut costs and suffer no consumer backlash. Some values are less like DNA and more like barnacles on the side of a whale: easy to knock off." For all of Stonyfield Farm's success on the food front, we have heard less about what the internal culture looked like and what plans were in place to preserve or build upon it. With all the best intentions, the world of a publicly held company can often move in strange and unpredictable ways. What would happen if Danone fell on hard times and ended up with a new CEO, who turned around and sold Stonyfield to Kraft or General Foods?

Kelly continued, "What is opening is a new era of institutionalizing the social mission. Entrepreneurs have met the challenge of how to manage in socially responsible ways, but few even recognize the new challenge ahead: How to create the architectural forms that can hold social mission for generation after generation to come."

Gary described himself as a Trojan Horse inside a food Goliath into which he now enjoys entrée. People from Danone came by all the time to look at his operations, and he was constantly envisioning ways that Danone could use organic methods on a larger scale. Given the growing interest in organic food in both Europe and the United States, launching an organic line would seem like a no-brainer for the company. "We will be launching a Danone organic product," he promised, "in the near future, although I'm not entirely sure under which brand."

Gary saw this as the inevitable path of the innovator—that the new ideas would be eventually accepted by the mainstream. "What we can be proud of, including you and me and all of us who have been talking about this stuff for a couple of decades, is that we have test-driven these concepts. We have taken these hypotheses and proven that they work in the real world. For me personally, the endgame has never been to change the world by just becoming a better company. The endgame, for me, has always been to change the way that big companies do business by forcing them to reexamine their practices and showing them a better way."

Working Assets

One socially responsible company that could never survive as a publicly owned operation is the San Francisco–based telecommunications company Working Assets, which is unique in the CSR community. Working Assets maintains a relentlessly tight focus on deploying itself as a platform for raising money for worthy environmental and social causes, as well as running activist campaigns on everything from the elimination of chlorine in the paper industry to fighting against the launch of our war with Iraq. The company was founded in 1983 as a socially responsible investment fund not unlike Calvert, and by 1990 it had grown its asset base to nearly $200 million, and boasted some 17,000 shareholders. Two years later it sought to distinguish itself from the rest of the SRI pack by issuing the first socially progressive donation-linked credit card. Every time the cardholder used the card, five cents was donated to a pool of nonprofit groups voted on by the cardholders.

Other nonprofit groups like the Sierra Club, the alumni organizations of several universities, and even the Catholic Church quickly got into the affinity-card act, creating a crowded marketplace with limited growth potential. Working Assets next branched out into a cause-related travel service, which donated 2 percent of all transactions to selected nonprofits. They really hit the jackpot, however, when they decided to hook up with U.S. Sprint to become a long-distance phone provider. The deal with Sprint provided for 1 percent of the customer's phone bill to be donated to environmental and social groups, and the brilliance of the concept was that 1 percent on every bill, every month, adds up to pretty big money.

How big? Since 1985, Working Assets has generated over *$30 million* in donations to a long list of progressive nonprofits, ranging from Greenpeace to Oxfam America, from the Rainforest Action Network to the National Gay and Lesbian Task Force, to Planned Parenthood, the Children's Defense Fund, the AIDS Action Council, and Amnesty International. In 2001 alone, Working Assets generated over $5 million for fifty-five nonprofit groups, which the company divided into five categories: Economic & Social Justice, Environment, Civil Rights, Peace & International Development, and Education & Freedom of Expression. In 2002, Working Assets gave sizable donations to Greenpeace, Sweatshop Watch, Amnesty International, American Civil Liberties Union, and Children's Defense Fund.

In 1991, the company created its Citizen Action program (actforchange.com), which provides its customers with information on causes of interest, and easy ways to communicate with "the powers that be" on those issues. In 2001, the tenth anniversary of the program, the issues addressed included organic food labeling, winning compensation from Daimler-Chrysler for World War II slave laborers, and securing increased government funding for family planning and civil rights enforcement. Every month, the company highlights two crucial national issues and tries to explain what's at stake and whom to contact. Customers get "action alerts" on their monthly phone bill or by e-mail, and in 2000 alone customers generated more than one million calls, letters, and e-mails to Congress, the White House, and other leaders. That makes Working Assets one of the most vocal progressive activist organizations in the United States, and virtually unique in the field as a for-profit business.

Founded by Peter Barnes, the company is now run by Laura Scher and Michael Keischnick, who has for some time served as something of a role model for me. His business has been extremely successful (over $200 million in sales) and has dramatically redefined the kinds of social good a company can do. None of it would be possible if they had ever gone public.

We spoke to Laura Scher about the issue of corporate independence. In her twelve years as CEO, Laura helped to guide the company's expansion and transformation from a socially responsible mutual fund company—Working Assets Funding Service—into a telecommunications-slash-for-profit-advocacy organization. "In 1991 we created our own phone bill and the product became much more interesting," she recalled, noting that the phone bill's unique design empowered customers to vote on donations and to communicate with the company in a variety of ways.

The early 2000s, she noted, have been a difficult time for the telecom business as a whole, and after experiencing very rapid growth between 1991 and 1997, the company is now just holding its own. With a customer base of around 400,000 long-distance and 100,000 credit card users, Working Assets' "churn rate"—the level at which people cancel the service to sign up with another carrier—is well below the industry average. The reason is that the company's customers are committed to its social mission, not just the best deal they were last offered on discounted weekend and evening phone minutes.

Needless to say, Working Assets could never have taken any of the controversial positions that it takes if it had been a publicly held company. If Working Assets were publicly traded, she pointed out, it would have been entirely possible for anti-choice activists to buy up a sufficiently large chunk of stock to prohibit the company from adopting a pro-choice position on abortion.

> If we were publicly traded, we would be responsible for producing quarterly earnings reports, which would mean that if we wanted to spend, let's say, an unusually large sum of money on marketing in a particular quarter, we would have to be concerned about balancing that expenditure—in that quarter—against profits, which would have meant that we were running the company for the benefit of stock analysts.

This is why so many socially responsible companies live in dread of being publicly traded. "Being socially responsible," Scher said, "often means that you need to make long-term investments in search of future payoffs, and not always tangible ones."

Design for Living

When Eileen Fisher was a young interior designer starting out in New York, she deeply resented the obligation to be *fashionable*—to track the ebb and flow of hemlines and necklines as closely as a financier might follow a stock. "Men's clothes look great year after year," she said to herself, "why shouldn't women's?" In 1984, she had a vision of a very basic wardrobe composed of just four separate pieces that would permit herself and her customers—assuming they ever turned up—to escape from the tyranny of fashion without giving up looking and feeling good in what they wore. With $350 in savings, she started designing an anti-fashion fashion line that was inspired by, of all things, the uniform she wore in high school. It was simple, versatile, practical, timeless, and surprisingly becoming—the very antithesis of superficial change for change's sake. Her basic idea, she later recalled, was as simple and straightforward as the clothes: "Just put on your clothes and *go*. You don't have to fuss, you don't have to think about them all day. You're just ready to do what you need to do."

Eileen designs clothes for women who are too busy to think about clothes. Her first four basic pieces were shown at a boutique in New York, and when those sold out, she expanded the line to eight pieces. Buyers immediately gave her $3000 in orders, and the following month, $40,000. Today, the Eileen Fisher label is carried in over 1000 specialty shops around the country, most major department stores, and the company also owns twenty-five of its own stores. With growth spikes of 47 percent in the mid-nineties, the company has been growing at an average rate of 20 percent every year.

Like Stonyfield Farm or Seventh Generation, the social focus at Eileen Fisher is deeply embedded in the product. Her mission is to design clothes that don't impose a vision but rather "invite every woman to express her own style." Everything that Eileen Fisher does is closely designed, with a very specific purpose in mind. And she has very carefully designed her own company according to her own deeply personal vision, which—according to her company's mission statement—expresses a corporate commitment to "individual growth and well-being," and to "nourish well-being through opportunities to learn and grow in mind, body and spirit." The statement also challenges the company "to support women through social initiatives that address their well-being," and "to practice business responsibly with absolute regard for human rights, and form partnerships to better working conditions globally."

To get a sense of how the company goes about converting this mission into practical day-to-day decisions, we interviewed Susan Schor, the Vice President for People and Culture, at Eileen Fisher's showroom-offices in New York. Susan is a Ph.D. in psychology and former professor of behavioral psychology, whose academic specialty was organizational behavior. After working for Eileen Fisher for four years as a consultant she agreed to leave academia and join the company full-time, in part because she was drawn to its commitment to its people, and in part because it was impossible to resist an opportunity to practice what formerly she had preached. She had spent years, she said, "looking at the way people foster each other's individual development, at the ways people support—or don't support—each other at work."

Eileen Fisher became her laboratory. In 1998, the year she took her job and her title and began spending her days in Tarrytown, New York, where the company has its main headquarters, Eileen Fisher was experiencing the turbulence that often strikes companies during periods of rapid growth. "We were moving very quickly," Susan recalled, "from a small company and a small group of people who were very culturally and values focused, to a bigger business."

She was brought in to help the company negotiate that transition, and to work with both long-time employees and new recruits on aligning the values of the people with those of the company. "With the growth we were experiencing," Susan continued, "we had to deal with the cultural impact of an influx of people who were more bottom line oriented." She began working very closely with Eileen "to get closer to the values-saturated environment she wanted."

"What makes it work is that this is Eileen's company and it all comes straight from Eileen's heart. This is what she cares about: understanding what you are, understanding what you care about, and finding people who care about the same things. Everything [in the mission statement] is all about Eileen." Yet the founder's special gift has always been that what she wants for herself is what she wants for others, which means that she tends to be intimately in tune with her customers. The employees, for this system of converting passion to work, also need to be in tune with these needs and desires.

It's a company that deeply believes in "inculcating spirit in business and spirit in work." And even though they put the quest for sales and profits last on their list of values, between 1998 and 2002, the company grew from $100 million in sales to $164 million.

"We have chosen to strengthen rather than grow," Susan Schor said. She knows of no real growth initiatives on the agenda, and though there is some desire to grow the retail business, that growth is carefully managed. The great thing about retail is that it gives the company a chance to send a message to its customers in a simple, direct way—the Eileen Fisher way.

The key here is cultural. "Service without a sales orientation, in a supportive environment, calm and un-pressured, simple and relaxing." One hears that fashion in Manhattan is a frenzied, high-stakes, white-knuckle, competitive business, but at Eileen Fisher's New York showroom and office in the heart of Manhattan's frenetic Garment District, the atmosphere radiates a quiet, Zen-like, country calm. "It's that same environment you see here that we strive to create in the retail environment."

"When hiring a retail manager," she said, "we want them to focus on creating that environment, not driving sales. Our feeling is that the environment drives sales by being not about sales. The store environment has to be comfortable, homey, welcoming—to make you feel easy and good about yourself, like the clothes."

Creating this atmosphere would likely be impossible in a publicly traded company. Being a private company, Eileen Fisher has no qualms about conducting what Schor politely calls "a values exploration" before making key hires. "We do like to make a natural match," Susan said simply. "Someone who is more authoritarian in style is not likely to be a good fit. And we believe that leadership is a different form of authority. We believe in leading by example."

It's not that a publicly traded company would be prevented from taking the same approach, but as Ben Cohen told us, when he tried to do the same thing at Ben & Jerry's, his board objected to "values-screening" on the somewhat vague grounds that it might seem discriminatory. While this is not a real issue from a legal perspective, "values-screening" is an integral part of the hiring process at Seventh Generation. Beyond simply ascertaining if a candidate has the experience, skills, and talent to do the job, we spend a lot of time trying to understand who the perspective candidate is as a person, what they believe in, how they will behave in the culture we have created, and what type of member they will be of our community. Among other things, since each and every member of our staff becomes a shareholder (or actually option-holder, which means they have the right to purchase stock at an agreed-upon price), we want to ensure that as we enlarge our shareholder pool, we all end up in the same pool for the same reasons.

While I am actively involved in the process, our Director of Community Development manages the programs and procedures to make sure it happens. At Seventh Generation we chose not to call this person the Human Resource manager and emphasize instead the development of our community. We also turn to organizational development experts like Worksmart, based in Rochester, New York, to ensure we have access to the very latest strategies on how to build our workplace community.

Even though Eileen Fisher doesn't have to, "we share financials with all employees at our company meetings," Shor admitted. "And we try very hard to give as accurate a portrayal as possible of our financial position, of our goals and objectives, of what we're doing and what we're not doing." This is another hallmark of privately held CSR companies.

Employee health and well-being rank very close to the top of the company's priority list, but this is not health and safety as interpreted by OSHA. Every employee is given an annual grant of $1000 to spend on health and fitness, whether it be on wellness, yoga, Pilates, exercise equipment, or for membership at a gym. Every employee is given an additional grant to spend on education. The chief worry: "Not enough of that money gets spent and we're looking into why it's not getting spent."

At the warehouse, Eileen Fisher workers pooled their fitness money to buy equipment for a workout room. At Seventh Generation, by the way, we do the same thing; and if you think it all sounds a bit touchy-feely, I can tell you it does wonders for worker morale and productivity. Every Thursday someone shows up to give us all a massage.

In the long run, ownership structure matters. Only when people are given time to clarify the values that lead up to making these types of investments, and are patient enough reap the benefits, can CSR do what it's supposed to do—revolutionize and revitalize an organization by aligning the values of all of its stakeholders.

It may be that the real reason so many large corporations have such a hard time becoming socially responsible has little to do with size, per se. Perhaps it's a result of the structure that companies of that size are generally obliged to adopt—that of a publicly traded corporation—which legally requires managers to report every 90 days on what they've done for you lately. Profits tend to drive that equation.

While socially responsible businesses increasingly outperform their non-CSR competitors financially, ultimately CSR demands a new level of involvement and commitment from shareholders as well as all stakeholders, and we as a society have simply not made the transition from the shareholder to the stakeholder model of the corporation.

We have seen the exploding participation in shareholder resolutions. Beyond religious investors and other "socially responsible" investment funds, labor and pension funds and other large institutional investors, led by groups such as Calpers in California, are beginning to gradually yet persistently transform the management agenda to focus more on the social concerns of shareholders.

At Seventh Generation, we discovered a few years back how difficult it was to sell our story of long-term, steady growth—with a strong social focus—to the public markets. After returning to private ownership, we had no problem at all (thanks to the help and experience of Peter Graham and long-term board member Arthur Gray) finding more than enough investors eager to put their money into a company that they can believe in—and that gives them the prospect of a reasonable return on their investment while also doing something valuable for society.

Since very few large companies have the luxury of going private, the only viable long-term solution for the big businesses is to persuade mainstream investors of the validity of the lessons learned by the SRI community: that social responsibility can be a growth driver as well as a predictor of superior profits—over time. As we have seen from the many examples of large companies that are making significant investments in this area, the most persuasive argument often seems to be a negative one: that not making these investments can expose a company to significant CSR risk, which in turns exposes the shareholders to increased liability.

That said, only companies pursuing CSR out of a sense of authentic conviction are going to succeed, in the long run—and it is the long run that matters. Investors are now realizing, to their regret, that *their* excessive focus on short-term performance led inevitably to the cycle of "infectious greed" that gave rise to the scandals that eroded the value of their portfolios. The logic of CSR as an antidote to that cycle of greed is inescapable. The real builders of long-term value and performance are values. Values such as respect—for employees, contract workers, customers, the community, the planet—trust, compassion, conviction, authenticity, fairness. As Johnson & Johnson CEO James Burke once put it, these are the things that are "bankable and palpable," a conviction echoed by Starbucks CEO Howard Schultz at a November 2001 BSR conference:

> The opportunity to do the right thing has never been as important as it is right now. Building a sustainable enterprise is about having a conscience and a heart. . . . As a business you care about doing the right thing because it is who you are, not because it is good press. Those with the backbone to do the right thing, even when it hurts, are sure to sustain greatness in their business.

Next

In August 2003, I returned with my family to the same stretch of Long Island beach where I'd spent just about every summer since I was a kid. Just as I had the summer before, and the summer before that, I naturally fell into a rhythm of rising with the sun and slipping out of our house to catch a few waves before breakfast. During those quiet pre-dawn hours, I often found myself thinking about the events of the past year, as they related to society, the economy, business, and life. And I found myself thinking about the events of many years, as part of an ongoing process to frame those events in a broader perspective.

At the age of fourteen, in a house not far from the beach where I now surfed, I founded my first company in partnership with my younger brother, Peter. The short-term sustainability of the Westhampton Window Washing Company largely depended on my powers of persuasion as CEO to charm (most often) the woman of the house into shelling out for an expensive window-cleaning job, conducted by a couple of kids who hadn't yet learned to shave. We earned $100 to $200 a day—an amount that I didn't earn again until my mid-twenties. Much as I enjoyed making the pitch (and the manual labor a little bit less), my favorite part of the job was the biweekly trips down to gritty Canal Street on Manhattan's Lower East Side to haggle with wholesalers for squeegees, natural sea sponges, and other cleaning supplies. Thirty-five years later, I find it a little fitting that Seventh Generation involves such intimate contact with surfactants and detergents, items that still take up a pretty large chunk of my thoughts every day.

In the summer of 1977, not long after dropping out of Hampshire College and settling in Toronto with my girlfriend Cynthia Pitts, I established a nonprofit organization called the Skills Exchange of Toronto, based on the alternative educational ideas of the social critic Ivan Illich. In his influential 1970 book *Deschooling Society*, Illich argued that the top-down management of schools renders students powerless, and that this top-down management style reflects our overly technological economy, which prevents people from learning the things they need to learn to live life.

In Illich's pristine system of free citizens sharing knowledge in an informal setting, little or no money ever changed hands. But we were practical enough to charge a nominal fee. To the *Toronto Globe & Mail* I confided shortly after the launch that I'd "grown up in the tail end of the sixties, and I knew I'd have to do something that benefited society. But I was always attracted to business, and it was hard to find something like that in business. I think the Skills Exchange achieves that balance." It is a balance that, successfully or not, I have been striving to achieve ever since.

There was also a certain irony that a twenty-year-old kid who had dropped out of college after only 18 months was devoting himself to adult education. As Illich suggested, the structure within which institutionalized learning took place, even at a famously liberal establishment like Hampshire College, was more than I could manage to work my way through. It made no sense to spend months pouring my heart and soul into writing a paper that only one person would read and alone decide on its value. I needed to find a way to make more of a difference and to be in a conversation with a broader audience.

After becoming disenchanted with the internal politics of the organization—which in predictable period style tore itself apart trying to become a Marxist collective—I simultaneously confronted my own flawed imbalance between my work life and my personal relationship with Cynthia. Work won out—all the time, which led her to threaten to leave me. At the same time I was arrested in my own office for having failed to acquire the proper papers to work in a foreign country.

Last but not least on the list was my father's endless insistence that running a nonprofit organization made no sense at all. The business I was building was ultimately owned by the Canadian government, he claimed. I was creating no equity for myself. This was no way for the son of an Eisenhower Republican, former advertising executive-turned venture capitalist to be spending his time. While I ardently disagreed with virtually everything he said, there was one thing with which I had to agree: It seemed like time for a change.

I moved back to my hometown of New York in 1980 to launch a for-profit version of the skills exchange. We called our venture the New York Network for Learning, and right from the get-go we gleefully followed the cut-throat commercial instincts of a Harold Robbins more than those of our former idol, Ivan Illich. Instead of "Introduction to Meditation" and "Marxist Thought" we offered an impressive smorgasbord of courses, ranging from "How to Break into Broadcasting" to "How to Meet Men" (taught by notorious pick-up artist Eric Weber) and its inevitable corollary, "How to Meet Women."

Two of my personal favorites were "Wrinkles, Wrinkles"—we billed it as a "one-night face-lift"—and "How to Lose Your Brooklyn Accent." We cleverly combined light entertainment with more nuts-and-bolts offerings in gardening, personal finance, and career advice. The company successfully rode the bucking bronco of what one magazine called the "roaring bull market in adult education" to a couple of million dollars a year in sales within two years. By the age of twenty-five, I had become a successful New York entrepreneur. A piece in *Time*—called "Fast Food for the Brain"—cheekily observed that "The Network's phenomenal success is due, in large measure, to Hollender's shrewd ability to live off the fad of the land."

At the peak of my success I found myself as a guest on the Phil Donahue Show, accompanied by one of our most popular lecturers, Joanna Steichen, the 48-year-old widow of famed photographer Edward Steichen, who'd married her late husband when he was half a century her senior, and had inherited the bulk of his estate. Her course—entitled "How to Marry Money"—sold out auditoriums, and not surprisingly garnered us a huge amount of media coverage.

On the Donahue show, Joanna and I experienced the dark under-side of our commercialism, when we were mercilessly heckled by irate audience members, most of them middle-aged women, who derided us for being mercenary, reprehensible, money-loving yuppie scum. After walking off the set and removing my make-up, I faced one of my periodic identity crises: Was this truly what I had become? How had it happened? I suddenly realized that achieving that delicate blend of sixties idealism and eighties materialism was becoming a tougher balancing act than I had ever imagined, and at the moment at least, I was failing miserably.

Shortly thereafter our adult-education business began to tank. This was the no doubt inevitable result of an aggressive expansion policy, combined with the entry of new competitors into an increas-ingly saturated market. Our fiercest competitor even sought to fran-chise the model, to become the McDonald's of higher education, and we unsuccessfully followed suit.

Things looked pretty bleak for a while. I even flirted with the no-tion of declaring bankruptcy—a course that my attorney and advisor sagely talked me out of. Fortunately, we had recently launched a suc-cessful line of audio books based on our most popular classes. With the help of Harry Hoffman, then president of Walden Books, we were able to move from recording classes to acquiring the rights to best-selling books. No one seemed to have any interest in purchasing these rights and within a comparatively short period of time we had amassed one of the largest portfolios of audio book rights in the world. This turned out to be an asset of intense interest to the deal-makers at Warner Books, the publishing division of Warner Commu-nications, who were looking to start up an audio book division. In time-honored corporate style, rather than start up one of their own, they decided they'd rather buy ours.

We ended up selling the company to Warner's for a few million dollars and change. This was not only a fabulous case of pulling the rabbit out of the hat before the hat burned, but more importantly a first step in establishing a successful track record of doing well by our investors. As part of the deal, I signed a contract to become head of Warner's audio book division for a specified number of years, at a generous salary and with plenty of perks. But the truth was I was ready to leave the day I started. While I had salvaged my business career with a high-profile deal that made everyone a fair amount of money, I was miserable. The conflict that I felt after walking off the Phil Donahue show had only deepened with time, and I was almost desperate to find a new path to redeem my soul, or at least my conscience. I was committed to the idea that—as Mahatma Gandhi once said—"We must be the change we want in the world."

Strange as it might sound, here I was lunching at the Warner corporate boardroom, enjoying all the perks of being the youngest divisional president at the company, and just about every step of the way feeling not much but guilty. Fortunately, I had just married a wonderfully accepting woman who didn't seem to care if I walked away from it all and stayed home taking care of our first child while she went to work every day in the Brooklyn courthouse pursuing her career as a real estate lawyer. Sheila has always let me follow my heart, even if she had no idea where it might take us. For that I am and will always be eternally grateful.

Part of what also caused me to leave Warner's in the end, strange as this might sound, was an increasing personal interest in a new wave of thinking about business and society, which went by the name "environmental economics." The chief proponent of this new school was the former World Bank economist Herman Daly, whose *Economic Growth: From Empty World to Full-World Economics* made a deep and lasting impression on me. Daly's 1989 book *For the Common Good*, written with the theologian John Cobb, proposed a new economic benchmark called the Index of Sustainable Economic Welfare, which took personal consumer spending as its base figure, and then factored in such negatives as the money spent to fight crime, respond to accidents, and mitigate the effects of pollution into an overall index of economic, spiritual, social, and environmental well-being.

I can't claim that reading Herman Daly caused me to leave my job at Warner's. But Daly's message did bolster a nagging feeling I'd had for some time that for all of its pleasures, the things that mattered most were missing from my job there. A search for a large sense of purpose and fulfillment, together with the arrival of our first child Meika, drove me to take a much-needed break from the corporate grind. When not changing environmentally designed disposable diapers that didn't work (after giving up on cloth diapers), I moved into the New York Public Library's main branch to write a book. *How to Make the World a Better Place: A Guide to Doing Good* was published by Morrow & Co. in 1990 and reissued by W. W. Norton in 1995. The book's essential premise was neatly summed up by Buckminster Fuller's adage that by changing the minds of 5 percent of the population, one could effectively change the way society operates. The book ended up selling over 110,000 copies in paperback, and though we never reached anything close to the 5 percent mark, I have since been advised that it inspired quite a few people to do something positive for the world with their lives and their work—including me.

During the fact-checking process for the book, I learned that a small Washington, D.C.–based environmental organization called Renew America—which produced a catalog of water and energy conservation products that I deeply admired, and had mentioned favorably in the book—was planning to shut down. As a nonprofit organization, Renew America could no longer afford to float the losses of a venture that, however admirable, was costing them a lot of money. When I spoke to the people at Renew America, I asked them what was going to happen to the catalog. They told me that they had agreed to turn over all rights to it to the fulfillment company in Burlington, Vermont, that handled the orders, doing everything from taking the phone calls to storing and shipping the product. On a whim, but also because I liked the products and was personally sorry to see a good thing disappear, I placed a call to Alan Newman, the principal of Niche Marketing, to see if he might be interested in working with me to relaunch the business on a firmer footing.

What was going on, of course—although this became much clearer in retrospect—was that I was trying to act on the central premise of my book: that each one of us, by taking individual actions tailored to our tastes and temperament, can make a positive change in the world. Saving the Renew America catalog from extinction seemed like a pretty good place to start, because every time someone bought one of their environmentally friendly and energy-saving products, it was a step in the right direction.

While Alan already had plans to get underway, it turned out that we had a mutual friend who also served on Alan's board. Over the next six months, he encouraged us to explore working together. After a little back and forthing, Alan and I agreed that it would take at least $300,000 to relaunch the catalog effectively under the new name: Seventh Generation. The name was suggested by a Native American woman who worked for Niche Marketing, who wisely counseled to draw our inspiration from the Great Law of Peace of the *Hau de no sau nee*, better known as the Six Nations Iroquois Confederacy. Providing wisdom to its people, along with the inspiration for our own country's constitution, the Great Law of Peace (*Gayaneshakgowa*) holds that "in our every deliberation we must consider the impact of our decisions on the next seven generations."

Poetry aside, we quickly came to the conclusion that we needed more like a million bucks to get off the ground, and as I prepared to drum up a first round of $850,000 from investors, we drew up a Private Placement Memorandum that—as we proudly noted on the front cover—was entirely printed on 100 percent recycled paper. We were bravely up front about disclosing to potential investors that our goals were something other than making money, although we insisted that if we fulfilled our goals as expected, we would also generate a handsome return on their investment—in the long term. I had no idea at the time that this seeming noble pursuit would take close to ten years to hit its stride. In 1989 we wrote:

> The Company will seek to successfully combine what it believes to be a variety of interrelated and mutually supportive goals. Financially, the Company will strive to achieve an above-average return for its shareholders . . . while [seeking] to spread its principles of social and environmental responsibility to other businesses with which it deals.
>
> It will, for example, request that vendors package their products with recycled materials and avoid over-packaging wherever possible. The Company will pursue a policy of not buying products from companies operating in South Africa or from companies who abuse the

environment, are major weapons contractors, or who treat their employees in an unfair or discriminatory manner.

The most interesting part came in paragraph 3, where we laid out a pretty persuasive pitch that a socially and environmentally responsible business could provide a net plus return on capital over time.

The Company believes that taking such an active role in being a responsible corporate citizen makes good business sense. This view is reported by the financial newsletter *Good Money* to be shared by James Burke, the chairman of Johnson & Johnson, who is quoted as having said that "companies with a superior reputation for ethical behavior will demonstrate superior results for the stockholder."

The pitch worked. We easily raised the seed money. Just as easily, we blew through it. On the plus side, we shot from selling a million dollars worth of product in 1989 to over $6 million in 1990, sending tens of millions of catalogs with our message of environmental responsibility out across the country. But what we did not fully take into account was the degree to which this spectacular growth was largely fueled by the publicity surrounding the twentieth anniversary of the first Earth Day. On the minus side, we were spending a truly amazing amount of money printing and mailing catalogs, had a warehouse full of merchandise, and over a hundred people ready to answer phones and pack boxes. Unfortunately only a small percentage of those catalogs were producing any sales, and certainly not the repeat sales that we needed to stay alive, let alone thrive.

We were successful at garnering tremendous media attention, because what we were doing at the time seemed like a genuine novelty. In November 1990, we were featured in a four-page spread in *People* magazine, which noted that "despite the hoopla surrounding Earth Day last April, the moment has yet to arrive when the American consumer can push a cart through a supermarket and hear the announcement: 'Special in aisle 7: dioxin-free diapers!'" (That moment finally came to pass fifteen years later, when we rolled out our first product line carried in supermarkets, chlorine- and dioxin-free diapers.)

"In doing good," *People* observed, "Newman and Hollender are doing well." They quoted Alan as being bewildered by our successful experiment in green marketing: "We didn't think we were going to make any money. Not in our wildest dreams did we imagine anything like this." I put in my two cents: "We wanted to sell products that would help solve environmental problems. And we also wanted to create a business model that was fundamentally different."

We had done both, and might have spent more time slapping ourselves on the back if we hadn't been under such intense pressure to achieve some level of profitability before we burned through our next financing round—the $5 million we had raised following our initial success. Of course, we could take credit for being one of the first companies—and certainly one of the first socially responsible companies—to institutionalize the notion of Having Fun. Having Fun meant playing lots of Ping-Pong and basketball games on our own court, and devouring, whenever we felt like it, an endless and free supply of Ben & Jerry's ice cream. We had no dress code or restrictions on relationships with our co-workers, which meant that on many occasions romance and work did mix. We had a nap room, and no shortage of after-work parties. Yet having fun can get difficult if you're too anxious about staying in business.

In 1991, based on overly aggressive projections that forecast a three-and-a-half-fold sales increase—from $6 to $20 million in sales, we embarked on another course of expansion. We leased new offices that included our own warehouse (but no air conditioning), bought fancy new office equipment (including Apple's first laptop computers), and lavished loads of perks on the staff. By the first quarter of 1991, we had missed our sales target by a healthy margin; by the second quarter, we had missed it by a long shot. By the beginning of the fourth quarter, we knew pretty much for a fact that our sales were going to stay flat at around $6 million. Which, if we hadn't gone out and geared up to sell $20 million, would have been fine. Instead, it was a total disaster.

Not long after we hit the panic button, I found myself deeply engrossed in renegotiating the lease on the copy machine. Alan Newman, our jovial Minister of Fun, and in many respects my first mentor in socially responsible business, found out that it wasn't as much fun letting good people go as it was hiring them. Facing the mounting stress, increasing disagreement about what direction the business should head in, and the constant question of what we would do next to save more money, he decided that it was time for him to eliminate his own job and salary until the future looked a little brighter. I found myself facing for the second time in my life the prospect of out-and-out business failure. The first time around, audio book sales had bailed us out. This time around, what would it be? Could it be possible that lofty social goals and financial success were simply incompatible? I refused to believe it.

For an answer to that question, I turned to our old friend Ben Cohen, the by then famous cofounder of Ben & Jerry's. I called Ben up and asked him to come in and give us a much-needed pep talk. Instead of handing out Peace Pops, Ben let us all have it right between the eyes. The first words he uttered certainly got our attention.

"You people are completely fucked up!"

With his balding head and gray beard quivering with righteous indignation, and sweat pouring profusely from his brow, Ben turned up the volume to painful levels, and said some pretty frank things that some of us did not want to hear. I have to admit, I was partly responsible for Ben's fire-and-brimstone tone, because a few days before, in a moment of weakness, I had confided in him that I was still a little disturbed by a run-in I'd had with the staff, some of whom had cornered me at a staff meeting and asked to explain why everyone in the company didn't make the same salary.

Disgruntled over recent layoffs and the hard times, someone had gotten hold of my most recent credit card statement and circulated it for all to see. Point by point, my own employees began asking me to justify every expense item on it. I bristled but kept cool. But Ben wouldn't let it go. To him, it symbolized some of the reasons that we were floundering. As an old West Texas saying goes, if you find yourself digging yourself deeper into a hole, the best thing to do is stop digging.

"You've been spending too much time asking why Jeffrey makes more money than you do and why we aren't having as much *fun* as we used to!" Ben shouted. "How can you keep criticizing the business plan when if you don't go out and sell some of this shit fast, you won't have a business to come back to!" A business that was out of business wasn't going to do any good for anyone, and that prospect became painfully real to us all.

More out of desperation than inspiration, we embarked on an entirely new strategic plan. The new thrust was a wholesale strategy centering on distributing our own brand name products to natural food stores and some of the smaller grocery chains. By branding and marketing our own proprietary products through the retail channel—starting with our perennial best-seller, unbleached bathroom tissue made from 100 percent post-consumer recycled fiber—we began to turn a corner that had eluded us for years. We followed up with our own branded ecologically friendly liquid dish detergent, All-Purpose Cleaner, and recycled, nonchlorine bleached paper towels and napkins. Within a short period of time we had gone broadly national with a new group of a few dozen products, which began selling in significant volume.

In late 1993, just as things were starting to get rolling again, we made another mistake. Needing additional capital to expand but hoping to keep ourselves out of the grasping hands of the venture capitalists, we took the company public at $5 a share. We raised close to $7 million in the process, but we should have realized that something was not quite right with this picture when we ended up turning over close to $2 million of that—almost 30 percent—in underwriting and other fees to the investment banking firm that raised the money for us with a basement full of twenty-year-olds pitching the company as a "get-rich-quick" scheme.

To my horror, I had to mail back checks to elderly women who had been convinced to part with their retirement nest eggs. We raised this money in the beginning of Alan Greenspan's period of "irrational exuberance." This form of financing should really be called "public venture capital." We raised money from many people who couldn't afford to lose it, and couldn't understand the risks they were taking. Our stock was sold by salesmen parading as investment advisors. I could say I didn't know better, and I didn't—but I should have.

In December 1993, I called on Peter Graham, an old friend from fifth grade who had become a successful investment banker in New

York, to help us out of our jam. Peter had gotten involved with the company a few years earlier when he bought out some of the stock that Alan Newman wanted to sell. Unlike my desire for quick solutions, Peter always took the long view. He was always able to see around the bend in the road that I didn't even know was coming.

Those first few years as a public company were exciting, exhausting, and confusing. Each quarter we painstakingly prepared our SEC filings, making sure to spell out the good, the bad, and the ugly, as we were advised by our lawyer, who guided us through the endlessly idiosyncratic laws governing public companies. No matter how well we thought we were doing, the price of our stock seemed to only be able to move in one direction—down. As I later learned, one significant factor in the stock's downward spiral was that the stockbrokers who were working at our underwriters firm needed to free up money in their clients' accounts so that they could buy into the next public offering their company was peddling.

Our wholesale business was beginning to grow, but the catalog hadn't responded to the additional money we poured into it using the funds we had raised in the public offering. With Peter's encouragement in 1995, we took a deep breath and sold off the mail-order catalog—responsible for 80 percent of our revenue stream—to focus on building up the Seventh Generation branded products in retail stores.

Selling off the catalog, our original reason for being, turned out to be liberating. We no longer had to meet the huge overhead of printing and distributing catalogs, or handle the complexities and frustrations of order fulfillment. The proceeds from the sale permitted us to establish and maintain a new set of key relationships with leading natural-food retailers, including Whole Foods and Wild Oats, and independent chains like Trader Joe's.

In 1999, once again under Peter's guidance, we took another huge plunge and decided to take the company private. There were virtually no benefits for us to remaining a public company, since it cost us over $250,000 a year to pay lawyers and accountants. Our hugely undervalued stock price also made us an easy takeover target, a prospect we dreaded. After Peter lined up a small group of new investors, we offered all our public stockholders a 40 percent premium over the price that the stock had been trading at, and voilà—everyone decided to sell. Within a matter of months, we were a private company again.

In the now nearly five years since we took the company private and focused exclusively on the retail side of the business, we've finally achieved a healthy balance between growing and deepening our business. Yes, we are growing robustly at a rate of upward of 20 percent per year. But we are also strengthening and clarifying what it means to be a socially responsible small business in the twenty-first century.

During the summer of 2002, when the corporate scandals were still dominating the headlines of the financial pages, every day seemed to bring a new story with titles ranging from "The Revenge of Gordon Gekko" (Paul Krugman, *New York Times*) to "Does the Rot on Wall Street Reach Right to the Top?" (Gretchen Morgenson, *New York Times*) to "Recycling Corporate Responsibility" (*Wall Street Journal*) to "Martha's $$$ Falling Like a Bad Soufflé" (*New York Post*).

The scandals were causing increasing anger and disgust among the public, as they began to wipe out billions of dollars of stock market value, most painfully in the pension accounts of people who had spent a lifetime building up savings that disappeared in a matter of weeks. Something had to happen, and while the situation was likely to generate some minor accounting changes from Congress, what this all might add up to was anybody's best guess.

Would the financial scandals touch off a major wave of regulatory reform, comparable to the one that followed the Great Depression of the 1930s, which gave birth to the SEC, the New Deal, and a host of government watchdogs? Or would the endgame be more like the one that followed the savings and loan scandals of the 1980s, when there was much noise and smoke, but little in the way of substantial reform was accomplished?

A year later, it's possible to say that as a society, we have—at the behest of an ultra-conservative administration unwilling and unable to provide any true leadership—steered a mostly pro-business, conservative middle course. John Cassidy, writing in the *New Yorker*, marked the one-year anniversary of the passage of the Sarbanes-Oxley Act in the Senate with an essay entitled "Business as Usual." President Bush's righteous insistence that "Every corporate official who has chosen to commit a crime can expect to face the consequences," he wrote, has barely been borne out by the facts. "No more easy money for corporate criminals," Bush vowed, in his by now predictable but ultimately laughable tough-guy style. "Just hard time."

Except for a few glaring exceptions to date, including the case of ImClone founder Sam Waksal—and the ambiguous charges brought against his close friend Martha Stewart—the only "hard time" being served by the corporate rogue's gallery of the 2002 line-up has been in a lawyer's chambers. The notorious Bernie Ebbers of WorldCom and Ken Lay of Enron have thus far mysteriously failed to face up to much of anything, except their constitutional rights to keep their lips sealed. Both Waksal and Stewart, Cassidy recalled, face insider trading charges, which though comparatively easy to prove, were really peanuts compared to the multibillion-dollar outrages committed by Ebbers and Lay, to name just a few of the more visible miscreants.

On the plus side, the Fed's interagency Corporate Fraud Task Force had helped to bring charges against Dennis Koslowski of Tyco International and John Rigas, chairman of cable operator Adelphia Communications—allegedly operated by the founding Rigas family as its own private piggy bank. Former Enron CFO Andrew Fastow and Bernie Ebbers' accomplice and protégé in crime at WorldCom, Scott Sullivan, had also been forced to sing to the music. But these were, quite clearly, medium-fry—the big names remained at large.

One has to conclude that in spite of campaign finance reform and other marginal efforts to free the government from the grasp of big business, no matter how bad the behavior gets, if the offender is a large corporation or highly visible tycoon, some unstated rule seems to operate in which the government's response is generally to turn the other cheek and wait for more dirt to fly. Perhaps in keeping with the new age we are living in, leadership in this situation seems to be only forthcoming from business itself. And not all business of course, but from just enough companies to finally make a difference.

Within the socially responsible business community, the overriding concern has always been that the corporate scandals would end up being defined too narrowly—as purely financial in scope, having to do with a "few bad apples." We hoped, or rather fantasized, that the scandals might provide the impetus to persuade managements of companies all over the country, if not the world, to adopt and embrace the stakeholder as opposed to the shareholder model of the corporation. We wanted them to internalize the idea that pursuing the CSR goals of sustainability, transparency, responsibility, and accountability would be the best way to restore the much-battered public trust, and would be the best way to deliver real value in the long term.

In August 2003, the Dow was no longer flipping about like a scared bait fish, but neither was it swimming ahead like a shark. Perhaps the most remarkable aspect of the summer was the exceptionally good and consistent waves, as well as the endless humidity and cloud cover. On the macro level, whether or not an economic recovery was actually under way remained very much an open question. At Seventh Generation, despite the ongoing economic doldrums, we had experienced our best year ever, as measured by revenue growth, profitability, and the continuing evolution of our internal culture. Of the various shocks administered to the system over the past couple of years, from terrorist attacks to sudden shifts in long-term interest rates to the enormous decline in the high-tech sector, none seemed capable of disturbing the long-term upward trend of the natural products category, the healthy food sector, and our own related if even narrower niche, the natural and healthy household products category.

Our own results certainly accorded with the conclusions of a study published in August 2003 by Innovest Strategic Value Advisors: "Global food companies with an above average commitment to sustainable development," the study reported, had "outperformed their peers with regard to revenues and increase in market value by more than 30 percent over the past three years." The report singled out Unilever and Danone as leading food firms that had deliberately capitalized on a number of environmentally driven business opportunities, with positive results for their bottom lines.

Most recently, Kraft announced that it intends to take on the worldwide obesity epidemic by reducing the fat in its snacks. The subhead in the *New York Times* gave some sense of the widespread reaction: "Experts Skeptical on Vow to Change." I was also struck by a full-page ad that had appeared a few days before in a number of national newspapers (including the *New York Times* and the *Wall Street Journal*) from Philip Morris—Kraft's corporate parent—with the banner headline: "Where Can You Find Information on Important Tobacco Issues?"

At philipmorris.usa, of course. Was a tobacco maker's placement of a section on "Health Issues" on its Web site a reflection of the new transparency, or yet another piece of PR spin? "We agree with the overwhelming medical and scientific consensus that cigarette smoking causes lung cancer, heart disease, emphysema and other serious diseases in smokers," the section began. "There is no 'safe' cigarette."

PR of course, yet this statement does represent a 180-degree advance from the company's long-held position, even if it was inspired as part of their settlement to a massive array of lawsuits. Anti-smoking advocates could easily be excused for questioning the motivation for the company to take out full-page ads purporting to provide consumers with impartial scientific information on the health issues raised by smoking.

Is this progress? I think so, if only of an incremental sort—I'd love to see a Philip Morris CSR report accurately present the number of deaths per year for which its products could actually be held responsible. At the very least, Kraft's stated commitment to reduce fat and Philip Morris's attempt to more directly confront the health issues demonstrate that sufficient pressure was brought to bear on these companies, by NGOs and a more educated public, to start the process of change. One of the most effective ways to tame bad companies into becoming good companies has been to shame them. CSR is a perfectly valid response to such pressures.

That CSR has gone mainstream is no longer in doubt. That business has begun to reassess its role and responsibility to society is also no longer in dispute. But where does it go from here? For Anita Roddick, the real revolution is occurring not in the executive suites, but in the "amazing rebirth of grassroots community, including community economic initiatives," which she sees as she travels the world, no longer tethered to the executive committee of the Body Shop. "Look at the burgeoning grassroots cooperative movement of women in India or Africa," she said, which she called "the biggest explosion of social solidarity in our entire history. This transformation is producing new forms of economic cooperation . . . [which] are allowing people to work outside the traditional relationship of dependency on America or the West."

But even Anita Roddick, who rightly regards herself as a free-spirited radical, freely conceded to us that she has been encouraged by the fact that CSR issues like transparency and social and environmental reporting are now considered legitimate subjects in business schools, and that the first generation of socially responsible entrepreneurs—like herself—are frequently called upon to be speakers at such forums.

When we spoke to Ben Cohen, despite his obvious disenchantment with Unilever's stewardship of his legacy, he was generally optimistic about the direction in which business is headed in the twenty-first century. "I think it's getting much better," he responded to a question asking him to give his opinion of the general business climate for socially responsible entrepreneurs. "The big businesses of tomorrow are the small businesses of today. There is now much more space available for the next generation of socially conscious entrepreneurs to get started, because we have proven that it can be done. There is a general recognition that social responsibility protects reputation, and promotes brand value. And there is a much greater acceptance of the notion that it is not only possible or desirable but actually profitable to build social consciousness directly into the core of the enterprise."

When we asked him to describe the biggest change under way today, he responded without hesitation that it was a broad-based shift of perceptions. "Conventional wisdom has always had it that if you needed to solve a social problem, you needed to set up a nonprofit social service agency and give them money to tackle the problem. If you needed to make money, the right tool to do that was business. I've always thought that that was a false dichotomy. We are in the process of creating a world, and creating a business climate, in which the right way to go about solving social problems is by founding and maintaining and sustaining a socially responsible business."

Bob Massie, the former executive director of CERES, noted that the most important cultural shift currently under way is a spiritual one, from a culture of competition to a culture of cooperation. "I think that for a variety of reasons the power of cooperation has been grossly underestimated and inadequately understood. Conventional economics tends to look at all social phenomena as a function of the firm, whose sole purpose is to engage in a never-ending series of transactions aimed primarily at bidding down costs and prices."

"But then take a walk through any airport," he said, "and take a look at the business books. They're all about teamwork and cooperation and making the firm more like a family. Look at the way that the stakeholder concept is taking hold, all over the world, which is truly a triumph of cooperation over competition. What CSR is really about in a larger sense is that arguing not just from a moral standpoint but from an efficacy standpoint, the best way to gain the most out of people is to inspire them."

As we as a society undergo this profound shift in the conventional wisdom, Massie contended, "We're entering into a debate that involves every institution in society evolving over time, from government to private enterprise to the church and the press. We tend to assume that the world is pretty much the way it is when we were born, but in fact that's not true. Look at the enormous speed of change as people have begun to redefine the roles of virtually every institution we know of."

Massie also sees this change reflected in the curriculum of business schools: "Whatever its motivation, business has adopted language that twenty years ago when I was at Harvard Business School would have been considered hopelessly, ridiculously out of touch with reality. The use of the term sustainability, the use of the term stakeholder, the use of the term transparency. The corporate rhetoric has fundamentally changed, and with it, action will follow."

For Robert Dunn, executive director of Businesses for Social Responsibility, the most important change has been "the sudden decline of the consensus that the Washington Model of a publicly traded company operating in a free market was the be-all and end-all of business." With that model now being called into question, "CSR has emerged as a most effective way for companies to address issues like global climate change and our industrial society's continuing reliance on nonrenewable resources."

With regard to transparency, Dunn said "companies traditionally have regarded all information as being better off not disclosed unless there was a compelling and overwhelming reason to disclose it. Today, information—if understood to have a potential effect or impact on stakeholders—tends to be seen as worthy of disclosure, unless some onerous legal or some other penalty is attached to its transmission." With regard to accountability: "The leaders of large corporations are still absorbing and digesting the notion that their interests may be better served by engaging with stakeholders, and the more proactively the better." With regard to responsibility: "People are just beginning to grasp the breadth and scope of this dramatic expansion. Companies are being asked to account for and make amends for historic wrongs, an enormous shift in the definition of responsibility that has enormous implications for public policy."

From Dunn's perspective, these changes are profound and far-reaching. "Companies are talking about how to change their systems of reporting, systems of data-gathering, adjusting to new requirements for communication, developing metrics in a field that does not yet have a lot of refinement built in." But speak to the NGO community, and they will—with good reason—ask three questions about these supposed profound transformations: How Far? How Deep? How soon?

Speak to Judy Wicks of the White Dog Café, and although she "applauds people who engage in what I think of as the reform-oriented side of the CSR movement," she sees herself as standing on "the other side, which is trying to engineer a more fundamental shift toward local economies as an alternative to corporate globalization. We're interested in a corporate model oriented around small businesses, small farmers, small buyers, small sellers. The sort of economy"—dryly dubbed by author David Korten "The Judy Economy"—"is more like the localized economies in so much of the Third World today, and in much of the First World prior to industrialization."

But is such a rustic vision of a golden return to the pastoral pre-industrial days of yore a realistic appraisal of our possibilities? According to Wicks's friend and fellow Social Venture Network member Gary Hirshberg of Stonyfield Farm, Judy and her cohorts are dreaming. "To these people who say that you should buy everything from your backyard, I say 'Great, I wish you lived in my backyard, but you probably don't.' By which I mean that most people live in urban areas and therefore don't have that choice, or that luxury. Thank god for Whole Foods and Wild Oats. Look at the impact that Whole Foods and Wild Oats have had on Safeway, Stop & Shop, Wal-Mart, and Costco. There is not a store in New England now that doesn't have natural shelves."

The fact that Whole Foods and Wild Oats are growing at a rapid rate is, in Gary's somewhat self-serving opinion, anything but a mixed blessing. "Waiting for capitalism to fail and waiting for the big companies to disaggregate into millions of little companies is kind of like waiting for Godot—it's certainly not going to happen within my lifetime, if it's going to happen at all."

In the end as in the beginning, we come down to this vexing issue of scale, which can be framed as a fourth question: Are the huge companies that currently dominate our worldwide economic system truly capable of reform? In the face of a government that won't acknowledge the reality of a problem that runs counter to the interests of the hands that feed it—leadership is left ironically to the energy and automobile companies that caused much of the problem to begin with. That companies like British Petroleum (which has committed itself to making no more political contributions anywhere in the world), Shell, Toyota, and Honda are providing any leadership at all should convince all but the most hardened skeptic that genuine change is afoot.

The Ford Motor Company, in the meantime, under embattled chairman William Clay Ford, announced in its 2002 CSR report that it had no new "green" initiatives on the drawing boards. The company did pledge to improve the fuel efficiency of its fleet by 20 percent before 2005, but Ford's seemingly never-ending economic woes further forced management to flatly state that its capacity to address the challenges posed by global climate change "will be tempered by our near-term business realities."

"This is a case of a company that's got one foot on the accelerator and one foot on the brakes," Bob Massie blasted Ford in the *Wall Street Journal*. Unfortunately, that is often the case with companies, and that is not about to change any time soon, and certainly not overnight. What is worth noting in this regard is that these often quite fractious debates are being carried out in a new atmosphere— one of greater transparency. Under the current climate, many companies feel obliged to engage with CERES, or its counterparts around the world, to produce and release CSR reports, to think in terms of their environmental and social footprints, and to take the heat when—

as is probably inevitable—they are forced to backpedal fiercely on those commitments, because their profitability is imperiled.

Despite the prevalence of this two-steps-forward-and-one-back phenomenon, I've been struck by the number of people we've met inside big companies who are truly sincere, articulate, and passionate proponents of change. These are the champions of change inside the beast, who often take strong positions on these issues that can only be described as courageous. It's one thing for someone who works at Environmental Defense or the Natural Resources Defense Council to take a strong stand on the subject of fleet fuel efficiency. It's quite another thing for someone whose livelihood depends on pleasing the management at Ford or GM to adopt an aggressive posture in this area.

One of the comments I was most impressed by during our discussions was one from Bob Massie, who pointed out (without naming names) that during a number of often bitter CERES campaigns to pressure companies to turn over all sorts of new leaves, he would receive phone calls and letters from people inside the hierarchies of these companies. These covert change agents deep within the "enemy" camp would furtively inform him that they would appreciate receiving "a little pressure" in a particular area, as a means of helping them make the internal case that some new initiative had to be approved, or there would be hell to pay from the "radicals."

That embarking upon a course of corporate social responsibility is a complex and conflicted process was clear to me before I ever started working on this book. Now, the fact that the picture and the way forward can often be murky is, paradoxically, clear as day. It is certainly a process more amenable to the asking of questions than the delivery of incisive, authoritative answers.

GDP (Gross Domestic Product) is a lousy benchmark for human happiness. Our society still fails to reconcile the costs of producing high living standards for the few while many endure the daily impacts of growing pollution, environmental degradation, congestion, and urban sprawl. And the world has yet to begin to come to terms with the social resentments that are arising from massive inequities in economic and social status, both within the most affluent nations on earth as well as between the international economic haves and have-nots. This is why so many of the CSR initiatives described in this book, from HP's efforts to bridge the digital divide to Chiquita's efforts to improve the lives of those living on and near its banana plantations, to Starbucks' efforts to put more money into the pocket of the coffee producers, have shared a theme of redressing this balance, which desperately needs to be addressed and redressed because it is simply unconscionable to tolerate the present state of affairs in which human suffering is callously chalked up to the cost of doing business.

A great debate continues—and may well never end—on the best means to solve the problems facing us all today, from global climate change to species depletion, from population increase to desertification to the ongoing destruction of the rain forest. We have widespread social disruption and an overreliance on nonrenewable sources of energy, an economic system that spends more on arms than on schools, oceans that are being scoured clean of fish, and chemicals disrupting and destroying our hormone systems. We have kids who are too fat because the fast-food industry is shoving itself down their faces in their schools. We have a heart hospital in which you can find a high-cholesterol fast-food restaurant serving the patients in the corridors. The list of challenges, as we all know, goes on and on, while the list of remedies is woefully short. One of the most pernicious problems that we all face is a kind of problem fatigue, which in turn generates widespread cynicism and a feeling of complete powerlessness.

While one school of thought passionately contends that only increased government regulation and structural economic change that redresses the balance between the small and the weak and the big and powerful will produce the results required for the long-term survival of our species, an opposing faction holds, with equally passionate conviction, that only the discipline and noncentralized action of the free market can produce the changes needed to improve our lot in life. I personally believe that for all the talk of metrics and guidelines and benchmarks and indices, the heart as opposed to the head may well be the best place to find the real drivers of change. Inspiring people to look to their passions and ideas, their mission and beliefs, that yes, we shall overcome—is the part of corporate social responsibility that I fervently hope survives its incorporation into the mainstream.

We can all make a difference. Whether as employees, managers, consumers, activists, regulators, parents, teachers, or students—the future lies in our hands. Our greatest peril is that we lose sight of our own power and responsibility. In this dance into the future we all have our parts to play.

One day a man was walking along the beach when he noticed a figure in the distance.

As he got closer, he realized the figure was that of a boy picking something up and gently throwing it into the ocean.

Approaching the boy, he asked, "What are you doing?"

The youth replied, "Throwing starfish in the ocean. The sun is up and the tide is going out. If I don't throw them in, they'll die."

The man said, "Don't you realize there are miles and miles of beach and hundreds of starfish? You can't possibly make a difference!"

After listening politely, the boy bent down, picked up another starfish, and threw it into the surf.

Then, smiling at the man, he said, "I made a difference for that one."

(Adapted from *The Star Thrower* by Loren Eiseley)

To learn more about what you can do to help your company
become a more responsible corporate citizen, find out
the latest news on what other businesses are doing,
and share your own ideas and thoughts, please visit:

www.whatmattersmost.biz

resources

The following resources include both those referenced in the book as well as numerous additional sources of information. Descriptions appear only for those that we discuss and have experience working with. Compilation of the resources section was aided by the work of greenbiz.com, one of the best reference sites on the Web. The resources are organized into the following sections:

Books on Sustainable Business and Best Practices

Alternatives to Economic Globalization: A Better World Is Possible, by John Cavanagh et al., Alternatives Taskforce of the International Forum on Globalization. San Francisco: Berrett-Koehler, 2002.
Ben and Jerry's Double Dip: Lead with Your Values and Make Money, Too, by Ben Cohen and Jerry Greenfield, with Meredith Maran. New York: Simon & Schuster, 1997.

Ben & Jerry's, the Inside Scoop: How Two Real Guys Built a Business with a Social Conscience and a Sense of Humor, by Fred "Chico" Lager. New York: Crown Publishers, 1994.

Beyond Growth: The Economics of Sustainable Development, by Herman E. Daly. Boston: Beacon Press, 1996.

Building Partnerships: Cooperation Between the United Nations System and the Private Sector, by Jane Nelson. New York: United Nations Department of Public Information, 2002.

Built to Last: Successful Habits of Visionary Companies, by J. C. Collins and J. I. Porras. New York: Random House, 1995.

Cannibals with Forks: The Triple Bottom Line of 21st Century Business, by John Elkington. London: Capstone Publishing, 1997.

The Chrysalis Economy: How Citizen CEOs and Corporations Can Fuse Values and Value Creation, by John Elkington. London: Capstone Publishing, 2001.

The Civil Corporation: The New Economy of Corporate Citizenship, by Simon Zadek. London and Sterling, Va.: Earthscan Publications Ltd., 2001.

Corporate Citizenship, by Malcolm McIntosh, Deborah Leipziger, Keith Jones, and Gill Coleman. London: *Financial Times* and Pittman Publishing, 1998.

Cradle-to-Cradle: Putting Eco-Effectiveness into Practice, by William McDonough and Michael Braungart. New York: North Point Press, 2002.

Dancing with the Tiger: Learning Sustainability Step by Natural Step, by Brian Nattrass and Mary Altomare. Gabriola Island, British Columbia: New Society Publishers, 2002.

The Ecology of Commerce: A Declaration of Sustainability, by Paul Hawken. New York: HarperBusiness, 1993.

Everybody's Business: Managing Risks and Opportunities in Today's Global Society, by David Grayson and Adrian Hodges. London: *Financial Times* and Dorling Kindersley Ltd., 2002.

For the Common Good: Redirecting the Economy Toward Community, the Environment, and a Sustainable Future, by Herman E. Daly and John B. Cobb, Jr. Boston: Beacon Press, 1994.

Good Business: Your World Needs You, by Steve Hilton and Giles Gibbons. London: Texere Publishing Ltd., 2002.

Good to Great: Why Some Companies Make the Leap—And Others Don't, by J. C. Collins and J. I. Porras. New York: HarperCollins, 2001.

Living Corporate Citizenship: Strategic Routes to Socially Responsible Business, by Malcolm McIntosh, Ruth Thomas, Deborah Leipziger, and Gill Coleman. London: *Financial Times* and Prentice Hall, 2002.

Mid-Course Correction: Toward a Sustainable Enterprise: The Interface Model, by Ray Anderson. Atlanta: Peregrinzilla Press, 1998.

Natural Capitalism: Creating the Next Industrial Revolution, by Paul Hawken, Amory B. Lovins, and L. Hunter Lovins. Boston: Little Brown, 1999.

The Planetary Bargain: Corporate Social Responsibility Matters, by Michael Hopkins. London and Sterling, Va.: Earthscan Publications Ltd., 2003.

Saving the Corporate Soul—& (Who Knows) Maybe Your Own: Eight Principles for Creating and Preserving Integrity and Profitability without Selling Out, by David Batstone. San Francisco: Jossey-Bass, 2003.

Say It and Live It: The 50 Corporate Mission Statements That Hit the Mark, by Patricia A. Jones and Larry Kahaner. New York: Doubleday, 1995.

Setting Global Standards: Guidelines for Creating Codes of Conduct in Multinational Corporations, by Prakash Sethi. New York: John Wiley & Sons, 2003.

The Soul in the Computer: The Story of a Corporate Revolutionary, by Barbara Waugh et al. Makawao, Maui, Hawaii: Inner Ocean, 2001.

The SRI Advantage: Why Socially Responsible Investing Has Outperformed Financially, by Peter Camejo. Gabriola Island, British Columbia: New Society Publishers, 2002.

The Tyranny of the Bottom Line: Why Corporations Make Good People Do Bad Things, by Ralph Eskes. Emeryville, Calif.: Berrett-Koehler, 1995.

Value Shift: Why Companies Must Merge Social and Financial Imperatives to Achieve Superior Performance, by Lynn Sharp Paine. New York: McGraw-Hill, 2003.

Walking the Talk: The Business Case for Sustainable Development, by Charles Holliday, Stephen Schmidheiny, and Philip Watts. Sheffield, UK: Greenleaf Publishing, 2002.

What We Learned in the Rainforest: Business Lessons from Nature: Innovation, Growth, Profit, and Sustainability at Twenty of the World's Top Companies, by Tachi Kiuchi and Bill Shireman. San Francisco: Berrett-Koehler, 2002.

When Corporations Rule the World, by David Korten. New York: Seven Stories Press, 1995.

Socially Responsible Business Networks

Businesses for Social Responsibility
609 Mission Street, 2nd Floor
San Francisco, CA 94105-3506

Ph: 415-537-0888
Fx: 415-537-0889
http://www.bsr.org
BSR Forum: http://www.bsr.org/BSRForum/index.cfm
BSR Global Alliances: http://www.bsr.org/BSRForum/GlobalAlliances.cfm
BSR is a global nonprofit organization that partners with member companies to pursue commercial success—in ways that respect ethical values, people, communities, and the environment. BSR provides advisory services, collaborative opportunities, information resources, and networking to make corporate social responsibility an integral part of business operations and strategies. Its Global Business Responsibility Resource Center offers consultations, seminars, strategic tools, and training. BSR's reports cover climate change, alternative energy and energy efficiency, green building, and product design.

CERES: Coalition for Environmentally Responsible Economies
Coalition for Environmentally Responsible Economies
99 Chauncy St., 6th Floor
Boston, MA 02111
Ph: 617-247-0700
Fx: 617-267-5400
http://www.ceres.org
A central player in efforts to standardize corporate reporting on environmental performance, CERES believes that more and better corporate environmental performance information is essential for improved corporate environmental management. Members voluntarily adhere to the CERES Principles, a set of practical, realistic paths toward corporate environmental responsibility. These principles focus on energy conservation, the sustainable use of natural resources, risk reduction, safe products and services, and other environmentally responsible actions. The CERES Report—the first standardized format for environmental reporting crafted through the collaboration of industry, environmental groups, and investors—is designed to lower pollution and improve management and stakeholder responsiveness at companies that complete it.

Conference Board
845 3rd Avenue
New York, NY 10022-6679
Ph: 212-759-0900
Fx: 212-980-7014

http://www.conference-board.org
Corporate Citizenship Working Groups: http://www.conference-
    board.org/expertise/workinggroups
Global Network: http://www.conference-board.org/International/index.cfm

Co-op America
1612 K Street, NW, Suite 600
Washington, DC 20006
Ph: 202-872-5307
Fx: 202-331-8166
http://www.coopamerica.org
Co-op America is a national nonprofit organization founded in 1982, provides the economic strategies, organizing power, and practical tools for small
businesses and individuals to address today's social and environmental problems. While many environmental organizations choose to fight important
political and legal battles, Co-op America is the leading force in educating
and empowering our nation's people and businesses to make significant improvements through the economic system.

CSR Europe
Rue du Prince Royal, 25
Brussels B-1050, Belgium
Ph: 32-2/502-8354
Fx: 32-2/502-8458
http://www.csreurope.org
SRI (Socially Responsible Investing) Compass: http://www.sricompass.org
Partners: http://www.sricompass.org/partners/default.asp

Eurosif (European Sustainable and Responsible Investment Forum)
P.O. Box 504
4100 AM Culemborg, The Netherlands
Ph: 31-345/523-332
Fx: 31-345/510-053
http://www.eurosif.org

Forum EMPRESA
Forum on Business and Social Responsibility in the Americas
Rue Francisco Leitao, 469-Conj. 1407
CEP: 05414-020

São Paulo, Brazil
Ph: 55-11/3061-5894
Fx: 55-11/3068-8539
http://www.empresa.org

Future 500
Global Futures Foundation
25 Maiden Lane
San Francisco, CA 94104
Ph: 415-248-0011
Fx: 415-821-2736
http://www.globalff.org/Future_500/
Future 500 provides businesses with tools and techniques for thriving in an environmentally responsible and resource-efficient economy. It provides workshops, roundtable discussions, and publications devoted to the principles of industrial ecology. Industrial ecology incorporates some of the following topics: design for the environment, sustainable building, industrial metabolism, eco-industrial parks, systems thinking, and life-cycle assessments. Future 500 publications provide instruction on management, accounting, product development, marketing, and public policy; its workshops and roundtable discussions help make these concepts applicable to real business practices.

International Business Leaders Forum
15-16 Cornwall Terrace, Regent's Park
London NW1 4QP, United Kingdom
Ph: 44-20/7467-3656
Fx: 44-20/7467-3610
Member, EMPRESA
http://csrforum.com

Social Venture Network
P.O. Box 29221
San Francisco, CA 94129
Ph: 415-561-6501
Fx: 415-561-6435
http://www.svn.org
The Social Venture Network brings together in two annual meetings businesses with a social conscience: Those interested in combining good busi-

ness with sustainability, livable workplaces, and social justice. Members of the network often work with each other on new ventures. The network's programs include the Urban Enterprise Initiative, the Standards for Corporate Social Responsibility Project, the Sustainable Trade Initiative, and the Social Action Initiative. The annual Social Venture Institute offers a forum on the challenges of doing socially conscious business. Mentors from the Social Venture Network are available to speak with other businesses and the media.

World Business Council for Sustainable Development
4 chemin de Conches
CH-1231 Conches, Switzerland
Ph: 41-22/839-3100
Fx: 41-22/839-3131
http://www.wbcsd.ch

World Resources Institute
10 G Street, NE, Suite 800
Washington, D.C. 20002
Ph: 202-729-7600
Fx: 202-729-7610
http://www.wri.org
World Resources Institute's (WRI) Business Center features extensive resources and environmental information for industry and business schools. Working with corporate partners like General Motors, BP Amoco, and Monsanto, WRI's Business Leadership efforts focus on climate change. The Climate Protection Initiative works to accelerate the business community's acceptance of climate change as a real, manageable problem as well as to encourage innovative private-sector solutions. "Safe Climate, Sound Business" is a collaborative effort between WRI and major corporations to find and demonstrate ways to reduce emissions and protect the climate system while ensuring a sound business future for industry. "Taking a Byte Out of Carbon" profiles electronics technologies used by companies that reduce or eliminate the need to burn fossil fuels.

Publications and Other Resources

Some of our favorites are marked with a triple asterisk:

Business and the Environment
Aspen Law & Business
1185 Avenue of the Americas
New York, NY 10036
Ph: 212-597-0200
http://www.aspenpublishers.com/environment.asp
Editor: William Dalessandro
Ph: 603-672-5811
Fx: 603-672-5212

***Business Ethics*
P.O. Box 8439
2845 Harriet Avenue, Suite 207
Minneapolis, MN 55408
Ph: 612-879-0695
Fx: 612-879-0699
http://www.business-ethics.com
For the past fifteen years *Business Ethics* has been the premier publication of the movement for greater social responsibility in business. You'll find thought-provoking articles like:

- Why stock options aren't real employee ownership
- Six changes to corporate governance after Enron
- Rating the best MBA programs for social and environmental responsibility
- The inside scoop on the forced buyout of Ben & Jerry's
- Labor claims the power of $7 trillion in pension funds
- Real-life case studies of challenges good people face inside corporations
- Annual ranking of the "100 Best Corporate Citizens"
- The untold story of the devastation caused by Jack Welch of General Electric
- A half-dozen bold new ideas for spreading capital ownership to regular folks
- Why company social innovations die after a company founder departs

Corporate Citizenship Company
5/11 Lavington Street
London SE1 0NZ, United Kingdom

Ph: 44-20/7945-6130
Fx: 44-20/7945-6138
http://www.ccbriefing.co.uk
Corporate Citizenship Briefing: http://www.ccbriefing.co.uk

Corporate Register
http://www.corporate-register.com
The Corporate Register Web site allows users to search for and view the published environmental and social reports of more than 1500 companies. After a quick—and free—registration, users can search by company name, sector, region, or country. While largely covering European countries, this site is a fairly comprehensive way to measure and compare corporate environmental performances.

***CSRwire
SRI World Group, Inc.
74 Cotton Mill Hill
Brattleboro, VT 05301
Ph: 802-251-0500
Fx: 802-251-0555
http://www.csrwire.com
CSRwire seeks to promote the growth of corporate responsibility and sustainability through solutions-based information and positive examples of corporate practices. They offer four core services:

- A free weekly email newsletter
- Links to Corporate Social Responsibility reports
- Press release distribution
- CSR events promotion and CSR resources

CSR Directory: Resources for Promoting Global Business Principles and Best Practices, a directory of worldwide organizations working on all aspects of corporate social responsibility. This interactive, Web-based tool provides contact information for more than 700 organizations, with listings of the senior leaders and Web sites for each organization.
http://www.csrwire.com/directory

***Ethical Corporation Magazine
FC Group
7/9 Fashion Street

London E1 6PX, United Kingdom
Ph: 44-20/7375-7561
http://www.ethicalcorp.com
Ethical Corporation Magazine is an independent business information provider and events producer on issues related to corporate social, financial, and environmental responsibility. It provides independent content and events on the subject of global corporate citizenship and corporate responsibility management.

Global Ethics Monitor
AFX News Ltd.
747 Third Street, 37th Floor
New York, NY 10017
http://www.globalethicsmonitor.com

green@work
L.C. Clark Publishing Co.
840 U.S. Highway 1, Suite 330
North Palm Beach, FL 33408
Ph: 561-627-3393
http://www.greenatworkmag.com
The *green@work magazine* and Web site are devoted to reinforcing sustainable initiatives by sharing success stories and profiling the individuals who are making them happen. green@work explores the social, ideological, economic, and political issues that advance green design strategies, as well as the intellectual and charismatic expressions of the visionaries who are fostering mainstream acceptance of ecological advocacy.

***GreenBiz.com
http://www.greenbiz.com
Ph: 510-451-6611
Fx: 510-451-6603
GreenBiz.com is a nonprofit, nonpartisan network and publisher that harnesses the power of technology to bring environmental information, resources, and tools to the mainstream business community. Its principal mission is: "To provide clear, concise, accurate, and balanced information, resources, and learning opportunities to help companies of all sizes and sectors integrate environmental responsibility into their operations in a manner that combines ecological sustainability with profitable business practices."

International Cleaner Production Information Clearinghouse
http://www.emcentre.com/unepweb/index.htm
Cleaner production refers to the continuous application of an integrated, preventive environmental strategy to processes, products, and services to increase efficiency and reduce risks to humans and the environment.

The International Cleaner Production Information Clearinghouse offers a treasure trove of case studies, which can be viewed by sector. Also discover the cleaner production policies of various countries and search for additional contacts and experts by world region. The clearinghouse was developed by UNEP's Division of Technology, Industry, and Economics.

International Corporate Environmental Reporting Site
http://www.enviroreporting.com
Though difficult to navigate, the International Corporate Environmental Reporting Web site houses useful information for tracking environmental performance. The site also lists environmental reporting resources and awards. In addition, the site addresses shareholder topics such as the relationship between environmental performance and financial results.

ISO 14000 Information Center
http://www.iso14000.com
The ISO 14000 Information Center explains what to expect during the ISO 14000 audit process and how to successfully become registered to ISO 14000. The resource section contains related journals, newsletters, publications, and discussion lists, plus links to other ISO 14000 organizations; the training section provides computer-based training and systems development tools and auditor training. The ISO 14000 Implementation Tools provide standard overviews, EMS articles, and information on eco-efficiency. Connect with others involved in the same process through the ISO 14000 Community Center.

The Journal of Corporate Citizenship
Greenleaf Publishing
Aizlewood Business Centre
Nursery Street
Sheffield S3 8GG, United Kingdom
Ph: 44/114-282-3475
Fx: 44/114-282-3476
http://www.greenleaf-publishing.com
http://www.greenleaf-publishing.com/jcc/jcchome.htm

U.S.-Based Business Policy Organizations

Center for Corporate Citizenship
1615 H Street, NW
Washington, D.C. 20062
Ph: 202-463-5517
Fx: 202-887-3402
http://www.uschamber.com/CCC/default.html

Center for Ethical Business Cultures
1000 LaSalle Avenue, Suite 153
Minneapolis, MN 55403
Ph: 651-962-4120
Fx: 651-962-4125
http://www.cebcglobal.org

Center for Small Business and the Environment
P.O. Box 53127
Washington, D.C. 20009
Ph: 202-332-6875
Fx: 202-638-1973
http://www.aboutcsbe.org

Ethics Resource Center
1747 Pennsylvania Avenue, NW, Suite 400
Washington, D.C. 20006
Ph: 202-737-2258
Fx: 202-737-2227
http://www.ethics.org

Global Futures Foundation
25 Maiden Lane
San Francisco, CA 94104
Ph: 415-248-0011
Fx: 415-821-2736
http://www.globalfutures.org

Interfaith Center on Corporate Responsibility
475 Riverside Drive
New York, NY 10115

Ph: 212-870-2293
Fx: 212-870-2023
http://www.iccr.org
Shareholder Resolutions information: http://www.socialfunds.com/index.cgi
(go to Activism)
Global Codes of Conduct (for comparison): http://www.iccr.org/issue_
groups/accountability/resources.htm

International Business Ethics Institute
1725 K Street, NW, Suite 1207
Washington, D.C. 20006
Ph: 202-296-6938
Fx: 202-296-5897
http://www.business-ethics.org

The Natural Step
P.O. Box 29372
San Francisco, CA 94129
Ph: 415-561-3344
Fx: 415-561-3345
http://www.naturalstep.org
The Natural Step is a nonprofit environmental education organization
working to build an ecologically and economically sustainable society. TNS
offers a framework that is based on science and serves as a compass for businesses, communities, academia, government entities, and individuals working to redesign their activities to become more sustainable. The program,
which originated in Sweden, has been adopted by several U.S. companies,
including Nike and Interface.

Redefining Progress
1904 Franklin Street, 6th Floor
Oakland, CA 94612
Ph: 510-444-3041
Fx: 510-444-3191
http://www.rprogress.org

Transparency International–USA
1615 L Street, NW, Suite 700
Washington, D.C. 20036

Ph: 202-682-7048
Fx: 202-857-0939
http://www.transparency-usa.org

Verite
49 South Pleasant Street, 3rd Floor
Amherst, MA 01002
Ph: 413-253-9227
Fx: 413-256-8960
http://www.verite.org

International Business Policy Organizations
and Resources

AccountAbility
Institute of Social and Ethical AccountAbility
Unit A, 137 Shepherdess Walk
London N1 7RQ, United Kingdom
Ph: 44-020/7549-0400
Fx: 44-020/7549-0400
http://www.accountability.org.uk
AccountAbility is an international, nonprofit institute dedicated to promoting social and ethical accountability across all organizations and sectors. The multistakeholder membership organization conducts and publishes research and holds training courses and discussion forums throughout the world.

Business for Africa
Secretariat
African Investment Advisory
63 Wilbury Road, Hove
East Sussex BN3 3PB, United Kingdom
Ph: 44-1273/732-262
Fx: 44-1273/722-902
http://www.africaaplc.com

Canadian Centre for Ethics and Corporate Policy
360 Bloor Street, Suite 408
Toronto, Ontario M5S 1X1, Canada

Ph: 416-348-8691
Fx: 416-348-8689
http://www.ethicscentre.com/welcome.html

Caux Round Table
Amaliastraat 10
The Hague 2514 JC, The Netherlands
Ph: 31-70/360-5260
Fx: 31-70/361-7209
http://www.cauxroundtable.org
Caux Business Principles: http://www.cauxroundtable.org

Centre for Innovation in Corporate Responsibility
342 MacLaren Street
Ottawa, Ontario K2P 0M6, Canada
Ph: 613-276-6080
Fx: 613-238-5642
http://www.cicr.net

Centre for Social Markets
38 Decima Street
London SE1 4QQ, United Kingdom
Ph: 44-20/7407-7625
Fx: 44-20/7407-7082
http://www.csmworld.org/public/balcc/balcc.htm

European Corporate Governance Institute
ULB CP 114
50, avenue FD Roosevelt
B-1050 Brussels, Belgium
http://www.ecgi.org
Corporate Governance Codes and Principles: http://www.ecgi.org/
    codes/index.htm

Forum EMPRESA
Forum on Business and Social Responsibility in the Americas
Rue Francisco Leitao, 469-Conj. 1407
CEP: 05414-020
São Paulo, Brazil

Ph: 55-11/3061-5894
Fx: 55-11/3068-8539
and
Ebro 2740, Of. 301
Santiago, Chile
Ph: 56-2/431-0310
Fx: 56-2/378-7290

Global Corporate Governance Forum
c/o The World Bank Group
1818 H Street, NW
Washington, D.C. 20433
Ph: 202-473-3604
Fx: 202-522-7588
http://www.gcgf.org

Global Reporting Initiative (GRI)
Secretariat
Keizersgracht 209
1016 DT Amsterdam, The Netherlands
Ph: 31-20/531-0000
Fx: 31-20/531-0031
http://www.globalreporting.org
The Global Reporting Initiative (GRI) is a multi-stakeholder process and independent institution whose mission is to develop and disseminate globally
applicable Sustainability Reporting Guidelines. These Guidelines are for
voluntary use by organisations for reporting on the economic, environmental, and social dimensions of their activities, products, and services. The GRI
incorporates the active participation of representatives from business, ac-
countacy, investment, environmental, human rights, research and labour
organisations from around the world. Started in 1997 by the Coalition for
Environmentally Responsible Economies (CERES), the GRI became independent in 2002, and is an official collaborating centre of the United Nations Environment Programme (UNEP) and works in cooperation with the
UN Secretary-General Kofi Annan's Global Compact.

Greening of Industry Network
950 Main Street
Clark University

Worcester, MA 01610-1477
Ph: 508-751-4607
Fx: 508-751-4600
http://www.greeningofindustry.org

Institute for Global Ethics
11 Main Street
Camden, ME 04843
Ph: 207-236-6658
Fx: 207-236-4014
http://www.globalethics.org

International Business Leaders Forum
15-16 Cornwall Terrace, Regent's Park
London NW1 4QP, United Kingdom
Ph: 44-20/7467-3656
Fx: 44-20/7467-3610
http://www.pwblf.org
http://www.csrforum.com
The Americas Region: Adrian Hodges, coauthor of *Everybody's Business*,
    2001; http://www.dkonline.co.uk/everybodysbusiness
Asia Network: http://www.corporatecitizenshipasia.net
Report: *Creating the Enabling Environment for Public–Private Partnerships and
    Global Corporate Citizenship*, 2000
Report: *Human Rights: Is It Any of Your Business?* 2000 (with Amnesty
    International–UK)

International Corporate Governance Network
Secretariat
16 Park Crescent
London W1N 4AH, United Kingdom
Ph: 44-20/7580-4741
Fx: 44-20/7612-7034
http://www.icgn.org

New Economics Foundation
Cinnamon House
6-8 Cole Street
London SE1 4YH, United Kingdom

Ph: 44-207/7407-77447
Fx: 44-207/7407-6473
http://www.neweconomics.org
The New Economics Foundation is a radical think tank. It is unique in bringing together the ideas, people, resources, and influence to challenge business-as-usual. It creates practical and enterprising solutions to the social, environmental, and economic challenges facing the local, regional, national, and global economies.

Resource Centre for the Social Dimensions of Business Practice
15-16 Cornwall Terrace, Regent's Park
London NW1 4QP, United Kingdom
Ph: 44-20/7467-3618
Fx: 44-20/7467-3615
http://www.rc-sdbp.org/main.asp

Social Accountability International
220 East 23rd Street, Suite 605
New York, NY 10010
Ph: 212-684-1414
Fx: 212-684-1515
http://www.sa-intl.org

Tomorrow's Company
The Centre for Tomorrow's Company
19 Buckingham Street
London WC2N 6EF, United Kingdom
Ph: 44-020/7930-5150
Fx: 44-020/7930-5155
info@tomorrowscompany.com
The vision of Tomorrow's Company is to create, with business, a future for business that makes equal sense to staff, shareholders, and society. It achieves this through four objectives: by acting as a leading and influential networking hub for organizations, by identifying and exploring the future of sustainable success, by undertaking and publishing agenda-setting research, and by promoting the adoption of new ideas and concepts.

In 2002, Tomorrow's Company researched and defined three key issues that, it believes, will be fundamental to business if they are to successfully face the challenges of the near and long-term future. Over the course of the next three years it will explore, with its members, three issues: 21st Century Investment—Tomorrow's Investment System: How can we make our current investment system more efficient? The Inclusive Company—Leadership and Governance: How can we restore trust and improve performance in all key relationships? Business and Society—Closing the Gap: What is the role of business in society at the local and global levels?

Transparency International
Otto-Suhr-Allee 97-99
D-10585 Berlin, Germany
Ph: 49-30/343-8200
Fx: 49-30/3470-3912
http://www.transparency.org

United Kingdom Department of Trade & Industry
1 Victoria Street
London SW1H OET, United Kingdom
http://www.dti.gov.uk
Minister for Corporate Social Responsibility: Stephen Timms, MP
Corporate Social Responsibility: http://www.dti.gov.uk/support/
    responsibility.htm
Report: *Business and Society: Developing Corporate Social Responsibility in the
    U.K.*, 2001
Report: *Business and Society: Corporate Social Responsibility*, 2002
http://www.societyandbusiness.gov.uk
http://www.societyandbusiness.gov.uk/2002/index.htm

World Business Council for Sustainable Development
4 chemin de Conches
CH-1231 Conches, Switzerland
Ph: 41-22/839-3100
Fx: 41-22/839-3131
http://www.wbcsd.ch

World Economic Forum
91-93 route de la Capite
1223 Cologny

Geneva, Switzerland
Ph: 41-22/869-1212
Fx: 41-22/786-2744
http://www.weforum.org
Report: *Responding to the Leadership Challenge: Findings of a CEO Survey on Global Corporate Citizenship*, 2003 (online)
CEO Statement on Corporate Citizenship, 2002: http://www.weforum.org/corporatecitizenship
Global Exchange for Social Investment: http://www.gexsi.org

Trends and Indexes Online

Business in the Community
http://www.bitc.org.uk
Index of Corporate Environmental Engagement (for UK Companies):
    http://www.business-in-environment.org.uk/s_b_engagement.html

Calvert Social Index
http://www.calvert.com/sri_calvertindex.asp
Calvert Group, a leading firm focusing on socially responsible investing, has developed the Calvert Social Index, a broad-based benchmark of large, socially responsible U.S. companies. The index consists of 468 companies that are weighted on a market capitalization basis. Calvert constructed the index by analyzing roughly 1000 of the largest publicly traded companies using its social criteria. To be included, companies must meet Calvert's standards on the environment, workplace issues, product safety, community relations, weapons contracting, international operations and human rights, and respect for the rights of indigenous peoples.

Environics International
Annual Corporate Social Responsibility Monitor survey:
    www.environicsinternational.com/sp-csr.asp
Environics International is a global public opinion and stakeholder research company with research partners in over fifty countries. Established in 1987, it specializes in providing continuous tracking, insights, and strategic counsel on global issues to multinational companies, national governments, multilateral agencies, and nongovernmental organizations.

Ethical Purchasing Index
http://www.co-operativebank.co.uk (go to Ethics, then to Ethical
    Consumerism Research Reports)

International Business Leaders Forum
http://www.csrforum.com
Emerging CSR Trends: http://www.csrforum.com (go to What's New)
Report on CSR Trends in Consulting Firms

Investment Responsibility Research Center
http://www.irrc.org
Shareholder Resolutions: http://www.irrc.org/press_releases/06292001_
    RecordVotes.html
Report: *Towards a Shared Agenda: Emerging Corporate Governance and Social
    Issue Trends for the 2002 Proxy Season and 2001 Issues Review* (IRRC and
    Social Investment Forum): http://www.socialfunds.com/news/article.
    cgi?sfArticleId=807

Leading Social Investment Report
http://www.ishareowner.com

New Economics Foundation
http://www.neweconomics.org

RoperNOP Corporate Reputation Scorecard
http://roperasw.com/products/reputation.html
RoperASW, a NOP World company, is a leading global marketing research
and consulting firm. The Corporate Reputation Scorecard is a survey of over
6500 adult Americans.

Social Investment Forum
http://www.socialinvest.org
Social Investment Trends Report: http://www.socialinvest.org/Areas/News/
    2001-trends.htm

Social Investing Trends
http://www.socialfunds.com/news/article.cgi?sfArticleID=750

SRI World Group, Inc.
http://www.sriworld.com

Transparency International
http://www.transparency.org
Corruption Perceptions Index: http://transparency.org/documents/cpi/
2001/cpi2001.html

Surveys Online

Boston College
Community Involvement Index: http://www.bc.edu/bc_org/avp/csom/ccc/
index.html

Davis Global Advisors
http://www.davisglobal.com
Leading Corporate Governance: http://www.davisglobal.com/
publications.lcgi

Echo Research
Corporate Social Responsibility Survey: http://www.echoresearch.com

Environics International
GlobeScan Survey: http://www.environicsinternational.com

Financial Times
http://www.ft.com
World's Most Respected Companies: http://specials.ft.com/wmr2001/
index.html

Harris Interactive
http://www.harrisinteractive.com/index.asp
Reputation Quotient: http://www.harrisinteractive.com/pop_up/rq/index.asp

Market & Opinion Research International
http://www.mori.com
Annual Corporate Social Responsibility Survey: http://www.mori.com/csr/
annual.shtml

PricewaterhouseCoopers
5th Annual Global CEO Survey: http://www.pwcglobal.com

SRI Compass
http://www.sricompass.org
European Survey on Socially Responsible Investment and the Financial
    Community: http://www.sricompass.org/trends/default.asp

World Bank
http://www.worldbank.org
World Bank Institute Survey on Corporate Social Responsibility: http://
    www.worldbank.org/wbi/governance/CSR/edialogue.html

News Online

CSRwire (daily)
http://csrwire.com

Ethical Corporation Magazine (monthly)
http://www.ethicalcorp.com

Ethical Performance (monthly)
http://www.ethicalperformance.com

Global Ethics Monitor (daily)
http://www.globalethicsmonitor.com

Global Reporting Initiative
http://www.globalreporting.org

GreenBiz.com
http://www.greenbiz.com

SRI-in-Progress (French and English)
http://www.sri-in-progress.com

SustainAbility
http://www.sustainability.com/news/radar/previous-editions.asp

SustainableBusiness.com
http://www.sustainablebusiness.com

UN Global Compact (weekly)
http://www.unausa.org

Nongovernmental Organizations

Friends of the Earth
1025 Vermont Ave., NW, 3rd Floor
Washington, DC 20005
Ph: 202-783-7400
Fx: 202-783-0444
http://www.foe.org
Friends of the Earth's activities include lobbying, litigation, and providing public information on a variety of environmental issues—including ozone depletion, river protection, and tropical deforestation. FOE's Economics for the Earth program promotes economic policies that promote sustainable development, strengthen communities, and provide economic security. Among its specific campaigns are efforts to cut government subsidies that hurt the environment and to promote environmental tax reform. Other FOE programs address sustainable communities, clean air and safe food, transportation, and global environmental protection. Its magazine is published quarterly.

Global Exchange
2017 Mission Street, Suite 303
San Francisco, CA 94110
Ph: 415-255-7296
Fx: 415-255-7498
http://www.globalexchange.org/
Global Exchange is an international human rights organization dedicated to promoting environmental, political, and social justice. Since their founding in 1988, they have increased the U.S. public's global awareness while building partnerships worldwide.

Greenpeace
1436 U St., NW
Washington, D.C. 20009

Ph: 202-462-1177
Fx: 202-462-4507
http://www.greenpeace.org
A well-known activist organization, Greenpeace is a good source for research, information, and news on climate change, toxics, nuclear power, renewable energy, oceans, genetic engineering, and forests. Businesses may be particularly interested in the resources on renewable energy and the chemical industry, as well as tips for reducing paper and wood-based product consumption.

Rainforest Alliance
65 Bleecker St.
New York, NY 10012
Ph: 888-MY-EARTH or 212-677-1900
Fx: 212-677-2187
http://www.rainforest-alliance.org
Rainforest Alliance is a partnership among business, government, scientists, and local communities to save the world's threatened tropical rain forests and promote economically viable and socially desirable alternatives. Its SmartWood eco-labeling program certifies forest products that come from sustainable or well-managed sources and companies that process, manufacture, or sell products made from certified wood. Their Web site provides a certified-products finder, lists certified operations by country and state, and offers certification guidelines and applications for businesses. Rainforest Alliance also publishes a bimonthly newsletter called *Canopy*.

Silicon Valley Toxics Coalition
760 N. First Street
San Jose, CA 95112
Ph: 408-287-6707
Fx: 408-287-6771
http://www.svtc.org/about/index.html
SVTC is a diverse grassroots coalition that engages in research, advocacy, and organizing around the environmental and human health problems caused by the rapid growth of the high-tech electronics industry. Their goal is to advance environmental sustainability and clean production; improve community health; promote environmental and social justice; and ensure democratic decision-making for communities and workers affected by the high-tech revolution in Silicon Valley and other high-tech areas of the United States and the world.

TrueMajority and Business Leaders for Sensible Priorities
http://www.truemajority.org
TrueMajority, started by Ben Cohen, provides a positive blueprint for moving forward in the post-9/11 world. These principles reflect the American values of compassion, charity, and justice—the same values we must adhere to in order to build a safer, more secure home and world. These principles are also revenue-neutral, meaning the investments proposed are entirely funded by reductions in unnecessary spending on Cold War–era weapons that no longer contribute to our national security.

TrueMajority Principles:

1. Attack poverty and world hunger as if our life depends on it. It does.
2. Champion the rights of every child, woman, and man.
3. End our obstructionism to the world's treaties.
4. Reduce our dependence on oil and lead the world to an age of renewable energy.
5. Close the book on the Cold War and ease the nuclear nightmare.
6. Renounce Star Wars and the militarization of space.
7. Make globalization work for, not against, working people.
8. Ensure equal treatment under law for all.
9. Get money out of politics.
10. Close the gap between rich and poor kids at home.

If you register at its Web site they will send you e-mail alerts on critical issues. With one click of a button you can either send a suggested fax or edit them yourself.

Corporate Social Responsibility Reports
for Companies Covered in the Book

Ben & Jerry's Homemade
http://www.benjerry.com/our_company/our_mission/

The Body Shop
http://www.thebodyshop.com/web/tbsgl/values_rep.jsp

British Petroleum
http://www.bp.com

Calvert Group
http://www.calvertgroup.com/aboutindex.html

Chiquita
http://www.chiquita.com

Danone
http://www.danonegroup.com/dev_durable/index_dev_durable.html

Eileen Fisher
http://www.eileenfisher.com

Hewlett-Packard
http://www.hp.com/hpinfo/globalcitizenship

Intel
http://www.intel.com/intel/finance/social.htm?iid=Homepage+IntelLinks_
   governance&

Interface Carpets
http://www.interfaceinc.com/goals

Johnson & Johnson
http://www.jnj.com/community/index.htm

Nike
http://www.nike.com/nikebiz/nikebiz.jhtml;bsessionid=F4YWWSOPQX1J
   ACQCGIUSF5AKAIZDOIZB?page=24.

Patagonia
http://www.patagonia.com/about/main_about_us.shtml

Proctor & Gamble
http://www.pg.com/about_pg/corporate/sustainability/substain_catmain.
   jhtml

Seventh Generation
http://www.seventhgeneration.com/page.asp?unitid=535

Shell Oil
http://www.shell.com/home/Framework?siteId=shellreport2002-en

Starbucks
http://www.starbucks.com/aboutus/csr.asp

Stonyfield Farm
http://www.stonyfield.com/AboutUs/CompanyProfile.shtml

Unilever
http://www.unilever.com/environmentsociety/

White Dog Café
http://www.whitedog.com

Working Assets
http://www.workingassets.com/aboutwa.cfm

appendix

Who Owns Who

Company	Which Makes	Now Owned By	Which Produces
Mad River Traders	Juices	Coca-Cola	Sprite, Minute Maid, Dasani Water, Hi-C
Odwalla	Organic juices		
Balance Bar	Energy bars	Kraft (subsidary of Philip Morris)	Oscar Mayer, Jello-O, Miracle Whip, Velveeta, Marlboro, Virginia Slims
Boca Burger	Vegi-burgers		
Cascadian Farm	Organic foods	General Mills	Pillsbury, Hamburger Helper, Cheerios, Chex
Small Planet Foods			
Muir Glen	Tomato sauce		
Ben & Jerry's	Ice cream	Unilever	Lipton, Slim-Fast, Skippy, Dove Soap,
Stonyfield Farm	Yogurt	Groupe Danone	Dannon Yogurt, Evian

Company	Which Makes	Now Owned By	Which Produces
Lightlife	Tofu dogs	ConAgra	Jiffy Pop, Reddi-wip, Swiss Miss, Hebrew National
Earth's Best	Baby food	Hain Celestial (20% owned by H. J. Heinz)	
Westsoy	Soy products		
Health Valley	Organic food		
Terra Chips	Chips & snacks		
Nile Spice Group	Soup		
Arrowhead Mills			
Yves Veggie Cuisine	Vegetarian food		
Celestial Seasonings	Tea		
Imagine Foods	Organic and natural foods		
Walnut Acres	Organic fruit juices, soups, pasta sauces and salsas		This was a North Castle Partners roll-up of: Mountain Sun, ShariAnn's, Millina's Finest, and Fruitti di Bosco into the Walnut Acres brand banner
Ethnic Gourmet	Frozen food	H. J. Heinz	
Alta Dena	Organic dairy	Dean Foods	Borden, Land O'Lakes, Veryfine
White Wave	Soy milk		
Horizon Organic	Organic dairy		
PowerBar	Energy bar	Nestlé	Carnation, Alpo, Stouffer's
Worthington Foods	Vegetarian food	Kellogg's	Pop-Tarts, Corn Flakes, Eggo
Morningstar Farms	Vegetarian food		
Kashi	Cereal & crackers		

Company	Which Makes	Now Owned By	Which Produces
Mother's	Cereal	Quaker Oat's (subsidary of PepsiCo)	Rice-A-Roni, Cap'n Crunch, Gatorade, Frito-Lay, Pepsi, Tropicana
After the Fall	Juices	J. M. Smucker	Jif, Crisco
Santa Cruz Natural	Juices		
R. W. Knudsen	Juices		
Solgar	Vitamins	American Home Products	
Walnut Acres	Organic food	North Castle Partners Note: all sold to Hain in June 2003	
Acirca	Juices	(North Castle Partners Venture Capital roll-up)	
Mountain Sun	Juices		
Avalon	Personal care		
Nantucket Nectars	Juices	Cadbury Schweppes	
Annie's Homegrown	Organic pasta	Solera Capital	

index